'Rights and Justice are arguably at the core of the Law School identity and curricula. Yet in recent years these concepts have been at the forefront of wider public discourse, and are increasingly contested and challenged. With this challenge arguably comes the opportunity to reflect, revaluate and renew their place within the Law School. This edited collection therefore provides a timely intervention to consider these questions and is a must-read for anyone who cares about what Law Schools teach and why.'

Professor Chris Ashford, *Professor of Law and Society at Northumbria University*

'Useful case studies to inspire and guide university law teachers keen to teach rights and justice in research-informed ways.'

Professor Rosemary Auchmuty FRSA, *Professor of Law Emerita, School of Law, University of Reading*

'Legal rights have never been more important but also never more contested. This book, which brings together contributions by a range of international and well respected legal scholars, is an important contribution to understanding how universities can best handle these difficult issues through calm and considered teaching that is well informed by research.'

Professor Sir Peter Scott FAcSS MAE, *Emeritus Professor of Higher Education Studies, University College London (IOE – UCL Faculty of Education and Society)*

'This engaging book offers a rich array of insightful accounts of research-led teaching in legal education. It will be of great value to those who want to give their students access to cutting edge debates in the field.'

Professor Paul Ashwin, *Lancaster University*

Teaching of Rights and Justice in the Law School

This book examines the challenges of bringing cutting-edge research in often controversial areas into the law syllabus and explores how academics can effectively adopt a holistic approach to research and pedagogy when teaching rights and justice. The collection brings together experts from all areas of legal scholarship to discuss how they fuse often controversial aspects of rights and justice into their teaching in a way that responds to and is ultimately led by academic research. As such, it advances legal education through the opportunity to explore the interplay between rights and justice and how scholars both ensure that their teaching is research-led, whilst responding to the needs and views of students and issues such as generational differences in viewpoints on controversial issues. This topical volume will appeal to academics and researchers interested in academic freedom, the challenges of research-led teaching and the pedagogy around the teaching of rights and justice.

Stephen Hurley is a Senior Lecturer in Employment and Equality Law at the University of Winchester. He is a solicitor and formerly an Employment Law Partner in private practice. For over a decade he has taught law at undergraduate and postgraduate level at a number of UK universities and is a Fellow of the Higher Education Academy. He has published in the area of disability harassment and fraud in the workplace.

Chris Monaghan is a Principal Lecturer in Law at the University of Worcester. He is the Director of the Constitutions, Rights and Justice Research Group at the University of Worcester. He has published on areas such as accountability, the Chagos Islands litigation, human rights, the UK constitution and impeachment.

Routledge Studies in Law, Rights and Justice

Routledge Studies in Law, Rights and Justice seeks to publish leading monographs and edited collections that explore the interplay between rights and justice across different areas of law and legal practice. The series serves as a home for scholars working in areas such as human rights, social justice, constitutional justice, business and human rights, equality rights and civil justice. It encourages authors to address the theoretical and practical aspects of the application of rights, the achievability of justice in these uncertain times and the methods available to individuals, organisations and states to achieve justice. *Routledge Studies in Law, Rights and Justice* embraces both scholarship from a national and international viewpoint and encourages authors to explore rights and justice from a global perspective. It strives to break down existing disciplinary silos and encourage collaboration, which offers the opportunity to publish thought-provoking, original and cutting-edge work. The aim is to foster debates, build bridges between different areas of scholarship and encourage a wider perspective on the underlying issues that might limit the applicability of rights, or render justice difficult to achieve.

Routledge Studies in Law, Rights and Justice primarily consider rights and justice from a legal perspective, but does however, welcome submissions that take a broader view and engage with the wider socio-economic, political, and social context. The series editor is very keen to consider works by established and early-career academics, and submissions are encouraged from scholars based all around the world.

Series Editor:
Chris Monaghan is the Head of Law and a Principal Lecturer in Law at the University of Worcester, and holds a PhD from the Dickson Poon School of Law at King's College London. He has published widely on aspects of public law.

Titles in this series:

The Evolution of International Criminal Procedure
From Nuremberg and Tokyo to the International Criminal Court
Giovanni Chiarini

Modern Slavery Survivor Pathways
Policy, Legislation and Practice in the UK
Anne-Marie Greenslade

Human Rights and Standard of Living in Sub-Saharan Africa
Challenges and Prospects
Augustine Edobor Arimoro

Teaching of Rights and Justice in the Law School
Challenges and Opportunities for Research Led Teaching
Edited by Stephen Hurley and Chris Monaghan

Teaching of Rights and Justice in the Law School

Challenges and Opportunities for Research Led Teaching

Edited by Stephen Hurley and Chris Monaghan

Routledge
Taylor & Francis Group
LONDON AND NEW YORK

First published 2025
by Routledge
4 Park Square, Milton Park, Abingdon, Oxon OX14 4RN

and by Routledge
605 Third Avenue, New York, NY 10158

Routledge is an imprint of the Taylor & Francis Group, an informa business

British Library Cataloguing-in-Publication Data
A catalogue record for this book is available from the British Library

Library of Congress Cataloging-in-Publication Data
Names: Hurley, Stephen, editor. | Monaghan, Christopher, editor.
Title: Teaching of rights and justice in the law school: challenges and opportunities for research Led teaching/edited by Stephen Hurley and Chris Monaghan.
Description: Abingdon, Oxon [UK]; New York, NY: Routledge, 2025. |Series: Routledge studies in law, rights and justice | Includes bibliographical references and index.
Identifiers: LCCN 2024047890 (print) | LCCN 2024047891 (ebook) | ISBN 9781032592121 (hardback) | ISBN 9781032601861 (paperback) | ISBN 9781003457985 (ebook)
Subjects: LCSH: Law–Study and teaching. | Justice, Administration of–Study and teaching. | Law schools.
Classification: LCC K100.T43 2025 (print) | LCC K100 (ebook) | DDC340.071–dc23/eng/20241010
LC record available at https://lccn.loc.gov/2024047890
LC ebook record available at https://lccn.loc.gov/2024047891

ISBN: 978-1-032-59212-1 (hbk)
ISBN: 978-1-032-60186-1 (pbk)
ISBN: 978-1-003-45798-5 (ebk)

DOI: 10.4324/9781003457985

Typeset in Galliard
by Deanta Global Publishing Services, Chennai, India

Contents

Preface

We hope that *Teaching of Rights and Justice in the Law School: Challenges and Opportunities for Research Led Teaching* will ignite debate, offer differing perspectives and provide a forum for thinking about how we as academics ensure that our teaching is research-led, whilst responding to the needs and views of students and issues such as generational differences in viewpoints on controversial issues. The contributors in their chapters show how they incorporate often controversial aspects of rights and justice (whether this controversy is political, religious or societal) into their teaching in a way that responds to and is ultimately led by academic research. We believe that *Teaching of Rights and Justice in the Law School: Challenges and Opportunities for Research Led Teaching* will help to advance legal education through the opportunity to explore the interplay between rights and justice and how scholars ensure that their teaching is research-led. We would like to thank our contributors who have made editing this book such an enjoyable and collaborative experience.

We would like to thank all those contributors who presented at the *Teaching of Rights and Justice in the Law School: Challenges and Opportunities for Research Led Teaching* Workshop in June 2023 at the University of Worcester. We are grateful for the help and support of our colleagues at the University of Worcester for helping us to convene the workshop, for coming along on the day to support us, and for encouraging us in pursuing this venture.

The team at Routledge have been fantastic and have supported us throughout the proposal, commissioning and publication process. In particular we would like to thank Alison Kirk and Anna Gallagher. We would like to thank Saraswathi Prasanthi (Project Manager) and colleagues at Deanta for all their help and support during the production process. We would also like to thank the two academic reviewers for kindly reviewing the proposal and for their helpful suggestions.

Stephen Hurley
University of Winchester

Chris Monaghan
University of Worcester

Contributors

Radu Cinpoes is Associate Professor of Politics and International Relations at the University of Greenwich.

Sarah Cooper is Professor of Interdisciplinary Criminal Justice at Birmingham City University's College for Law, Social and Criminal Justice.

John Dayton is a Professor of Education Law and Higher Education at the University of Georgia.

Bennett L. Gershman is a Distinguished Professor of Law, Elisabeth Haub School of Law, Pace University, New York.

Lissa Griffin is a Professor of Law, Elisabeth Haub School of Law at Pace University; Visiting Professor, Birmingham City University Faculty of Law.

Jessica Guth is Head of the School of Law at Leeds Trinity University.

Louise Hewitt is an Associate Professor, Director Innocence Project London, University of Greenwich.

Stephen Hurley is a Senior Lecturer in Employment & Equality Law at the University of Winchester.

Chris Monaghan is a Principal Lecturer in Law at the University of Worcester.

Sonya Onwu is an Assistant Professor of Law at the London School of Economics.

Anne-Alexa Stanica has an LLB Hons Law with American Legal Studies, LLM Master of Laws International Human Rights (expected 2024), Birmingham City University Faculty of Laws.

Alice Storey is Senior Lecturer in Law, Lead of the UPR Project at BCU, and Associate Director of the Centre for Human Rights, College of Law, Social and Criminal Justice, Birmingham City University.

Josie Welsh is a Senior Lecturer in Law at the University of Worcester.

1 Introduction

Chris Monaghan and Stephen Hurley

Academics as Teachers, Teachers as Researchers

Teaching is a core part of being an academic. Whether this teaching is to undergraduates or postgraduates, we are tasked with as legal scholars to explain often complex and uncertain areas of law to people who may have no prior knowledge of the subject-matter. Teaching within higher education offers the prospect of enriching the lives of those we teach, and building a rapport with your students, and ultimately constructing a community of learners, from which the teacher can learn from the students on a collegial basis. Whatever the demands on academics within higher education (in the United Kingdom this is the Research Excellence Framework, or in the United States the criteria to obtain tenure) which requires our research to have impact, to influence society, our peers, and decision makers beyond academe, and to ultimately result in outputs and research funding, we are teachers and our research enables us to use our research as a tool for how we teach. 'Rights and justice' is a broad term and those who teach subjects that fall within this term will be acutely aware of the research within their particular specialism and how this research will play a pivotal role in how they will teach their subject. For example within a field such as Employment Law the Equality Act 2010 continues to receive fresh judicial determination and this case law will then receive academic analysis, both the case law and academic analysis are important and play a key role in our own and our students' understanding.

This book came out of a workshop held at the University of Worcester in June 2023. The workshop was organised by the Constitutions, Rights and Justice Research Group and had the aim of giving researchers the space to think about, and articulate, how they taught areas of law that were often controversial and highly sensitive, in a way that encouraged student debate and academic freedom, and taught in a way that was research-led.

We believe that teachers who are researchers can offer their students an opportunity to engage in cutting edge debate, to question the law, to challenge authority and the preconceptions of society. Research does not have to mean academic in a traditional sense, as it can extend to practice, work placements, clinical legal education, or pedagogy. The value of the research-led teacher

DOI: 10.4324/9781003457985-1

is not intended to diminish academics who may not consider themselves as researchers or research active, as research encapsulates scholarship, such as following legal developments within one's specific discipline, and engaging in academic enquiry. We are clear that research is inclusive and belongs to all academics, hence our teaching will encapsulate the exploration of research, enquiry, and engagement with traditional or new viewpoints. *Teaching of Rights and Justice in the Law School: Challenges and Opportunities for Research Led Teaching* is intended to serve as a tool (both as case studies within each chapter, and as a way to stimulate debate) and as a rallying cry for academics interested in academic freedom, the challenges of research-led teaching, and the pedagogy around the teaching of rights and justice.

Our contributors are mainly drawn from legal academia, although the book benefits from a contribution by a political scientist. The book is very much situated in terms of contributors within the United Kingdom and United States, as three of our authors are based at universities within the United States. This offers a transatlantic perspective. Some of our contributors in their chapters also expressly draw upon legal and academic practice in the United States to inform some of the current debates ongoing in the United Kingdom.

What Is Research-Led Teaching

A search on the internet reveals the prevalence of universities marketing their courses as having research-led teaching. Some variants of the term are used, but ultimately it is the idea that undergraduate students will benefit from attending the X University because they will have the advantage of learning about a subject from someone who is engaged in research. This is the language of the university website, but what does this mean to the academics who teach at the X University? Griffiths is clear that the term serves a clear purpose in higher education, namely, to justify the place of research and why it should be funded,

> In the highly charged debate surrounding the research funding dilemma, ideas about the relationship between research and teaching have played a prominent part. In their defence of a policy of concentrating research funding, many of the older universities have invoked the notion of 'research-led teaching'. This term has been used to refer to a supposedly distinctive form of teaching in which research-intensive universities are able to excel.[1]

Given the perceived importance of research-led teaching, it is an ambiguous term across the higher education sector. Observing this, Griffiths states that,

1 Ron Griffiths, 'Knowledge Production and the Research–Teaching Nexus: The Case of the Built Environment Disciplines' (2004) 29(6) *Studies in Higher Education* 709, 720.

'while research-led teaching, research-based teaching and similar terms have been actively deployed by universities in order to highlight the distinctive forms of teaching and learning available in certain institutions, it is not always exactly clear what such terms mean.'[2]

Griffiths saw that there were four 'models of the research–teaching nexus.' These were firstly '*research-led*,' where 'the curriculum is structured around subject content, and the content selected is directly based on the specialist research interests of teaching staff'; secondly, '*research-oriented*' where 'the curriculum places emphasis as much on understanding the processes by which knowledge is produced in the field as on learning the codified knowledge that has been achieved'; thirdly, '*research-based*' where 'the curriculum is largely designed around inquiry-based activities, rather than on the acquisition of subject content'; and finally, '*research-informed* in the sense that it draws consciously on systematic inquiry into the teaching and learning process itself.'[3] For the purposes of *Teaching of Rights and Justice in the Law School: Challenges and Opportunities for Research Led Teaching* we take research-led teaching to mean the broadest engagement with research as part of an academic's teaching practice. It is vital to prevent research being viewed as belonging to a few, or not something that is part of an academics practice if they focus on pedagogy. Teaching and research are interlinked – those teaching rights and justice will either bring in their own research or expose their students to the research of others – either way both require research even if only the former generates an original output.

A problem within higher education is the perception at some institutions that research is paramount and that teaching is secondary. Tony Harland was critical of this approach:

> In the research university this message is clear from the start of a career as new academics are usually hired after a research apprenticeship and on predictions about future research potential. In terms of valuing academic roles, it seems that teaching only has to be good enough.[4]

In England, the Teaching Excellence Framework is an indicator from the government on the importance of teaching, as it sits alongside the Research Excellence Framework. According to the Office for Students, which regulates higher education, '[t]he [Teaching Excellence Framework] is a national scheme run by the Office for Students (OfS) that aims to incentivise excellence

2 ibid, 720.
3 ibid, 722.
4 Tony Harland, 'Teaching to Enhance Research' (2016) 35(3) Higher Education Research & Development 461, 469.

in teaching, learning and student outcomes.'[5] The Office for Students is clear about what students expect from a university, as the Teaching Excellence Framework 'aims to encourage higher education providers to improve and deliver excellence in the areas that students care about the most: teaching, learning and achieving positive outcomes from their studies.'[6] Failure to 'deliver excellent teaching and learning for all their students' will mean that 'if they don't, this will affect their ability to achieve the highest ratings,' which will impact the university's ability to increase tuition fees in line with inflation.[7]

What does this mean for research-led teaching? There is a danger that was outlined by Wei Pan, Debby Cotton, and Paul Murray, who found as a result of their research that 'there was also a perceived trade-off between the time committed to research and teaching activities, where highly research-active staff might not spend enough time on their teaching, or might not be fully aware of industry standards and professional practices.'[8] Those academics who devote a lot of time and attention to research must be alive to the requirements of teaching, although within the academy many colleagues can successfully combine both. According to Ian M Kinchin and David B Hay, '[o]ne of the keys to a good researcher becoming a good teacher is an understanding of the significance of pedagogical content knowledge.'[9] This is because

> An experienced teacher's knowledge is organized from the learners' perspective and is used as a basis for helping students to understand specific concepts. However, a researcher's knowledge is organized from a research perspective and is used as a basis for developing new knowledge in the field.[10]

Thus there is a need for reflection and self-awareness.

The natural connection between teaching and research is relatively new. Mick Healey notes that '[t]he general growth of research in universities did not take off until the beginning of the twentieth century.'[11] This new approach

5 'Regulatory Advice 22: Guidance on the Teaching Excellence Framework (TEF) 2023,' Office for Students, 7 October 2022, available at: https://www.officeforstudents.org.uk/media/77d4955c-4165-4f8f-94cf-315544b6cf25/ra22-tef-framework-guidance-final.pdf, 6.

6 'What Is the TEF,' Office for Students, 24 June 2020, available at: https://www.officeforstudents.org.uk/advice-and-guidance/the-tef/about-the-tef/.

7 'What Is the TEF,' Office for Students, 24 June 2020, available at: https://www.officeforstudents.org.uk/advice-and-guidance/the-tef/about-the-tef/.

8 Wei Pan, Debby Cotton, and Paul Murray, 'Linking Research and Teaching: Context, Conflict and Complementarity' (2014) 51(1) *Innovations in Education and Teaching International* 3, 10.

9 Ian M Kinchin and David B Hay, 'The Myth of the Research-Led Teacher' (2007) 13(1) *Teachers and Teaching: Theory and Practice* 43, 48.

10 ibid, 48.

11 Mick Healey, 'Linking Research and Teaching to Benefit Student Learning' (2005) 29(2) *Journal of Geography in Higher Education* 183, 185.

originated in Germany at the start of the 1800s whereby 'the idea that universities should do anything more than teach' first originated.'[12] Modern academics (dependent on the type of contract on which they are employed) are expected to research and to show that their teaching is research-led. But how do academics and students understand this? Barbara Zamorski offers an empirical perspective on how research-led teaching is viewed by both academics and students.[13] Zamorski's research is based on the Research-led Teaching and Learning Project that she undertook. Her research is clear as to the ambiguous understanding of research-led teaching within higher education:

> Lecturers and students understood 'research-led teaching and learning', in terms of practice, in a variety of ways. Academics discussed this phrase in terms of two principal pedagogical models: as teaching that is heavily informed by their or others' recent research, or where research with or by students forms part of the pedagogy or content of a course. This key distinction was characterised by one senior academic as practices that either 'place students as audiences to the research carried out by their tutors' or those that 'engage students directly in research activity.'[14]

One of the academics whose views were captured by Zamorski summed up this ambiguity, '[i]t's a bit hard to know where teaching and research sort of connect, because they connect in different ways with different people and with different subjects.'[15]

Herein lies the problem – how can we draw a clear line between what to do within and outside of the classroom. Academics may be reticent to claim that they engage in research-led teaching, as to them what they are doing is teaching (albeit underpinned by their own research, writing, and academic experiences) and to add in 'research-led' might make them feel like an imposter or a tad too self-important. This is not a criticism of those academics who confidently assert that their teaching is research-led, but rather it is an acknowledgment about the mysticism of research, the uncertainty about whether what one does counts as research, and the ambiguity concerning the meaning of research-led teaching.

Helen Carr and Nick Dearden's empirical research on what academics understand by research-led teaching revealed the ambiguous and broad understanding of the term amongst legal scholars. Carr and Dearden observe that based on the 32 legal scholars that they surveyed,

12 ibid, 185.
13 Barbara Zamorski, 'Research-Led Teaching and Learning in Higher Education: A Case' (2002) 7(4) *Teaching in Higher Education* 411.
14 ibid, 415.
15 ibid, 415.

> Our analysis of responses revealed that there was no consensus about the meaning and role of [research-led teaching]. Nonetheless certain themes emerged from the data which we examine below; the pedagogic case for [research-led teaching]; [research-led teaching] as something given meaning by the teacher; [research-led teaching] as a marketing tool; and the view that research and teaching are difficult to combine.[16]

As Carr and Dearden note, the people they surveyed could on the whole see a pedagogic benefit for research-led teaching. Yet this revealed more ambiguity and differing of opinion,

> [E]ven the pedagogic enthusiasts found it difficult to be coherent about [research-led teaching], claiming different and perhaps irreconcilable meanings for the term: that research done by others can be used in teaching, alternatively that teachers in higher education not only must seek to be 'research informed' but must be researchers themselves.[17]

The former is inclusionary and would result in a faculty where all colleagues could feel confident in subscribing to research-led teaching, whilst the latter is arguably exclusionary and acts implicitly as a gatekeeper. Interestingly, though not unsurprisingly, Carr and Dearden found that,

> Some participants wanted to shift the focus of discussion to the experience of the teacher and were keen to express that individual academics are passionate about their teaching and would not wish to be regarded only or even primarily as researchers.[18]

From a student perspective, what does research-led teaching mean and what purpose does it serve? As Zamorski notes, the '[s]tudents' understanding of research-led teaching and learning was, to a large extent, configured by their understanding of "research" itself, as well as an expression of their experiences of studying in the university.'[19] The views of the students who took part in Zamorski's research are telling, with one commenting, 'I knew that research went on in universities, it's what they are really famous for, isn't it … But I don't really take much notice of it.'[20] However, research and its role in teaching could also be viewed as a given, 'if they didn't do research, they'd have nothing to teach us would they? I mean, every book you pick up and every,

16 Helen Carr and Nick Dearden, 'Research-Led Teaching, Vehicular Ideas and the Feminist Judgments Project' (2012) 46(3) *The Law Teacher* 268, 272.

17 ibid, 272.

18 ibid, 273.

19 Barbara Zamorski, 'Research-Led Teaching and Learning in Higher Education: A Case' (2002) 7(4) *Teaching in Higher Education* 411, 416.

20 ibid, 417.

like, journal article you look at is based on somebody's research.'[21] It is interesting to observe Zamorski's point that 'a number of the respondents in this study understood research-led teaching in terms of their lecturers' references to their own and others' research and literature with which they were directly familiar.'[22]

Academics themselves could often allude to their own research, but perhaps not necessarily communicate its importance to those they taught. Zamorski gives the example of one student who told her,

> [My teacher] used to come in very excited about it if he had found something out. I remember ... he brought this manuscript in, plonked it down on the table and he was really excited because he'd just finished writing it and it was ready to go to the publishers, or something. I think he just wanted to tell someone. He picked it up and gave it a great big smacking kiss, so you knew it was really important. Mind you, he didn't really tell us what was in it. I would have liked to have known how you go about doing something like that.[23]

Carr and Dearden are clear on the benefits of research-led teaching as it, 'provides a means of avoiding over-reliance on textbooks and an over-emphasis on the delivery as opposed to outcomes, enables a dialogue between research and teaching, and a means for reintegrating the student into the academic endeavour.'[24] But does this exclude academics who may not perceive themselves as research active? The university sector increasingly distinguishes between academics on teaching focused, teaching and scholarship, and traditional academic contracts where research is a large component. Whilst this distinction serves a practical and financial purpose, it reinforces the perception that research-led teaching is not something that can be undertaken by all academics. The hierarchy point is made by Jan Schapper and Susan E Mayson who argue that, 'despite wide recognition of a reciprocal relationship between universities' core activities of research and teaching, relations between them are often experienced by academic staff as quite distinct and differentially rewarded activities.'[25] This is a perception issue where research and teaching are viewed differently by universities, and 'bringing research and teaching closer together' is difficult because of the 'context and process through which relations between research and teaching are structured and practiced are

21 ibid, 417.

22 ibid, 417.

23 ibid, 417.

24 Helen Carr and Nick Dearden, 'Research-Led Teaching, Vehicular Ideas and the Feminist Judgments Project' (2012) 46(3) *The Law Teacher* 268, 278.

25 Jan Schapper and Susan E Mayson, 'Research-Led Teaching: Moving from a Fractured Engagement to a Marriage of Convenience' (2010) 29(6) *Higher Education Research and Development* 641.

highly complex and political.'[26] As Jan Schapper and Susan E Mayson observe, there is an incentive for universities to strengthen this link: namely that 'government funding models ... demand high performing teaching and research academics.'[27]

Challenges

As academics we are evaluated and graded by a range of individuals, institutions, and processes. Our research is peer-reviewed during the publication stage, horror stories abound about the dreaded reviewer two, and if our research is published then this is reviewed and assessed by our peers. This does not touch upon departmental reviews, the appraisal process, and the demands on the Research Excellence Framework in the United Kingdom. Universities have an incentive for academics to engage in research-led teaching.[28] Academics gain much for doing this, and so do students. There is however a potential downside as Lynsey Mitchell notes, '[a]s legal academics we aim to inspire and empower our students. The proliferation of student evaluations and feedback means that there is a greater need to teach content that meets student expectations and concerns.'[29] What happens if our research is controversial and requires us (when engaging in research-led teaching) to touch upon sensitive or controversial issues that have proved so divisive within popular discourse (more often than not through social media)? Should we ensure our teaching is led by this research, or is there a need to take the safest option and skirt around the controversy? 'Rights and Justice' is a broad concept, but given the material covered within it (the rights of children, gender, equality, human rights, and criminal justice, etc.), this is an area of law (and political science) that will always prove most controversial.

What does this mean for the teaching of rights and justice in the law school? Lynsey Mitchell argues that

> While the human rights curriculum offers a vast array of opportunities through which to explore human rights law in such a way that students wish to engage with it, there is a perception that many academics shy away from some issues because they are considered 'controversial' and they wish to avoid controversy in the classroom. Certainly, there is some evidence that academics in the USA have chosen to avoid certain topics

26 ibid, 648.
27 ibid, 648.
28 See 'What Is the REF,' Research Excellence Framework 2029, available at: https://www.ref.ac.uk/about/what-is-the-ref/.
29 Lynsey Mitchell, 'Courting Controversy: the Use of Trigger Warnings in Teaching Human Rights Law' (2024) *The Law Teacher* 1.

> in class to avoid courting controversy. However, it is less clear whether this is the case in UK law schools.[30]

One solution is to pre-warn the students through a content or trigger warning. The use of warnings have been akin to a red rag to a bull in terms of how some sections of the media have reacted to them. As Lynsey Mitchell warns, 'warnings used in UK higher education have attracted an avalanche of negative comment from various newspapers and online commentators, who have borrowed from American media to deride them as pandering to the "snowflake generation."'[31] The labelling of students as the snowflake generation is cruel and a reaction to younger generations' unwillingness to accept cultural standards that were tolerated before (albeit reluctantly). It could be said that this is defensive, but also used as a weapon against those who have a different opinion to their own. In law we will often teach material that has the ability to cause discomfort (if not worse) amongst our students. Lynsey Mitchell observes the dilemma faced by academics – if we know that students might be offended or upset by the material – then do we choose 'the safest option, which often manifests itself as self-censorship through removing any potentially problematic content from modules,' issue a content warning, or do nothing.[32] Reviewing their own empirical research, Lynsey Mitchell writes that several participants noted that they were reluctant to issue an explicit content warning because they considered it problematic to label some subjects as potentially triggering or problematic, and not others.[33] The research carried out by Lynsey Mitchell

> [P]erhaps suggests that academics are more tolerant of content warnings when they are used for material that academics themselves deem problematic, but less tolerant when used where an academic does not consider it so. This is more likely to be seen as a threat to academic freedom.[34]

There may also be a significant distinction to be drawn too between use of trigger warnings regarding potentially upsetting images/case facts/stories of suffering (arguably more easily justified) and those regarding potentially upsetting ideas or viewpoints e.g. 'God exists/God doesn't exist' or 'white privilege exists/white privilege doesn't exist' (arguably less easily justified).

Beth Burkstrand-Reid, June Carbone, and Jennifer S Hendricks offer an American perspective on the considerations when teaching Family Law. They argue that:

30 ibid, 1, 2.
31 ibid, 1, 4.
32 ibid, 8.
33 ibid, 1, 11.
34 ibid, 15.

> The most easily recognizable controversial topics are those that are heavily politicized. Most professors planning a general course in family law will expect reproductive rights, especially abortion, to be controversial. Because abortion is frequently discussed in politics and religion, the grooves of the standard arguments are already worn into many students' minds. Students easily fall back onto talking points and fixed positions rather than remaining open to intellectual exploration of the legal regime surrounding this topic. Politicized topics and rigidity in thinking often go hand-in-hand. This complicates efforts to use controversial topics such as abortion, for example, as a vehicle for teaching in an intersectional manner, such as by incorporating feminist theoretical analyses of legal regimes into case-method teaching.[35]

Another issue identified by Beth Burkstrand-Reid, June Carbone, and Jennifer S Hendricks is that classroom composition may result in '[a] topic [… becoming] controversial or personal not because the issue inherently has resonance for particular students, but because of a lack of diversity in the classroom.'[36] Furthermore, individual students can have an impact on the class environment and disrupt academic debate and discussion amongst their peers, 'one or two students may have extreme or idiosyncratic views and be particularly unwilling to engage respectfully with other views. A few polarizing students can co-opt a discussion or even a course.'[37]

Their advice to academics when teaching potentially controversial or divisive material is to not attempt to treat every class the same and to acknowledge that each cohort is different. This is not designed to intimidate academics to cause them to steer clear of such matters, but rather to not simply follow precedent. As they observe,

> Teaching controversial topics can be the most rewarding aspect of teaching the law. Each class and each student present different challenges. Professors should not be surprised when techniques that were effective in one class are ineffective in the next. Therefore, teaching controversial topics requires a toolbox of techniques and a willingness to engage in honest self-reflection and pedagogical re-examination.[38]

They advise that

35 Beth Burkstrand-Reid, June Carbone, and Jennifer S Hendricks, 'Teaching Controversial Topics' (2011) 49(4) *Family Court Review* 678.

36 ibid, 679.

37 ibid, 679.

38 ibid, 684.

> When it comes to presenting a topic that you expect (or have just discovered) to be controversial, you will want to present all sides of the argument. There are several approaches to doing so. Many professors begin with an opening lecture giving primacy to the side that they do not align with, although this can backfire if the view is a minority in the class. There are many techniques, however, for presenting the controversial topic in its entirety and in context.[39]

Opportunities

Teaching allows us as academics to share ideas, ignite debate, and to learn from our students as colleagues. No one who teaches will ever forget the feeling when a class achieves these. This is part of the privilege of teaching the next generation of lawyers. It is true that debating rights and justice can become controversial, and that there can be significant ramifications for academics when using research-led teaching, given the often contentious nature of the wider debate and how this feeds into using research and a wide spectrum of differing opinion. Academics operate in the 'real world' and not in isolation, and factors such as political ideology influencing the law relating to education do have real consequences when academics risk pushback for teaching and debating areas that are deemed too controversial or too political (i.e., the teaching of Brexit in the United Kingdom and the request for teaching materials from all universities by a member of parliament (MP) from the governing party). The chapters within this book demonstrate the opportunities that are available for academics when teaching rights and justice.

In Chapter 2, Bennett L. Gershman explores the challenges of 'Teaching Constitutional Law When the Constitution Is in Peril.' As Gershman observes,

> [T]eaching Constitutional Law involves more than the study of doctrines, tests, and methodologies. The Constitution is the nation's secular scripture, the grand charter that organizes and implements government power as well as a repository of the values and aspirations of its Founders.

To those teaching Constitutional Law there is a challenge, namely that 'the United States faces its greatest constitutional crisis since the Civil War 185 years ago.' As a teacher of Constitutional Law, Gershman asks how he and his fellow teachers should approach teaching Law School students. He asks key questions such as 'should the teacher always be neutral and objective? Should the teacher refrain from interjecting her personal views about contentious constitutional events?' Gershman ponders whether given the controversy a teacher of Constitutional Law should play it safe and teach a course that will avoid

39 ibid, 681.

'explosive issues,' but is clear that to take such an approach, 'may misrepresent the place of constitutional law today.'

In Chapter 3, John Dayton considers 'Church-State Law: Navigating Culture Wars in Politically Controversial Areas of Law with Research Informed Teaching.' Dayton is clear that this is a topic which is difficult to teach in light of the current culture wars, and thus the teacher has the challenge of how to engage in research informed teaching 'in politically controversial areas of law.' As a case study, Dayton considers how he approaches research informed teaching when discussing 'the U.S. Supreme Court's highly controversial decision in *Kennedy v. Bremerton*.'[40] *Kennedy* offers an example of church-state law in action, as Kennedy was employed by the School District to coach football. However, as Dayton notes '[d]uring this time Kennedy had been leading students in locker-room prayers in violation of well-established law.' The prayers were not universally welcome, as '[a]lthough Kennedy's prayers received enthusiastic support from some, others saw his public prayers as a self-aggrandizing spectacle and as abusing his public position as a coach.' Dayton demonstrates how a law teacher can teach cases like *Kennedy* and offer a critique, and by using 'research informed teaching [ensure] that criticism is based on research, facts, and logical theories.' Thus, Dayton shows how research-informed teaching is so critical within the law school as it 'helps reveal the complexities of issues, in contrast to the overly simplified and politicized talking points from popular media sources.'

Louise Hewitt in Chapter 4 explores 'Clinical Legal Education, Just Not as You Know It: Innocence Work and Its Pedagogical Benefits and Challenges.' Hewitt highlights that clinical legal education offers an important tool to help students gain a 'critical perspective of the criminal justice system,' but through the Innocence Project to also expose 'students to an environment where they are motivated by the hope that they can effect change.' Hewitt's chapter considers the work of the Innocence Project London, where Hewitt is the Director, and how research underpins the work that the students do whilst working as part of the Innocence Project London. Hewitt is clear that the Innocence Project London, and the work that the students do, places an 'emphasis on presenting research concisely and accurately.'

In Chapter 5, Lissa Griffin and Anne-Alexa Stanica look at the role of academics in 'Teaching (In)Justice: Navigating the Fault Lines in Criminal Procedure.' They consider the challenges in teaching criminal procedure and note that when teaching criminal proceedings in US Law School, it is apparent that, '[s]tudents, like others, often have an emotional reaction to the question of what to do with people suspected of breaking the law: they may have themselves been a victim of crime or may know others who have been victimized.' The chapter offers an exploration of a key fault line in the United States, that is the problem of 'prosecutorial suppression of exculpatory evidence.' They then

40 142 S. Ct. 2407 (2022).

consider how this approach varies in the United Kingdom and Spain, and then offer a contrast to the United States, and importantly what does this mean for when teaching law students. The comparative approach will mean that 'students should be able to appreciate that prosecution disclosure of evidence that would be helpful to the defense falls neatly into a continuum from the limited disclosure in the United States, to the broader disclosure in the United Kingdom, to the even broader disclosure in Spain.'

In Chapter 6, Alice Storey explores 'Teaching Law Students to Advocate for Human Rights and Global Justice through the UPR Project at BCU.' Storey is clear about the importance of 'clinical human rights teaching and advocacy within higher education institutions.' The chapter looks at the Centre for Human Rights at Birmingham City University's use of the Universal Periodic Review (UPR) and how scholars use the UPR to 'teach law students to advocate for human rights and global justice.' Storey outlines and analyses how her students can develop their own research through engaging with the Universal Periodic Review Project.

Chris Monaghan in Chapter 7 focuses on 'The Changing Experience of Teaching Public Law since 2010: New Labour, a Novel Coalition Government, the Scottish Referendum, Brexit and the Trampling of Constitutional norms.' His chapter looks at how teachers of Public Law need to respond to the challenges of rapid constitutional change, controversy, and increased political polarisation. This needs to be confronted alongside the changing landscape of higher education in England and Wales, and the need to engage students in a way that is accessible, and avoids 'student fatigue given the dominance of the issues in the press and media.'

In Chapter 8, Sarah Cooper explores intercultural competency as a critical skill for law students using her level 6 law module *American Legal Practice*, as a case study. In her chapter, 'International Internships: Preparing Students for Rights and Justice in Action,' she argues that international internships can have a profound effect on the educational journey of students. She notes that: '[a]s educators, we can maximize our students' potential to thrive as "multicultural beings," ensuring they are well-prepared for the complexities of rights and justice in action on a global stage.' She considers techniques to foster students' intercultural competency prior to their US internment starting and also analyses student-led module design and institutional strategies that may be used. Cooper concludes that: 'Modules like *American Legal Practice* offer a dynamic space to trial innovations, refine good practices, and emphasise the need to cultivate inclusive institutions.'

Chris Monaghan and Josie Welsh in Chapter 9 look at the teaching of 'UK Politics and Human Rights' with reference to the changing political landscape and the attempts by the previous government to repeal the Human Rights Act 1998.

In Chapter 10, Sonya Onwu considers the key issue of legal study skills. In her chapter, 'Upholding the Racial Hierarchy: The so-called Perspectivelessness of Legal Study Skills,' she examines how 'the racist norms and values of

Euro-modern law and hence legal thinking and legal reason, forces global majority students to deny their lived experiences in pursuit of the perspectivelessness of thinking like a lawyer.' She explains how this idea of perspectivelessness is a myth designed to avoid a proper consideration of the racism inherent in Euro-modern law. In a detailed examination of the problems with concepts such as 'reason' and 'thinking like a lawyer,' she shows how this feeds into an overall problem with current law schools seen as 'white spaces' which reinforce racial hierarchies. Onwu draws widely upon her own experiences, academic literature, and also the operation of her own module in Legal Study Skills to consider the best way forward to '[counteract] the problematic that is Euro-modern law.'

In Chapter 11, Radu Cinpoes considers the issue of how teaching on human rights issues should be handled when dealing with 'hot button' topics such as refugees. His chapter, 'Human Rights Education in Times of Adversity: UK Government Agenda on Refugee Issues,' 'aims to engage with questions about the language of the international human rights legal documents compared with that in current government policy, and about how the (over-)use of the word "illegal" shapes the public understanding of refugee issues.' This then influences how human rights issues should be taught. Cinpoes explains how an understanding of current practices of anti-intellectualism and post-truth politics shapes the epistemic paradigm. He emphases the need to address the balance between neutrality and objectivity when teaching and argues that 'a fallible epistemological relativism' should be used to counteract the effects of post-factualism.

In Chapter 12, Stephen Hurley considers the challenges involved in 'Teaching and Debating the Legal Protection of Philosophical Belief in the Workplace in a University Law School.' As an aspect primarily of equality law, the subject naturally lends itself to spirited classroom discussions about whose beliefs should be protected, for what reasons and who should be the arbiter of such questions. Hurley explains how the parallel worlds of philosophical belief in the workplace and the realm of permissible university teaching and research often intertwine. The landmark decision of the Employment Appeal Tribunal in the case of *Forstater* involved a think-tank worker and the controversial issue of gender critical beliefs. The case provided a major clarification of which beliefs are likely to attract legal protection and has informed later decisions involving the conduct of other academics/educators in the United Kingdom. Hurley also notes how issues of academic freedom and philosophical belief protection may be impacted by concepts such as safe spaces, cancel culture, micro-aggressions, and debates around employer/institutional neutrality. He concludes by offering some practical suggestions for better, more respectful teaching taking into account recent legislative changes following the Higher Education (Freedom of Speech) Act 2023.

Finally, in Chapter 13, Jessica Guth looks at, '"But It's All about Women Though" Socio-Legal and Gender Research in the Core cCurriculum' and outlines her journey as a law teacher in teaching Public Law and the Law of the European Union and how she has sought to introduce socio-legal, interdisciplinary, and empirical research. Guth's chapter is based on her attempts to introduce research and debates on gender into her teaching, though using her own and other academic's research.

References

Burkstrand-Reid, B., Carbone, J., and Hendricks, J. S. 'Teaching Controversial Topics' (2011) 49(4) *Family Court Review* 678

Carr, H., and Dearden, N. 'Research-led Teaching, Vehicular Ideas and the Feminist Judgments Project' (2012) 46(3) *The Law Teacher* 268

Griffiths, R. 'Knowledge Production and the Research–Teaching Nexus: The Case of the Built Environment Disciplines' (2004) 29(6) *Studies in Higher Education* 709

Harland, T. 'Teaching to Enhance Research' (2016) 35(3) *Higher Education Research & Development* 461

Healey, M. 'Linking Research and Teaching to Benefit Student Learning' (2005) 29(2) *Journal of Geography in Higher Education* 183

Kinchin, I. M., and Hay, D. B. 'The Myth of the Research-led Teacher' (2007) 13(1) *Teachers and Teaching: Theory and Practice* 43

Mitchell, L. 'Courting Controversy: The Use of Trigger Warnings in Teaching Human Rights Law' (2024) 58(2) *The Law Teacher* 1

Pan, W., Cotton, D., and Murray, P. 'Linking Research and Teaching: Context, Conflict and Complementarity' (2014) 51(1) *Innovations in Education and Teaching International* 3

Schapper, J., and Mayson, S. E. 'Research-led Teaching: Moving from a Fractured Engagement to a Marriage of Convenience' (2010) 29(6) *Higher Education Research and Development* 641

Zamorski, B. 'Research-led Teaching and Learning in Higher Education: A Case' (2002) 7(4) *Teaching in Higher Education* 411

2 Teaching Constitutional Law When the Constitution Is in Peril

Bennett L. Gershman

Introduction – The Challenge for Teachers

Teaching Constitutional Law is a challenge, even in the best of times. The subject is vast and complex. There are no easy cases. There are nuanced and hyper-technical distinctions abound. To the public, the Constitution is an inscrutable document. To law students, the Constitution provokes curiosity, anxiety, and occasional passion.[1]

Studying the United States Constitution offers rich insights into America's legal system. It features the authority of legislatures to create laws and executive officials to enforce laws, the role of the judiciary in reviewing the laws, the relationship between the national government and the states, the identification of fundamental rights and the basis for protecting these rights, and the methodologies used by the U.S. Supreme Court to interpret and apply Constitutional rules.

But teaching Constitutional Law involves more than the study of doctrines, tests, and methodologies. The Constitution is the nation's secular scripture, the grand charter that organizes and implements government power as well as a repository of the values and aspirations of its Founders.[2] The Constitution's Preamble announces its great mission:

1 I would like to thank my students Madison Powers, Daniel Von Statts, and Andy Garcia for their helpful comments; my colleagues Lissa Griffin and Vicky Gannon for insights and advice; Hirem Chhiba, a student at Birmingham City University, for his citation assistance; to Dr. Sarah Cooper, for encouraging my participation in the University of Worcester symposium, and Dr. Chris Monaghan, who led the symposium and invited me to participate.

I have talked to many of my students in preparation for this chapter. My sense is that most students prior to taking the course view the subject as simply reading the text of the Constitution and studying how the Supreme Court applies the textual rules to fact-based situations. However, as the course progressed, students learned that the process was not so simple; they did not foresee the complexity of the issues, the importance of the procedural context, the often ambiguous factual record, and the politics of decision-making.

2 Benjamin Franklin, one of the Constitution's most renowned founders, is said to have responded to Elizabeth Willing Powel's question: 'Well, Doctor, what have we got, a republic or a monarchy?' with the famous quote: 'A republic, if you can keep it.' National Park Service, 'September

DOI: 10.4324/9781003457985-2

> We the People of the United States, in Order to form a more perfect Union, establish Justice, insure domestic Tranquility, provide for the common defense, promote the general Welfare, and secure the Blessings of Liberty to ourselves and our Posterity, do ordain and establish this Constitution for the United States of America.

Probing the Constitution's sparse text and selecting from the thousands of Supreme Court cases is only one facet of the teacher's agenda. Context is critical. Law students need to be exposed to the history, politics, economics, and social setting that underlie and dramatize the Supreme Court's work. And this exposure hopefully can elucidate for students the norms and values that have been the rich amalgam of constitutional law for over two centuries: liberty, equality, justice, human rights, pluralism, security, and the rule of law.

But these are not the best of times. As of this writing, the United States faces its greatest constitutional crisis since the Civil War 185 years ago. Consider these recent headlines: 'A Trump Dictatorship is Increasingly Inevitable. We Should Stop Pretending.'[3] 'Why a Second Trump Presidency May Be More Radical Than his First.'[4] 'A Second Trump Term Will Be Far More Autocratic Than the First. He's Telling Us.'[5] 'A Warning.'[6] Comparisons are made with the unrest and agitation in Weimar Germany during the rise of Hitler ('Make Germany Great Again'). There are dire warnings that if Trump is elected president, he will not be constrained by the U.S. Constitution or the Rule of Law. And it is feared that neither Congress nor the courts will be an impediment to his authoritarian rule. The terms 'Fascism' and 'Dictatorship' increasingly are used to describe a potential Trump presidency.

How should a teacher of Constitutional Law confront these turbulent times? Despite the Constitution's Preamble, the United States never was a 'perfect union;' social and racial 'justice' for too many Americans was always a distant dream; 'domestic tranquility' is an illusion; the 'welfare' of many Americans is in jeopardy. And while the 'liberty' to own a gun may be 'blessed,' the 'liberty'

17, 1787: A Republic, If You Can Keep It' (*National Park Service*) <https://www.nps.gov/articles/000/constitutionalconvention-september17.htm> accessed 16 February 2024.

3 Robert Kagan, 'The Trump Dictatorship: How to Stop It' (*The Washington Post*, 7 December 2023) <https://www.washingtonpost.com/opinions/2023/12/07/robert-kagan-trump-dictatorship-how-to-stop/> accessed 16 February 2024.

4 Charlie Savage, Johnathan Sawn & Maggie Haberman, 'Why a Second Trump Presidency May Be More Radical Than His First' (*N.Y. Times*, 4 December 2023) <https://www.nytimes.com/2023/12/04/us/politics/trump-2025-overview.html> accessed 16 February 2024.

5 Jan-Werner Müller, 'A Second Trump Term Will Be Far More Autocratic than the First. He's Telling Us.' (*The Guardian*, 4 December 2023) <https://www.theguardian.com/commentisfree/2023/dec/04/a-second-trump-term-will-be-far-more-autocratic-than-the-first-hes-telling-us> accessed 16 February 2024.

6 Jeffrey Goldberg, 'A Warning' (*The Atlantic,* 4 December 2023) <https://www.theatlantic.com/magazine/archive/2024/01/warning-second-trump-term/676117/> accessed 16 February 2024.

of women to control their bodies and the right of individuals to make decisions about their gender is not.

Most importantly, consider the teacher's audience. Law students are extremely intelligent people. They have accumulated many years of academic study, from high school to college. They are mature and thoughtful. They are likely to be highly motivated and capable of undertaking the rigorous analysis and conceptualization that are critical for law school success.[7]

But law students also mirror the unrest and division in American society in general. And Constitutional Law is not an anodyne subject. In fact, it may be the most volatile and visceral subject in law school. The teacher must tread carefully in navigating this potential landmine. Given that virtually all the Supreme Court's most contentious decisions include strong dissenting opinions, the teacher can guide students to analyze the correctness of the Justices' contrasting positions without taking sides.

But should the teacher always be neutral and objective? Should the teacher refrain from interjecting her personal views about contentious constitutional events? Consider the 6 January, 2020, insurrection in which a mob, incited by President Trump, attacked the U.S. Capitol, causing destruction and death and terrorizing government officials who fled the building believing their lives were in danger. Would it not be appropriate for the teacher to express her view that President Trump, as Article II commands, did not 'faithfully execute the Office of President of the United States' and did not 'preserve, protect, and defend the Constitution'?[8] Or should the teacher merely assert an equivalence; that Trump, the mob, and members of Congress were all trying to defend the Constitution?[9]

Teachers are aware of their considerable impact on the learning process. Teachers are often seen by students as role models. But most students probably expect the teacher to teach, not to proselytize. It is therefore vital, especially in Constitutional Law, for the teacher to maintain some semblance of neutrality, particularly when the nation is so polarized. The teacher can thereby create a more comfortable environment in which students may feel more confident to express their views. Students surely know that the decisions of a bitterly divided Supreme Court can ignite intense passion not only in the streets but in classrooms as well. Teaching responsibly and effectively in this volatile time while not undermining student trust is a daunting challenge.

7 Whether Constitutional Law is a useful subject to teach in high school or at a university is a valid question. A course in civics, government, or political science likely would be beneficial. Constitutional Law should be a prerequisite for lawyers. Without studying and understanding constitutional principles and doctrines would deprive future lawyers of a bedrock legal foundation to the practice of law.

8 U.S. Constitution (1787) art 2, s 1.

9 For an excellent discussion of this dilemma, see Sean Kammer, 'Reflections on Teaching Constitutional Law in the Midst of Constitutional Crisis' (2022) 67 *South Dakota Law Review* 194.

Constitutional Law and Constitutional Politics

Given the scope of Constitutional Law and its sizeable impact on democracy in a time of political and social discord, it is particularly challenging for the teacher to identify what subjects to emphasize, what decisions to select, and how to guide the discussion. The following sections present several areas that pose difficult challenges to constitutional doctrine and constitutional justice. The areas are race, presidential power, and the role of the U.S. Supreme Court.

Race

Consider the Constitution's treatment of race. Should the teacher assign cases in which the Supreme Court rendered notoriously racist opinions?[10] How should the teacher present the landmark affirmative action case decided last Term?[11] The case is extremely long and produced six separate opinions.[12] The arguments of the Justices capture the complexity of discussing the role of race in American society. Even the term 'racism' eludes clear meaning.[13] Should the teacher ask students whether they see a distinction between discrimination that burdens a race and discrimination that benefits a race? Are college admissions policies a zero-sum process? If a minority applicant is admitted, does it automatically follow that a non-minority applicant will be rejected? Should racial discrimination be analyzed in terms of the motive of the person alleged to have discriminated? Or should an alternative approach give less consideration to the purpose of the discriminator and more to the impact on the person discriminated against?[14] The critical impasse in the affirmative action case mirrors this divide.

Consider the case of *Trump v. Hawaii.*[15] A divided Supreme Court upheld President Trump's proclamation instituting a 'total and complete shutdown of Muslims entering the United States.' Trump had openly called for such a ban and then to deflect attacks at his bigoted order, directed his advisor to 'show me the right way to do it legally.' Would it be appropriate for the teacher to question the majority's reliance for upholding the ban on Trump's argument

10 The most notorious are *Dred Scott v. Sanford* (1857) 60 U.S. 393, *Plessy v. Ferguson* (1896) 163 U.S. 537, and *Korematsu v. United States* (1944) 323 U.S. 214.

11 *Students for Fair Admissions, Inc. v. President and Fellows of Harvard College* (2023) 600 U.S. 161.

12 See Bennet L Gershman, *Modern Constitutional Law – Cases, Notes and Questions* (13th edn, West Academic 2023). As some examples, the *Dobbs* opinion is 213 pages; the *Students for Fair Admissions* is 237 pages; the *Bruen* decision is 135 pages. I have attempted to compress these opinions to a manageable length while trying to remain faithful to the authors.

13 See Jiannbin Shiao & Ashley Woody, 'The Meaning of 'Racism' (2020) 64 *Sociological Perspective* 495.

14 This essentially is the critical issue in *Washington v. Davis* (1976) 426 U.S. 229 and *Village of Arlington Heights v. Metropolitan Housing Development Corp* (1977) 429 U.S. 252.

15 *Trump v. Hawaii* [2018] 138 S. Ct. 2392.

that national security, not religious animus, motivated the ban? The dissent makes this point emphatically. Or would it be appropriate for the teacher to point out that only a few months earlier, the same majority, in *Masterpiece Cakeshop v. Colorado Civil Rights Commission*,[16] chastised the state civil rights commission for criticizing a baker who refused on religious grounds to bake a cake for a gay couple seeking to get married? Would the teacher be acting irresponsibly in pointing to the Supreme Court's infamous decision in *Korematsu v. United States*,[17] in which a bitterly divided Court, also based on national security, upheld the forcible detention of Japanese-Americans during World War II?

By the same token, would it be appropriate for the teacher to contrast *Trump v. Hawaii* with one of the landmark decisions in Constitutional Law, *Youngstown Sheet & Tube Co. v. Sawyer*,[18] which addresses the scope of a president's power during a national crisis and considers whether the Constitution can function effectively during an emergency. President Truman, at the height of the Korean War, when American and allied troops were being slaughtered, took possession of steel factories and kept them running when a labor dispute arose between steel companies and the steel unions that threatened to halt the production of steel. The Supreme Court, 6-3, held that the president's action was unconstitutional.[19] Would the teacher be acting responsibly in posing this question to the class: If President Trump did the same thing today, would the current Court let him get away with it? Should the students see *Youngstown* as a constitutional outlier? Or does teaching that case highlight Trump's abuse of power? Since there likely will be strong views in the classroom on both sides of the issue, should the teacher engage students in this discussion at all?

Presidential Power

Donald Trump's conduct as president had and continues to have a huge impact on Constitutional Law. Below are some of the areas that a teacher may believe are appropriate for classroom discussion.

For example, early in his presidency, Trump's mental health became a focus of concern for critics. They questioned whether the Constitution's Twenty-Fifth Amendment should be activated. This Amendment, enacted after the assassination of President John F. Kennedy in 1963, provides for the transition process if a president is unable or unfit to serve. Section 4 describes the process, which is complicated. It requires the cooperation of the vice president and most of the cabinet and thereafter, if the president contests the result,

16 *Masterpiece Cakeshop v. Colorado Civil Rights Commission* [2018] 138 S. Ct. 1719.
17 *Korematsu v. United States* (1944) 323 U.S. 214.
18 *Youngstown Sheet & Tube Co. v. Sawyer*, [1952] 343 U.S. 579.
19 Congress had not authorized the President's action and there was no basis in the Constitution that authorized the President to commandeer private property for government use.

two-thirds of Congress. Indeed, as Trump's presidency early in his tenure appeared to unravel, constitutional scholars debated whether Trump's chaotic behavior made him ripe for removal under this Amendment.

Consider Trump's attack on a central theme in Constitutional Law, checks and balances. The Framers feared power from a despotic ruler and provided for shared power by three separate branches of government, each able to check the others. Some checks were built into the Constitution, such as the president's veto power, and others were assumed, such as the Supreme Court's power of judicial review and Congress's oversight over executive actions. The Framers did not foresee a president such as Trump essentially mocking the authority of Congress by filling Executive Branch vacancies with temporary appointees, thereby evading the Senate's confirmation process; diverting $3.8 billion that Congress had appropriated for the Defense Department to build a border wall between the United States and Mexico; holding up congressionally-appropriated funding for Ukraine's military defense as leverage in his scheme to extort favors from Ukraine's president; and obstructing congressional investigations by barring executive branch officials from testifying before Congress.

Nor did the Framers foresee a president who would politicize the concept of federalism, or the principle that states are equal players in our federal system. The Constitution mandates popular representation for the House of Representatives and equality in state representation for the Senate. To the Framers, the idea that a president would reward states that voted for him and punish states that did not was never contemplated. But that is exactly what Trump did with respect to health care, tax cuts, immigration, and environmental laws. Trump's famous remark that 'blue states are responsible for the coronavirus death toll' and that 'if you take out the blue states, we're at a very low level,' says it all.

The Framers also feared that a republican government would be vulnerable to a despotic or corrupt president with an authoritarian impulse.[20] They believed that the nation's stability would suffer without a mechanism for the lawful removal of a president. 'No man should be above justice,' James Madison argued. Trump's two impeachments – the only president to be impeached twice – describes for students the constitutional process,[21] but also highlights the inherent weakness of this unique constitutional check on presidential overreach. Trump's impeachment 'trials' featured rules and procedures

20 The Framers most specific anti-corruption provision appears in Article I, section 8, the so-called Emoluments Clause, which prohibits any official from accepting an 'emolument' – judicially-interpreted to mean any profit, gain, or advantage – from any foreign or domestic government. Trump, when he took office, and despite public outcry, retained ownership and control of his business empire. Two lawsuits accused Trump of violating the Emoluments Clause by profiting from his hotels and restaurants in New York and Washington. Lower courts upheld these lawsuits but after Trump lost the election the Supreme Court dismissed the cases as moot.

21 U.S. Constitution (1787) art 2, s 1(6).

that many students might find confusing and arguably unfair – dispensing with witnesses and evidence and requiring a super-majority for conviction despite powerful evidence of Trump's abuse of power.

By the same token, although many presidents have misused the pardon power, which in Article II, section 2, allows a president 'to grant Reprieves and Pardons for Offences against the United States,' no president abused this power as much as Trump. In his final day in office, Trump granted 70 pardons and 74 commutations, almost all to persons who had close connections to him.[22] Indeed, some of these individuals might have given incriminating evidence against him. Constitutional scholars have debated reforming this power, either through a constitutional amendment, or legislative limits such as outlawing self-pardons and prohibiting pardons given in exchange for bribes.

Moreover, as we painfully learned on 6 January, the president is not elected by the people but by obscure 'electors' chosen by the states. Article II, sections 2, 3, and 4 of the Constitution describe the process for appointing state electors to certify the votes for president and then transmitting the certifications to Congress where the vice president 'opens the Certificates,' counts the votes, 'and the person having the greatest number of votes shall be the President.' Only once in American history, in 1860, did states refuse to accept the results. After Abraham Lincoln defeated three presidential candidates, Southern states viewed the selection of a president who would not protect slavery as illegitimate and fought a losing Civil War, resulting in 600,000 deaths, to vindicate their anti-democratic stand. The 6 January insurrection, incited by Trump's challenge of Congress's electoral count, may not seem as catastrophic, but may prove just as costly to our democracy.

Also, although the Constitution protects peaceful protests and not violent insurrections, Trump's response to protests appears to have blurred the line. When mostly peaceful protests erupted after George Floyd's murder, Trump announced that 'I will deploy the United States military and quickly solve the problem.' To do that constitutionally, he would have needed to invoke the Insurrection Act of 1807. Commentators have debated the mechanics of invoking that Act: Must a state first request the presence of military forces? Can a president invoke the Act unilaterally? Does he first have to issue a proclamation ordering insurgents to disperse? Can he simply issue an executive order to send in troops? Finally, Trump's own incitement to the mob on 6 January to storm the Capitol renewed debate over the constitutional test for free speech and incitements to violence.[23]

Trump's actions to save his presidency and undermine the peaceful transfer of power after the 2020 election have produced significant constitutional

22 For the official list of pardons granted by Trump 2017–2021, see https://www.justice.gov/pardon/pardons-granted-president-donald-j-trump-2017-2021

23 See *Brandenburg v. Ohio* (1969) 395 U.S. 444.

questions. The Supreme Court ruled in *United States v. Nixon*[24] that a president could not refuse to comply with a grand jury subpoena for records related to a criminal trial, and in *Clinton v. Jones*,[25] that a president enjoys no immunity for conduct unrelated to his official duties. Trump challenged a subpoena issued by the New York County District Attorney for his tax records and other documents unrelated to his official duties. In *Trump v. Vance*,[26] the Supreme Court emphatically rejected Trump's claim of absolute immunity. The Court also ruled that there is no need for any heightened showing to obtain the materials.[27]

Finally, lawyers, academics, and commentators have focused on section 3 of the Fourteenth Amendment which forbids any person to hold federal or state office who engaged in an 'insurrection or rebellion against the United States,' or gave 'aid and comfort' to others similarly engaged. If Trump is found to have fomented the 6 January insurrection, he could be constitutionally disqualified from seeking the presidency.[28] This provision was enacted by Congress in 1868 to counter efforts by the Confederate states to enact Black Codes to keep the newly emancipated Black Americans subservient to white citizens and to ensure that the Confederate leaders did not obtain amnesty for their attempt to destroy the nation. The House 6 January committee's final report states explicitly that Donald Trump instigated a criminal insurrection to overturn the lawful results of the 2020 presidential election by the mob attack on the Capitol to prevent enforcement of the Constitution's election protocols. Trump has been indicted by federal and state authorities for several conspiracies and obstructions in trying to overturn the results of the 2020 election by illegally trying to stop the constitutional process to certify the 2020 electoral votes and defraud voters of their legitimate votes.[29]

24 *United States v. Nixon* (1974) 418 U.S. 683.

25 *Clinton v. Jones* (1987) 520 U.S. 681.

26 *Trump v. Vance* (2020) 140 S. Ct. 2412.

27 As I write this piece, Trump is again claiming absolute immunity from being prosecuted by the Justice Department for conspiring to undermine the 2020 election.

28 Lawsuits have been filed in several states seeking to disqualify Trump from the presidency. The Colorado Supreme Court, in a landmark decision, ruled that under section 3 of the Fourteenth Amendment Trump is disqualified from seeking the presidency and may not appear on the Colorado ballot in the 2024 presidential election. See (2023) *Anderson v. Griswold*, 2023 WL 8770111. A few days later Maine's Secretary of State ruled that Trump's name could not appear on the presidential ballot.

29 After Trump's several indictments, a New York court and a federal court issued gag orders restricting Trump's public comments disparaging judges, prosecutors, court personnel, and their families. Questions were raised over whether the orders are constitutional under the First Amendment either because they are too broad or unduly vague. The courts have not yet specified exactly how the orders will be enforced or what punishment Trump could face if he decides to violate them. The gag orders seek to balance Trump's right of free speech against his intimidation of courts, staff, and witnesses as well as ensuring that his statements do not affect how the case is presented. Additionally, the orders express concerns that Trump's statements could stoke violence and harassment toward the targets he mentions.

The Supreme Court

The most contentious subject in Constitutional Law today is the legitimacy and reputation of the Supreme Court. The concept of legal justice cannot be divorced from the integrity of the judges who administer the law. Should a teacher discuss the Court's reputation? Should the teacher raise questions about whether the six Justices in the current majority (three of whom were appointed by President Trump) may be the most politically partisan and ideologically driven group in the Court's history? Should the Court's ethical problems be discussed? Should the leak to the media of *Dobbs v. Jackson Women's Health Organization*, arguably the most contentious opinion in the Court's history, be raised? Should the teacher demonstrate that many of the Court's recent decisions, notably on abortion and guns, are significantly out of touch with public opinion?

Public confidence in the Supreme Court and the methodology which the Court uses to interpret the Constitution are low. The Court is perceived by many Americans as heavily hyper-partisan and ethically challenged.[30] It is also seen as demonstrating a cavalier disregard for public opinion. The death of former Supreme Court Justice Sandra Day O'Connor highlights the sense that the conservative majority functions today in a bubble and has no clue or simply doesn't care about the destructive consequences their decisions have on society. Justice O'Connor, the first woman to serve on the Court, was a conservative but not an ideologue. She was always cognizant of the real-world consequences of the Court's decisions and was willing to reassess her views to try to locate a middle position.[31]

The partisanship of the Justices is one reason for the Court's unpopularity. Should the teacher point out to students the radically conservative approach to judging by several of the Justices? Should the teacher through questions and comments suggest that these Justices decide cases based not on legal principle but on political and ideological motivation? Should the teacher note Justice Amy Coney Barrett's widely quoted remark, 'We're not a bunch of partisan hacks.' Should the backgrounds of Supreme Court Justices be noted? The six conservative Justices are acolytes of the Federalist Society – the most conservative legal organization in America – and owe their judgeships in large part to

30 According to a recent poll, only 25% of Americans have confidence in the Court. Legislative efforts have sought to impose term limits on the Justices and add more Justices to the Court. See Jeffrey M. Jones, 'Confidence in U.S. Supreme Court Sinks to Historic Low'(Gallup, 23 June 2022) <https://news.gallup.com/poll/394103/confidence-supreme-court-sinks-historic-low.aspx

31 See *Planned Parenthood of Southeastern Pennsylvania v. Casey* (1992) 505 U.S. 83; *Grutter v. Bollinger*, [2003] 539 U.S. 306. Justice O'Connor served in the Arizona state legislature for five years before becoming its majority leader. She understood how judicial decisions can affect people's lives. Many other Justices have held elective office before their elevation to the Court. Since Justice O'Connor's resignation there have been no Justices on the court with her elective experience and since her departure the court has swung hard to the right.

support from that group. Is a Justice's background relevant to studying the Justice's opinions?

It should be clear by now to students that rulings by these conservative Justices are easily predictable. The teacher will likely discuss pending cases. Should the teacher make predictions about the outcome? Did anybody doubt the result of the Court's landmark Affirmative Action case last Term? The class will have studied Supreme Court precedents strongly upholding affirmative action programs in higher education, including Justice O'Connor's powerful opinion in *Grutter v. Bollinger*.[32] The conservative majority held such programs unconstitutional, reiterating numerous times that the Constitution is 'color-blind.'

Similarly, how should the teacher present the landmark abortion decision, *Dobbs v. Jackson Women's Health Organization*,[33] in which the Court for the first time in its history struck down as unconstitutional a fundamental right that had existed for several generations. The majority asserted that *Roe v. Wade* was 'manifestly wrong.' The teacher should challenge students to articulate the legal principle forming the basis for the *Dobbs* decision. And in articulating that principle, students should be challenged to explain how ten Justices since *Roe* – Republicans and Democrats alike – supported a woman's fundamental right to an abortion. Needless to say, however, the teacher is treading into dangerous constitutional territory.

Should the teacher refrain from or minimize the ethical quagmire in which several of the Justices find themselves? Some of these Justices look more like a group of corrupt politicians than Justices of the highest court in the land. Chief Justice John Roberts never even thought of disqualifying himself after his wife made millions of dollars recruiting top lawyers who argued cases before the Court;[34] Justice Neil Gorsuch sold real estate property to the chief executive officer of a law firm that argued at least 22 cases before the Court but he never disclosed that information which was legally required;[35] Justice Clarence Thomas, the most conspicuously compromised Justice of all, was treated to millions of dollars in luxury vacations and lavish travel from a billionaire Republican megadonor who also renovated for free the home of

32 *Grutter v. Bollinger* [2002] 539 U.S. 306.

33 *Dobbs v. Jackson Women's Health Organization* [2022] 597 U.S. 215. The leak of the majority draft abortion opinion by Justice Samuel Alito overturning *Roe v. Wade* and the failed efforts to find the culprit did not sit well with many Court watchers, especially after the Justices themselves reportedly were given special dispensations from being interrogated aggressively or having to sign affidavits.

34 Steve Eder, 'At the Supreme Court, Ethics Questions Over a Spouse's Business Ties' (*N.Y. Times* 31 January 2023) <https://www.nytimes.com/2023/01/31/us/john-roberts-jane-sullivan-roberts.html> accessed December 12 2023.

35 Amy Wang, 'Gorsuch Property Sale Renews Calls for Supreme Court Ethics Reform' (*The Washington Post*, 25 April 2023) <https://www.washingtonpost.com/politics/2023/04/25/neil-gorsuch-property-sale-law-firm-ethics/> accessed December 11 2023.

Thomas's mother and paid the tuition for a young man Thomas referred to as his son.[36] Thomas never reported these expenditures, which likely were in violation of the law, nor did he report the half million dollars in income his wife received from the ultra-conservative Heritage Society.[37] Whether the Court's recent adoption of an ethics code will be a meaningful restraint is unclear.

Moreover, little attention has been given to the unprecedented dilution in the Court's workload. It used to be commonplace for the Court each Term to decide between 150–200 cases. The Court last Term decided less than 60 cases, fewer cases than the Court has handed down since 1864, in the middle of the Civil War. There has been a steep downward trend since Congress several years ago gave the Court exclusive authority to manage its case docket, and not to have to accept mandatory appeals. Since then, the Court has gradually reduced the number of cases it reviews annually. What might students think about this trend?

Along with the reduction in cases in which the Court grants review is the significant upward trend in the Court's so-called 'shadow docket' in which the Court disposes of cases of overriding significance – abortion, congressional redistricting, Covid vaccination mandates, restrictions on social media platforms – without having to read briefs, hear oral arguments, or have lengthy conferences. What might students think about this trend?

And these trends have important consequences for constitutional law. If far fewer cases involving important constitutional questions are being decided, then lower courts have the last word, for good or bad. There are less criminal procedural cases on the docket, virtually no military appeals, and fewer death row interventions. Some might say this is good news; the less involved the Court is, the less damage it can do.

But the Court's retreat from deciding more cases, and more important cases, tends to freeze constitutional law in areas that need review. To many observers the Court looks like an imperial majestry, a privileged institution that makes its own rules, does less work, cares little for transparency and the appearance of ethical uprightness, and does not appear committed to serving the public interest and the cause of justice.

There is another concern over the Court's methodology which the teacher should share with students. The conservative majority's new methodology is to interpret the Constitution's text as it supposedly was intended to be understood by the Framers. This so-called 'originalist' approach is relatively recent.

36 Alison Durkee, 'Clarence Thomas: Here Are All the Ethics Scandals Involving the Supreme Court Justice Amid Unpaid RV Loan Revelations' (Forbes, 26 October 2023)<https://www.forbes.com/sites/alisondurkee/2023/09/22/clarence-thomas-here-are-all-the-ethics-scandals-involving-the-supreme-court-justice-amid-koch-network-revelations/?sh=740ddd085df7> accessed 16 February 2024.

37 Darragh Roche, 'Clarence Thomas Failing to Note Wife Ginni's $680 K Side Income Resurfaces' (*Newsweek*, 29 September 2022)<https://www.newsweek.com/clarence-thomas-wife-ginni-680k-side-income-1747449> accessed 16 February 2024.

It is a peculiar way of reading the Constitution since it is virtually impossible to infer any specific intent of the Framers or ratifiers with respect to any Constitutional provision.[38] Several of the most consequential decisions of the Court have been based almost exclusively on the 'original intent' of the Framers.

The 'originalist' approach appears to have been a conservative reaction to the Court's expansion of fundamental rights in the 1960s and 1970s. How should the teacher deal with the subject? A good teacher would certainly want students to be conversant with the historical context of a decision. For example, in *District of Columbia v. Heller*,[39] Justice Scalia relied exclusively on history to argue that the Framers recognized an individual right to own a gun to protect 'hearth and home,' not merely to have a gun to serve in a militia, as the Second Amendment provides. But Justice Scalia also recognized that gun regulations that are intended to protect public safety are permissible.

However, in the landmark case of *New York State Rifle & Pistol Assn. v. Bruen*,[40] Justice Thomas arguably misused history to conclude that gun regulations that had no analog in 1787 were unconstitutional. But regardless of whether students may applaud the result, they should be forced to confront Thomas' methodology. Rather than using the Court's familiar approach to fundamental rights analysis by weighing the right against the government's interest, Thomas virtually ignored 'public safety.' He did not consider whether New York's law, written over 100 years ago, was enacted to protect the public safety of the citizenry from unregulated guns. In fact, no other fundamental rights analysis rests exclusively on history. As Justice Breyer commented in his mocking dissent,

> Some of the laws New York has identified are too old. But others are too recent. Still others did not last long enough. Some applied to too few people. Some were enacted for the wrong reasons. Some may have been based on a constitutional rationale that is now impossible to identify. Some arose in historically unique circumstances. And some are not sufficiently analogous to the licensing regime at issue here.[41]

Thomas's distortion of history did not sit well with one of the most conservative members of the Court. In a constitutional case involving the interpretation of the Sixth Amendment.[42] Thomas asserted that 'longstanding practice' and 'considerable authority' supports the practice of admitting a confession of

38 The following comment of Chief Justice John Marshall is frequently cited: '[W]e must never forget that it is a *constitution* we are expounding.' *McCullogh v. Maryland* (1819) 17 U.S. 316, 407 (emphasis in original).

39 *District of Columbia v. Heller* [2008] 554 U.S. 570.

40 *New York State Rifle & Pistol Asson. v. Bruen* [2022] 597 U.S. 1.

41 *New York State Rifle & Pistol Asson. v. Bruen*, 142 S. Ct. at 2190.

42 *Samia v. United States* [2023] 599 U.S. 635.

one defendant at a joint trial. For this 'longstanding practice,' Thomas cited four cases, all written over a century ago, and all resting exclusively on a rule of evidence, not the Constitution. Thomas's misuse of history was ridiculed by Justice Amy Conery Barrett.[43] 'Why drop it in 1896,' she asked rhetorically. The claim of 'longstanding practice' is overstated; at most it describes a 'snapshot.' The Court overclaims, she wrote. 'While history is often important and sometimes dispositive, we should be discriminating in its use. Otherwise, we risk undermining the force of historical arguments.'

Conclusion

Teachers of Constitutional Law face hard choices. The subject is extensive and complex; the principles are elusive; and the subject matter incites strong feelings. The teacher should be very clear about her objectives. What exactly does the teacher want to accomplish in the classroom? A teacher seeks to cover as much of the material as possible given time constraints and the capacity of students to absorb the material. The teacher may prepare a syllabus that is relatively safe – staying away from explosive issues like abortion, guns, race, and presidential power.

But such restraint may misrepresent the place of Constitutional Law today. Given the turbulent times, the teacher needs to confront objectively the myriad issues that percolate in the Supreme Court and are passed on to society. With a heavily partisan Court whose popularity is low, and writing high-profile decisions that will be vilified by many students, the teacher's task is difficult. The teacher should mediate the discussion so that diverse and sometimes hostile points of view are considered, strive to find common ground and some mediating principles, and all the while hoping that students will approach the subject with patience, common sense, and open minds.

If the teacher has provoked the students to think long and hard about the role of law and justice in American society without suggesting any 'right answers,' and use the Constitution as the legal context for that investigation, then the teacher should feel somewhat less uneasy and perhaps even feel a certain measure of success.

Bibliography

Durkee A, 'Clarence Thomas: Here Are All the Ethics Scandals Involving the Supreme Court Justice Amid Unpaid RV Loan Revelations' (*Forbes*, 26 October 2023)

Eder S, 'At the Supreme Court, Ethics Questions Over a Spouse's Business Ties' (*New York Times*, 31 January 2023)

Gershman B, *Modern Constitutional Law – Cases, Notes and Questions* (13th edn, West Academic 2023)

43 ibid, 655–657.

Goldberg J, 'A Warning' (*The Atlantic*, 4 December 2023)

Jones J, 'Confidence in U.S. Supreme Court Sinks to Historic Low' (*Gallup*, 23 June 2022)

Kagan R, 'The Trump Dictatorship: How to Stop It' (*The Washington Post*, 7 December 2023)

Kammer S, 'Reflections on Teaching Constitutional Law in the Midst of Constitutional Crisis' (2022) 67 *South Dakota Law Review* 194

Müller J, 'A Second Trump Term Will Be Far More Autocratic than the First. He's Telling Us' (*The Guardian*, 4 December 2023)

National Park Service, *September 17, 1787: A Republic, If You Can Keep It* (National Park Service 2023)

Office of Pardon Attorney, U.S. Department of Justice, https://www.justice.gov/pardon/pardons-granted-president-donald-j-trump-2017-2021 (accessed 9 January 2024).

Roche D, 'Clarence Thomas Failing to Note Wife Ginni's $680 K Side Income Resurfaces' (*Newsweek*, 29 September 2022)

Savage C, Sawn J & Haberman M. 'Why a Second Trump Presidency May Be More Radical Than His First' (*New York Times*, 4 December 2023)

Shiao J & Woody A, 'The Meaning of "Racism"' (2020) 64 Sociological Perspective 495–517

Wang A, 'Gorsuch Property Sale Renews Calls for Supreme Court Ethics Reform' (*The Washington Post*, 25 April 2023)

3 Church–State Law

Navigating Culture Wars in Politically Controversial Areas of Law with Research-Informed Teaching

John Dayton

Introduction

Politically controversial issues often end up in our courts for resolution. Accordingly, in research and teaching, law professors necessarily address issues that are politically controversial. Teaching law has always been challenging. It has become even more difficult, however, in an increasingly post-fact, post-truth culture where classroom discussions may too often devolve into socially popular political tribalism and shallow repetitions of media talking points.

This chapter provides an example of navigating culture wars in politically controversial areas of law with research informed teaching.[1] Research informed teaching can help broaden discussions beyond the exchange of shallow media talking points through deeper examinations of, for example, the history of the law in the area; the unique facts and issues presented by the case; the political, social, economic, and demographic factors in which the case occurred and was decided; and research-based analyses of the case's impact and meaning going forward. As an example case in research informed teaching, this chapter reviews the U.S. Supreme Court's highly controversial decision in *Kennedy v. Bremerton*[2] by providing a brief history of U.S. church-state law; a fact-based summary of *Kennedy*; placing *Kennedy* in a broader context; and an analysis of the legal impact and meaning of *Kennedy*.

A Brief History of U.S. Church–State Law

The United States is a nation of immigrants. Many immigrants came to the United States to escape religious oppression and seek religious freedom. The result is that the United States is among the most religiously diverse nations, making it difficult for any single religious denomination to control government. European Age of Enlightenment principles of secularism further shaped U.S. governance structures to formally separate the state from the church,

1 See, e.g., University of Plymouth, *Research Informed Teaching*, https://www.plymouth.ac.uk/about-us/teaching-and-learning/guidance-and-resources/research-informed-teaching.
2 142 S. Ct. 2407 (2022).

DOI: 10.4324/9781003457985-3

with the goal of safeguarding the integrity of both institutions. In contrast to nations founded on religious identities, religion is only mentioned twice in the U.S. Constitution. Both mentions are prohibitions against government involvement in religion.[3]

By setting reasonable boundaries between the church and state, the United States avoided many of the religious conflicts other nations faced when government powers were misused to force religious beliefs and practices on citizens. The U.S. Supreme Court played an important role in clarifying and defending constitutional boundaries between church and state, especially in the post-World War II era, as the United States was becoming increasingly religiously diverse.

Nonetheless, despite over 60 years of relative stability in church-state law, the United States is now in an existential struggle over the role of religion in government and society. One side in this culture war seeks to protect the U.S. tradition of separation of church and state and advance religious pluralism. The other side seeks to use the power of government to advance Christian Nationalist views.

At the core of this debate is the First Amendment to the U.S. Constitution which declares: 'Congress shall make no law respecting an establishment of religion, or prohibiting the free exercise thereof.'[4] The dual commands of the First Amendment's religion clauses, the Establishment Clause and the Free Exercise Clause, prohibit government from establishing religious preferences; and require the government to respect the free exercise of religion. Together these clauses have been interpreted as requiring official neutrality by government concerning religion.[5]

The First Amendment was seen as establishing a reasonable 'wall of separation' between church and state for the mutual protection of religion and government.[6] The wall of separation between church and state is not, however, an absolute wall of separation. The Court has recognized that religion plays a central role in many people's lives, and that it has been a driving force of societal change throughout much of human history.[7] Religion cannot be banned from the public square without also banning the free expression of people who hold religious beliefs.[8]

History proves, however, that in a religiously diverse nation few issues are more divisive, and potentially dangerous, than whose religion will be officially recognized and favored in the public square.[9] These concerns are especially

3 U.S. Const. art. VI; amend. I.
4 U.S. Const. amend. I.
5 School District of Abington Township v. Schempp, 374 U.S. 203 (1963).
6 See generally John Dayton, *Education Law: Principles, Policies and Practice* (John Dayton 2019).
7 ibid.
8 ibid.
9 ibid.

heightened in public schools where impressionable children under compulsory attendance laws and the authority of school employees are subject to peer pressure and separated from the guidance and protections of their own parents, ideal conditions for aggressive religious proselytizers to indoctrinate and coerce vulnerable children. For these reasons the Court has sent a clear message concerning religion in public educational institutions: School employees may not use their official powers to endorse or coerce religion.[10]

The Court consistently rejected arguments for public school sponsored prayer, whether direct or indirect, 'voluntary' or involuntary, noting that the First Amendment 'tried to put an end to governmental control of religion and prayer.'[11] The Court has consistently held that private religious choices belong to parents, students, and the clergy, and not to public school officials and employees.[12] Being elected to the public school board or hired to work in a public school does not authorize anyone to assume religious control over other peoples' children. By accepting a position in a public school, school officials and employees are required to honor the commands of the U.S. Constitution, including the First Amendment, while acting in their official capacities.[13]

For over 60 years the law was clear: Public school employees must remain neutral concerning religion while acting in their official capacities, and not use their official positions and powers to religiously coerce students under their authority.[14] Nonetheless, Establishment Clause violations continued in far too many public schools, in clear violation of well-established law, as was the case in *Kennedy v. Bremerton* where an assistant football coach had a long history of violating well-established law and school policy through on-duty religious activities with students.[15]

A Summary of *Kennedy v. Bremerton*

Bremerton School District (BSD) is a small school district in a religiously diverse community near Seattle, Washington, USA.[16] Joseph Kennedy, the plaintiff in *Kennedy v. Bremerton*, was employed by BSD as an assistant football coach from 2008 to 2015. During this time, Kennedy had been leading students in locker-room prayers in violation of well-established law. BSD

10 *Lee v. Weisman*, 505 U.S. 577 (1992).

11 *Engel v. Vitale*, 370 U.S. 421, 435 (1962).

12 *Engel v. Vitale*, 370 U.S. 421 (1962); *School District of Abington Township v Schempp*, 374 U.S. 203 (1963); *Lee v Weisman*, 505 U.S. 577 (1992); *Santa Fe Independent School District v Doe*, 530 U.S. 290 (2000).

13 U.S. Const. art. VI.

14 Above (n 12).

15 See, e.g., *Freedom From Religion Foundation, Pray to Play: Christian Coaches and Chaplains are Converting Football Fields into Mission Fields* (2015), available at: https://ffrf.org/images/PraytoPlayReport.pdf, accessed on 16 February 2024.

16 869 F.3d 813 (9th Cir., 2017), *rehearing en banc denied*, 880 F.3d 1097 (9th Cir., 2018), *cert. denied*, 139 S. Ct. 634 (2019).

claimed it was unaware of this practice.[17] Controversy in the community escalated when Kennedy announced that after watching a film about a public school coach leading students in prayers, he was religiously called to 'take a knee at the 50-yard line and offer a brief, quiet prayer of thanksgiving for player safety, sportsmanship, and spirited competition' immediately following the game and in full public view of students and others in attendance.[18] Kennedy initially appeared alone under the stadium lights for his 50-yard line prayers, then some team members joined him, and eventually he was joined by a majority of the team. Kennedy claimed his 'prayer lifts up the players and recognizes their hard work and sportsmanship during the game.'[19]

Not everyone in this religiously diverse community welcomed Kennedy's dramatic public prayers. Although Kennedy's prayers received enthusiastic support from some, others saw his public prayers as a self-aggrandizing spectacle and as abusing his public position as a coach to proselytize and coerce vulnerable students into his personal religious beliefs, causing division in the school and community.[20] Kennedy, however, was not deterred by these concerns, and instead kept pushing the boundaries in his 50-yard line prayers.[21]

In response to reports of unlawful religious proselytizing by an employee, BSD Superintendent Leavell investigated whether Kennedy was complying with BSD's 'Religious-Related Activities and Practices' policy which required compliance with the Establishment Clause.[22] The investigation revealed that the 'coaching staff had received little training regarding the District's policy.'[23] Leavell sent Kennedy a letter clarifying BSD policy and finding that Kennedy's conduct was 'problematic' under the Establishment Clause.[24]

Kennedy initially ceased his public prayers and instead gave only secular motivational speeches to the students and crowd, waiting until the crowd had left to go to the 50-yard line to pray alone.[25] No one objected to this practice. A few weeks later, however, Kennedy's lawyer sent a letter to Leavell stating that Kennedy must be allowed to resume his post-game prayers to the crowd as a reasonable accommodation of his free exercise of religion, asserting that Kennedy's official duties ended when the game ended, and that Kennedy was acting as a private citizen in his 50-yard line prayers.[26] It should be noted, however, that Kennedy's job description and supervisors at BSD confirmed that he was still on duty; public school employees do not define their own

17 ibid, 834 (Smith, J., concurring).
18 ibid, 816.
19 ibid.
20 ibid, at 817 note 1.
21 ibid, 816.
22 ibid, 817.
23 ibid.
24 ibid.
25 ibid.
26 ibid, 818.

work duties; Kennedy continued to present himself as a BSD coach during prayers; and private citizens did not have access to the field at that time nor access to a captive audience of students and spectators.[27]

Meanwhile, Kennedy's 50-yard line prayers were receiving growing national attention, including through his own social media and public appearances.[28] This included support from then presidential candidate Donald Trump.[29] The situation quickly escalated into full culture-war chaos when Kennedy resumed his 50-yard line prayers attracting large crowds including supporters from outside the school district. School officials received complaints of students being knocked over as Kennedy's supporters jumped barriers and ran among the cheerleaders, band members, and players to join Kennedy on the 50-yard line.[30] Reacting to Kennedy's prayers a 'Satanist' group announced it would also conduct post-game ceremonies on the BSD field if others were allowed to pray at that time and place.[31] In response, school officials tried to prevent anyone from entering the field post-game by posting signs, publicizing the new policy, and working with local police to stop people from jumping barriers and entering the field.[32]

Leavell sent Kennedy a second letter thanking him for his initial compliance but noting that subsequently his conduct was inconsistent with BSD policy. Leavell emphasized BSD respected religious expression by employees but that 'such exercise must not interfere with the performance of job responsibilities, and must not lead to a perception of District endorsement of religion.'[33] Leavell further noted that contrary to the opinion of Kennedy's attorney, Kennedy was still on duty during his post-game public prayers as 'paid assistant coaches in District athletic programs are responsible for supervision of students not only prior to and during the course of games, but also during the activities following games and until players are released to their parents or otherwise allowed to leave.'[34]

School officials offered to work with Kennedy to find a reasonable accommodation. They suggested making a private room available to Kennedy for prayer immediately before and after games and allowing Kennedy to pray on the 50-yard line after the students and spectators dispersed. BSD officials expressed concern to Kennedy that otherwise 'any reasonable observer saw a District employee, on the field only by virtue of his employment with the District, still on duty, under the bright lights of the stadium, engaged in what

27 ibid, 818–819.
28 ibid, 818.
29 See e.g., Michael Gryboski, *Trump Meets Coach Kennedy: Suspension for Praying After Games 'Outrageous, Very Sad'*, Christian Post (4 October 2016).
30 869 F.3d 813, 818 (9th Cir., 2017).
31 ibid.
32 ibid.
33 ibid, 818–819.
34 ibid, 819.

was clearly, given your prior public conduct, overtly religious conduct.'[35] School officials reminded Kennedy that 'while on duty for the District as an assistant coach, you may not engage in demonstrative religious activity, readily observable to (if not intended to be observed by) students and the attending public.'[36] Because Kennedy continued to violate BSD policy, even after receiving a clear letter of direction, Kennedy was placed on paid administrative leave.

At the conclusion of the season the BSD Athletic Director did not recommend renewing Kennedy's coaching contract because Kennedy failed to follow BSD policy and 'failed to supervise student-athletes after games due to his interactions with [the] media and [the] community.'[37] Kennedy filed suit against BSD claiming violations of the First Amendment and Title VII, and that BSD retaliated against him for his exercise of free speech. Kennedy sought an injunction against BSD ordering the district to cease discriminating against him; reinstate him as a coach; and allow him to kneel and pray on the 50-yard line immediately following games.[38]

The federal district court rejected Kennedy's request for a preliminary injunction.[39] The court found that BSD's actions were justified in order to avoid violating the Establishment Clause as 'Kennedy was dressed in school colors ... chose a time and event [that] ... is a big deal for students, and used that opportunity to convey his religious views while he was still responsible for the conduct of his students.'[40] The court further noted the coercive impact of Kennedy's conduct finding 'if you are an athlete, you are impressionable, and you ... want to please your coach to get more playing time, to shine.'[41] The court concluded that reasonable observers 'would have seen Kennedy as a coach, participating, in fact, leading an orchestrated session of faith' in open violation of the Establishment Clause.[42]

Having lost at both the trial court and the court of appeals in his effort to obtain a preliminary injunction, Kennedy appealed to the U.S. Supreme Court. The U.S. Supreme Court denied certiorari and the case was returned to the trial court for resolution.[43] The trial court granted summary judgment for the school district.[44] The court of appeals affirmed.[45] Kennedy sought certiorari from the U.S. Supreme Court again. The Court, with three new members,

35 ibid.
36 ibid.
37 ibid.
38 ibid, 820–821.
39 ibid, 821.
40 ibid.
41 ibid.
42 ibid.
43 139 S. Ct. 634 (2019), *cert. denied*.
44 443 F. Supp. 3d 1223 (W.D. Wa. 2020).
45 991 F.3d 1004 (9th Cir. 2021).

Justices Gorsuch, Kavanaugh, and Barrett, all appointed under President Trump who publicly supported Kennedy, granted certiorari the second time.[46]

Contrary to every court that had previously reviewed the case, the Court's new Trump appointed conservative supermajority ruled in favor of Kennedy in a 6-3 opinion written by Justice Gorsuch and joined by Chief Justice Roberts and Justices Thomas, Alito, Kavanaugh, and Barrett.[47] Justice Gorsuch began his opinion with a statement that directly contradicted both the facts of the case and well-established law:

> Joseph Kennedy lost his job as a high school football coach because he knelt at midfield after games to offer a quiet prayer of thanks. Mr. Kennedy prayed during a period when school employees were free to speak with a friend, call for a reservation at a restaurant, check email, or attend to other personal matters. He offered his prayers quietly while his students were otherwise occupied. Still, the Bremerton School District disciplined him anyway. It did so because it thought anything less could lead a reasonable observer to conclude (mistakenly) that it endorsed Mr. Kennedy's religious beliefs.[48]

Justice Sotomayor, in dissent, and joined by Justices Breyer and Kagan, objected that the majority opinion portrayed a very different set of facts than the established record in the trial court.[49] For example, Justice Gorsuch's majority opinion described Kennedy's conduct as 'a quiet prayer of thanks' and asserted that Kennedy 'offered his prayers quietly while his students were otherwise occupied.'[50] Justice Sotomayor's dissenting opinion included photographs from the evidence admitted in the trial court showing Kennedy's prayers at BSD were in fact dramatic public religious performances, directly and purposely engaging students and others in his prayers, with Kennedy under the stadium lights at the 50-yard line ritualistically holding up team helmets and leading proselytizing prayers while surrounded by students, and not just 'a quiet prayer of thanks ... while his students were otherwise occupied' as Justice Gorsuch claimed.[51]

Justice Sotomayor's dissenting opinion objected to more than just the majority's misrepresentation of the facts, stating:

> Today's decision goes beyond merely misreading the record. The Court overrules *Lemon v. Kurtzman*, and calls into question decades of

46 142 S. Ct. 857 (2022).
47 142 S. Ct. 2407 (2022).
48 ibid, 2415–2416.
49 ibid, 2434 (Sotomayor, J., dissenting).
50 142 S. Ct. 2407 (2022).
51 ibid, 2436 (Sotomayor, J., dissenting).

> subsequent precedents that it deems 'offshoots' of that decision. In the process, the Court rejects longstanding concerns surrounding government endorsement of religion and replaces the standard for reviewing such questions with a new 'history and tradition' test. In addition, while the Court reaffirms that the Establishment Clause prohibits the government from coercing participation in religious exercise, it applies a nearly toothless version of the coercion analysis, failing to acknowledge the unique pressures faced by students when participating in school-sponsored activities. This decision does a disservice to schools and the young citizens they serve, as well as to our Nation's longstanding commitment to the separation of church and state.[52]

The dissenting opinion concluded:

> Today's decision is particularly misguided because it elevates the religious rights of a school official, who voluntarily accepted public employment and the limits that public employment entails, over those of his students, who are required to attend school and who this Court has long recognized are particularly vulnerable and deserving of protection. In doing so, the Court sets us further down a perilous path in forcing States to entangle themselves with religion, with all of our rights hanging in the balance. As much as the Court protests otherwise, today's decision is no victory for religious liberty. I respectfully dissent.[53]

Putting *Kennedy v. Bremerton* in Context

As a nation of immigrants, the religious, racial, political, and social context of the United States is always changing. Those changes have been accelerating since World War II. Especially in the last few decades, the United States has seen dramatic changes in religious and racial/ethnic demographics. Fears related to these changes have fueled reactionary political movements that were at the core of how *Kennedy v. Bremerton* got to the U.S. Supreme Court and the resulting opinion from the Court. *Kennedy* cannot be fully understood without understanding the context in which the case occurred and was decided.

Changing Religious Demographics

Just after the World War II, 76% of Americans were members of a house of worship. That number was still 70% in 1999. But by 2020, most Americans

52 ibid, 2434 (Sotomayor, J., dissenting) (citations omitted).
53 ibid, 2453 (Sotomayor, J., dissenting) (citations omitted).

were not members with only 47% retaining membership.[54] This change is generational, with mostly younger Americans rejecting traditional religious roles.[55] The change is also regional/political with northern Democrats in progressive states less likely to be church members than Republicans in southern conservative states.[56]

The U.S. has seen a rapid decline in the numbers of citizens identifying as White Christians. Among the findings from a 2017 national study were that White Protestant Christians, who dominated U.S. politics from the founding of the nation, were no longer a majority in the United States. The number of Americans identifying as White and Christian was 43% (down from 81% in 1976) and 30% as White and Protestant (down from 55% in 1976). Religiously unaffiliated is now the largest group in 20 states, states in the more progressive coastal and northern Great Lakes regions, with younger Americans throughout the nation more likely to be non-Christian and non-White.[57]

Changing Racial/Ethnic Demographics

From 1790 through 1900 between 80% to 90% of Americans identified as White.[58] Black Americans made up most of the remainder of citizens living mostly in the southern United States. There were few citizens of other races. In the last century, however, the United States has become increasingly racially and ethnically diverse. Based on immigration rates, birth rates, and other factors, White Americans are projected to become a minority race by 2043 when the United States becomes a majority minority nation.[59]

Most Americans understand that the United States is rapidly changing, becoming far more diverse in terms of religion and race/ethnicity. But Americans are sharply divided on what this means, and what should be done in response. Progressive Americans generally welcome a more diverse America and believe U.S. laws, institutions, and communities must embrace these changing realities and work to assure equality for all persons. More conservative

54 Jeffrey M. Jones, 'U.S. Church Membership Falls Below Majority for First Time' *Gallup* (2021), available at: https://news.gallup.com/poll/341963/church-membership-falls-below-majority-first-time.aspx, accessed on 16 February 2024.

55 ibid.

56 ibid.

57 See Public Religion Research Institute (PRRI), 'America's Changing Religious Identity' (2017), available at: https://www.prri.org/research/american-religious-landscape-christian-religiously-unaffiliated, accessed on 16 February 2024.

58 U.S. Census Bureau Data, 'United States-Race and Hispanic Origin: 1790 to 1990' (2023), available at: http://www.census.gov/population/www/documentation/twps0056/tab01.pdf, accessed on 16 February 2024.

59 U.S. Census Bureau Data, 'U.S. Census Bureau Projections Show a Slower Growing, Older, More Diverse Nation a Half Century from Now' (2012) available at: https://www.census.gov/newsroom/releases/archives/population/cb12-243.html, accessed on 16 February 2024.

Americans, however, generally take a darker view of these changes, with many believing that 'their nation' (i.e., a White Christian nation) is being taken away from them, and the remedy is to fight these changes and take 'their' nation back. Fears of White Christians losing social relevance and political control are fueling reactionary political movements, including White Christian Nationalism, an ideological belief that God gave the United States to White Christian Protestants who have a Divine right to control the United States.[60]

Although the political battles are generally fought over issues like abortion; school prayer; LGBTQ+ equality; book banning; gun rights; etc., the real fight is over who will control government and the authority to enforce their views on others through laws and police powers. Candidate Trump captured the U.S. presidency in 2016 by building a coalition of voters over issues including building walls to stop immigration; an alleged 'war on Christmas'; Christianizing the nation; and the passive-aggressive normalization of neo-fascism and political violence. Trump rejected U.S. democratic norms and international alliances, e.g., attacking NATO and other democratic institutions and praising authoritarians. Fascist rhetoric and threats of political violence became the energizing force of the 'Make America Great Again' (MAGA) political movement. The movement embraced White supremacists, Confederate sympathizers, and neo-Nazis, with a common thread of threats of political violence. It was not coincidence that many of the January 6 insurrectionists who attacked the U.S. Capitol to keep Trump in power after he lost reelection in 2020 were displaying Confederate and Nazi symbols in opposition to U.S. democratic norms.

The Rise of White Christian Nationalism

In alliance with fundamentalist Christians and a coalition of authoritarian groups, President Trump attempted to reshape government institutions to support his agenda, including the U.S. Department of Justice and federal courts. Trump and other far-right politicians increasingly embraced the rhetoric and agenda of White Christian Nationalism, tapping into deep fears of demographic change. White Christian Nationalism quickly went from a fringe belief to a central principal of one of the two major political parties in the United States.[61]

60 See e.g., Philip Gorski & Samuel L. Perry, *The Flag and the Cross: White Christian Nationalism and the Threat to American Democracy* (Oxford University Press 2022).

61 See e.g., Stella Rouse & Shibley Telhami, 'Most Republicans Support Declaring the United States a Christian Nation,' Politico (Sept. 21, 2022) available at: https://www.politico.com/news/magazine/2022/09/21/most-republicans-support-declaring-the-united-states-a-christian-nation-00057736, accessed on 16 February 2024.

One theory of what was fueling this reactionary political movement is 'terror management theory.'[62] According to this theory humans live in a perpetual unresolvable tension between their instinct for self-preservation and the inevitability of death, creating a deep existential paradox, i.e., survival is essential, but death is inevitable. People turn to identities they believe are more enduring than themselves for comfort, e.g., immortality promised by religion and identities and ideologies that will live on past their deaths. Driven by fear and fear-based anger, they will support leaders who champion these ideas and attack anyone challenging these ideas. Supporting ideological leaders is equated to self-preservation. Facts that undermine this support are disregarded. If leaders can defend your tribe and its dogma nothing else matters, explaining the cult-like following of White Christian Nationalist politicians like former President Trump.

In empowering Trump, religious fundamentalists had two items at the top of their political agenda: Abortion and school prayer. By overturning well-established law in these areas, evangelicals would send a clear message to their culture wars opponents that they were now in charge, and they are able to use the force of government, including laws and police powers, to enforce compliance with their beliefs. Although he was only a one-term president, Trump stunningly placed three new members on the Supreme Court creating a 6-3 conservative supermajority, all Christian, which promptly overturned *Roe v. Wade*[63] in *Dobbs v. Jackson*,[64] ending legal protections for abortion rights, and endorsed Kennedy's proselytizing prayers in *Kennedy v. Bremerton*, both contrary to well-established law.[65]

An Analysis of the Meaning and Impact of *Kennedy v. Bremerton*

Through research informed teaching, professors may provide a deeper understanding of the meaning and impact of a case by, for example, analyzing its impact on the legal system and in practice. This section provides a review of cases and law review articles citing the Court's decision in *Kennedy* to assess the impact of the decision on the legal system. An analysis of the likely impact of *Kennedy* on practice is also provided.

In the year following the Court's decision in *Kennedy*, 148 cases and 194 law review articles cited *Kennedy*.[66] The 148 reported cases citing *Kennedy*

62 See e.g., Sheldon Solomon, Jeff Greenberg & Tom Pyszczynski, '*A Terror Management Theory of Social Behavior*' (1991) 24 *Advances* in *Experimental Social Psychology* 93.

63 410 U.S. 113 (1973).

64 142 S. Ct. 2228 (2022).

65 142 S. Ct. 2407 (2022).

66 A search of the Westlaw database was conducted October 23, 2023, for all cases, law review articles, and administrative letters in the database citing *Kennedy v. Bremerton*, 142 S. Ct. 2407 (2022). The search results were analyzed using a process of legal analysis and synthesis. See John Dayton, *Legal Research, Analysis, and Writing* (John Dayton 2020). This section

covered a broad range of legal issues ranging from religious free speech to objections to COVID-19 mandates.[67] But none of the reported cases citing *Kennedy* were factually on all fours with *Kennedy*, i.e., none of these cases were focused on public school employees praying while on duty. In the cases citing *Kennedy*, the most cited points of law were related to burdens of proof and how they may be met.[68]

A total of 194 law review articles cited *Kennedy*.[69] Most of the law review articles cited *Kennedy* incidentally and did not directly focus on *Kennedy* or the subject of public employees praying while on duty. The law review articles that directly addressed *Kennedy* generally fell into two categories: Articles critical of the Court's decision;[70] and articles supportive of the Court's decision.[71] Articles critical of the Court's decision in *Kennedy* commonly included themes such as: 'The Court's holding is erroneous because it distorted precedent, misconstrued the facts, and disregarded the heightened First Amendment challenges in public schools to improperly reduce Joseph Kennedy's demonstrative prayer to "private," constitutionally protected speech.'[72] Articles supportive of the Court's decision in *Kennedy* commonly included themes such as 'out of a misguided reverence to neutrality ... lower courts attempted to sanitize all religion from the public square. But secularism is not neutrality. This is not required or permitted by the First Amendment.'[73]

builds on research for a forthcoming publication: John Dayton, 'One Year After *Kennedy v. Bremerton*: An Analysis of the Impact of the Court's Decision on Church–State Law in Public Schools' *Education Law Reporter* (in-press).

67 ibid.

68 ibid.

69 ibid.

70 See e.g., Martha M. McCarthy, '*Kennedy v. Bremerton*: Farewell to the Establishment Clause' (2022) 402 *Education Law Reporter* 557; John Dayton, 'An Analysis of the U.S. Supreme Court's Decision in *Kennedy v. Bremerton School District*: What is the Status of Church–State Law After *Kennedy*?' (2022) 402 *Education Law Reporter* 1; Isabella Henry, '*Kennedy v. Bremerton School District*: Throwing a Red Flag for the Public-Employee Speech Arena to Challenge the Court's Hail Mary' (2023) 82 *Maryland Law Review* 1067; Justin Driver, 'Three Hail Marys: *Carson, Kennedy*, and the Fractured Détente over Religion and Education' (2022) 136 *Harvard Law Review* 208; Ann L. Schiavone, 'Mere Shadow' of a Conflict: Obscuring the Establishment Clause in *Kennedy v. Bremerton*' (2023) 61 *Duquesne Law Review* 40.

71 See e.g., Stephanie H. Barclay, 'The Religion Clauses after *Kennedy v. Bremerton School District*' (2023) 108 *Iowa Law Review* 2097. (2023); Mallory B Rechtenbach, 'Personal Foul—Encroachment: How Kennedy v. Bremerton School District Blurs the Line Between Government Endorsement of Religion and Private Religious Expression' (2023) 35 *Regent University Law Review* 295; Samantha Thompson Lipp, 'The Rise of Public School Prayer with the Demise of Lemon v. Kurtzman' (2023) 74 *Mercer Law Review* 1221.

72 Isabella Henry, '*Kennedy v. Bremerton School District*: Throwing a Red Flag for the Public-Employee Speech Arena to Challenge the Court's Hail Mary' (2023) 82 *Maryland Law Review* 1067, 1101–1102.

73 Mallory B Rechtenbach, 'Personal Foul—Encroachment: How Kennedy v. Bremerton School District Blurs the Line Between Government Endorsement of Religion and Private Religious Expression' (2023) 35 *Regent University Law Review* 295, 336–337.

In summary, despite dramatic reactions to the Court's decision in *Kennedy*, the impact of the decision on the legal system, as reflected in published cases and law review articles one year after the decision, was surprisingly limited. This may reflect confusion about the holding in *Kennedy* given the narrow version of facts in the Court's opinion, i.e., the Court did not actually rule on the highly disruptive conduct that caused the litigation, and instead answered a far more narrow question for which there was no real controversy: Whether Kennedy had a right to a brief, private, personal prayer alone and not in the presence of students or a captive audience.[74] No one contested that claim. To the contrary, the school district offered Kennedy that option as a reasonable accommodation.[75]

Kennedy was not the wrecking ball that sent Jefferson's wall of separation between church and state tumbling down, which some had feared, and others had hoped for. It is important to note that the Court did not endorse any state sponsored prayer in *Kennedy*.[76] The Court did not endorse coach-led locker room prayers or post-game religious talks with students;[77] inviting members of the clergy to lead prayers;[78] or broadcasting prayers through school forums.[79] The Court recognized limits on employee speech rights including religious speech.[80] The Court also recognized religious coercion is unlawful[81] although the current Court's definition of coercion is narrower than the standard previously recognized as well-established law.[82] Nonetheless, the Court recognized the continued validity of *Lee* and *Santa Fe*.[83] It should also be noted that the pre-*Lemon* school prayer cases were not overruled in *Kennedy*, although their teachings were largely ignored by the *Kennedy* Court.[84] The Court did not even directly overrule *Lemon*, but instead asserted *Lemon* had been abandoned long ago.[85] On closer examination, the Court's opinion in *Kennedy* did little beyond affirming an individual right to a 'brief, quiet, personal religious observance[86] ... while his students were otherwise occupied' which wasn't contested;[87] abandoning *Lemon*; and replacing the *Lemon* test with a history and tradition test, a stunning opinion at the time, but not the end of

74 142 S. Ct. 2407, 2415 (2022).
75 869 F.3d 813, 825 (9th Cir., 2017).
76 142 S. Ct. 2407 (2022).
77 ibid, 2423.
78 ibid, 2431.
79 ibid.
80 ibid, 2423.
81 ibid, 2429.
82 ibid, 2434 (Sotomayor, J., dissenting).
83 ibid, 2442–2443. *Lee v. Weisman*, 505 U.S. 577 (1992); *Santa Fe v. Doe*, 530 U.S. 290 (2000).
84 142 S. Ct. 2407 (2022).
85 ibid, 2427.
86 ibid, 2433.
87 ibid, 2415.

church–state separation in the United States. Handing a highly public school prayer victory to Trump and his Christian Nationalist supporters may have been more important than the technical legal scope of the victory.

The deeper dangers of *Kennedy* are the chilling direction that it signals for the Court, and its impact on practices in public schools. Concerning the trajectory of the Court, *Kennedy* is another step down a deeply troubling path. It is clawing back rights and imposing minority Christian Nationalist political views on the nation through judicial fiat:

> It does not take a Religion Clause scholar to see what has been going on at the Supreme Court over the last dozen years. Religion always wins. Sometimes religion is on the side of challengers, like those in *Kennedy* and *Carson*. Sometimes religion is on the side of government, as in cases like *Town of Greece* and *American Humanist*. And in almost every case the religion in the case is Christianity. The Christian Nationalists among us, and among the Justices, must be thrilled. For those of us who know and fear the consequences of a state dominated by a single faith, the Court's trajectory is chilling.[88]

The Court's decision in *Kennedy* no doubt emboldened religious proselytizers in public schools to use their public positions and unique access to other people's children as Kennedy did. And discouraged administrators from responding to complaints, after seeing the fate of school officials in *Kennedy*, who in good faith attempted to enforce the Establishment Clause and school policies, consistent with well-established law, but still lost the case.[89]

The conservative supermajority in *Kennedy* also disturbingly ignored some dark realities documented by lower courts. School officials reported that with Trump championing coach Kennedy 'the District began receiving a large number of emails, letters, and calls, many of them threatening'[90] and:

> [t]he head coach himself also resigned after 11 years in that position, expressing fears that he or his staff would be shot from the crowd or otherwise attacked because of the turmoil created by Kennedy's media appearances. Three of five other assistant coaches did not reapply.[91]

Kennedy's years of locker room proselytizing also no doubt caused great stress for minority faith students as they wrestled with turning their backs on their

88 Ira C Lupu & Robert W Tuttle, '*Kennedy v. Bremerton School District* – A Sledgehammer to the Bedrock of Nonestablishment', *Expert Forum: Law and Policy Analysis* (28 June 2022), available at: https://www.acslaw.org/expertforum/kennedy-v-bremerton-school-district-a-sledgehammer-to-the-bedrock-of-nonestablishment, accessed on 16 February 2024.

89 142 S. Ct. 2407 (2022).

90 ibid, 2437 (Sotomayor, J., dissenting).

91 ibid, 2440 (Sotomayor, J., dissenting).

own family's faith to join Kennedy's prayers or confronting the intimidating realities of being 'outed' as a member of a minority faith for not participating in the coach's prayers with their peers.[92] In *Kennedy* the Court opened the door to the very dangers the Establishment Clause was intended to prevent, although much of the harm is likely to go unreported because victims fear retaliation and administrators may be reluctant to act even when blatant violations are reported.[93]

For decades Christian Nationalists had at the top of their political agenda creating a Court that opposed abortion and favored school prayer, objectives they had failed to achieve politically because a growing majority of Americans support abortion rights and oppose school sponsored prayer.[94] Nonetheless, the Court's new conservative supermajority delivered victories on these issues to Christian Nationalists in *Dobbs* and *Kennedy*.[95] By continuing to impose an unpopular Christian Nationalist political agenda under the guise of law, however, the Court is on a collision course with political and cultural reality in an increasingly religiously diverse nation.[96]

In *Dobbs* and *Kennedy*, for the first time in its history, the Court clawed back rights previously recognized by the Court as well-established law, i.e., rights of reproductive freedom in *Dobbs*[97] and rights of religious freedom in *Kennedy*.[98] Justice Thomas suggested in *Dobbs*, that the clawing back of rights by the Court was only beginning and the current Court had a duty to 'correct the error' concerning prior Courts recognizing rights to obtain contraceptives in *Griswold*; rights to engage in private consensual sexual acts in *Lawrence*; and rights to marriage equality in *Obergefell*.[99]

92 See e.g., Mary Beth Tinker, *Foreword: Special Issue of the Education Law & Policy Review Free Speech in Public Educational Institutions*, 2 (2015) *Education Law & Policy Review* 10 (public school coach attempted to coerce participation in team prayer; family received anti-Semitic death threats; the family was terrorized for months; their home was vandalized; and a fire was set on their property).

93 ibid.

94 See e.g., Aaron Blake, 'Abortion Rights Have Long Been Ballot Winners but Post-Roe, Even More So', *Washington Post* (9 November 2023), available at: https://www.msn.com/en-us/news/politics/abortion-rights-have-long-been-ballot-winners-but-post-roe-even-more-so/ar-AA1jFL46, accessed on 16 February 2024; Pew Research Center, 'In U.S. Far More Support Than Oppose Separation of Church and State' (28 October 2021), available at: https://www.pewresearch.org/religion/2021/10/28/in-u-s-far-more-support-than-oppose-separation-of-church-and-state, accessed on 16 February 2024.

95 142 S. Ct. 2407 (2022).

96 See e.g., Pew Research Center, 'How U.S. Religious Composition Has Changed in Recent Decades' (13 September 2022), available at: https://www.pewresearch.org/religion/2022/09/13/how-u-s-religious-composition-has-changed-in-recent-decades, accessed on 16 February 2024.

97 142 S. Ct. 2228 (2022).

98 142 S. Ct. 2407 (2022).

99 142 S. Ct. 2228, 2301 (2022) (Thomas, J., concurring). *Griswold v. Connecticut*, 381 U.S. 479 (1965); *Lawrence v. Texas*, 539 U.S. 558 (2003); *Obergefell v. Hodges*, 576 U.S. 644 (2015).

Ultimately, the power of the Court is based on broad respect for the opinions of the Court. If the Court continues to impose minority Christian Nationalist views on a majority that has rejected those views, limits will be imposed on the Court's reach, including limits from voters. Following the Court's decision in *Dobbs* last year, voters rejected the result of the Court's decision in every state voting on access to abortion, including voters in deep red conservative states.[100] Similarly, Christian Nationalist affiliated groups experienced big loses in school board elections, school boards that will control the future selection, hiring, and retention of coaches and other public school employees.[101] Six Justices may now control the Court. But one year after *Dobbs* and *Kennedy* we are seeing emerging evidence that they cannot control the nation.[102]

Conclusion

This chapter provided an example of navigating culture wars in politically controversial areas of law with research informed teaching in the context of U.S. church–state law. The goal is not to avoid passionate debates in the classroom, but rather to have those debates informed by research and refereed by facts. Further, the goal is not to avoid taking 'sides' on issues, but to base opinions on research, facts, and logical theories, and not political posturing and talking points.

Law professors taking positions on issues is hardly novel. Taking a position on controversial issues can be highly useful in stimulating discussions and examining the complexities of issues and cases. This chapter is critical of the Court's opinion in *Kennedy*, but with research informed teaching, that criticism is based on research, facts, and logical theories. Controversial issues can powerfully fuel learning, but only when minds are open to new perspectives. Research informed teaching can help open minds and push students out of comfortable but shallow talking points and into authentically wrestling with the challenging realities in which controversial cases arise, are adjudicated by courts, and shape future law.

Research informed teaching, especially when drawing on interdisciplinary research, promotes critical thinking and helps students to better understand the broader context of issues and conflicts, as well as the seamless nature of

100 Kate Zirnike, 'Ohio Vote Continues a Winning Streak for Abortion Rights', *New York Times* (7 November 2023), available at: https://www.nytimes.com/2023/11/07/us/politics/ohio-abortion-amendment.html, accessed on 16 February 2024.

101 See e.g., Tori Otten, 'Moms for Liberty Falls Flat on Its Face in School Board Races', New Republic (8 November 2023), available at: https://newrepublic.com/post/176746/moms-liberty-falls-flat-face-school-board-races-iowa, accessed on 16 February 2024.

102 Above (n 100) and (n 101); see e.g., Mark Murray, 'Poll: 61% of Voters Disapprove of Supreme Court Decision Overturning Roe', NBC News (22 June 2023), available at: https://www.nbcnews.com/meet-the-press/first-read/poll-61-voters-disapprove-supreme-court-decision-overturning-roe-rcna90415, accessed on 16 February 2024.

learning and practice. Clarifying a common set of facts helps students to focus on making arguments firmly grounded in facts. Introducing students to relevant theories and theoretical lenses can help students in viewing issues and cases from different perspectives and in developing deeper understandings of the issues and cases.[103] Data-based analyses of the impact of cases on the legal system, through analyses of cases, law review articles, etc., can help students more clearly see the impact of cases on legal scholarship, courts, and in practice. Research informed teaching helps reveal the complexities of issues, in contrast to the overly simplified and politicized talking points from popular media sources. While the news cycle may be driven by soundbites, legal studies classrooms must prepare students to understand greater depth and breadth in important issues and cases so that they may find better solutions for disputes in practice.

Bibliography

Barclay, Stephanie H. 'The Religion Clauses after Kennedy v. Bremerton School District' (2023) 108 *Iowa Law Review* 2097–2113

Dayton, John. 'An Analysis of the U.S. Supreme Court's Decision in Kennedy v. Bremerton School District: What is the Status of Church-State Law After Kennedy?' (2022) 402 *Education Law Reporter* 1–22

Dayton, John. *Education Law: Principles, Policies and Practice* (Wisdom Builders Press 2019)

Dayton, John. *Legal Research, Analysis, and Writing*. Athens (Wisdom Builders Press 2020)

Dayton, John. 'One Year After Kennedy v. Bremerton: An Analysis of the Impact of the Court's Decision on Church-State Law in Public Schools' (2024) 416 *Education Law Reporter* 729–748

Driver, Justin. 'Three Hail Marys: Carson, Kennedy, and the Fractured Détente over Religion and Education' (2022) 136 *Harvard Law Review* 208–261

Gorski, Philip and Samuel L. Perry. *The Flag and the Cross: White Christian Nationalism and the Threat to American Democracy* (Oxford University Press 2022)

Henry, Isabella. 'Kennedy v. Bremerton School District: Throwing a Red Flag for the Public Employee Speech Arena to Challenge the Court's Hail Mary' (2023) 82 *Maryland Law Review* 1067–1102

Lipp, Samantha Thompson. 'The Rise of Public School Prayer with the Demise of Lemon v. Kurtzman' (2023) 74 *Mercer Law Review* 1221–1257

McCarthy, Martha M. 'Kennedy v. Bremerton: Farewell to the Establishment Clause' (2022) 402 *Education Law Reporter* 557–569

Rechtenbach, Mallory B. 'Personal Foul—Encroachment: How Kennedy v. Bremerton School District Blurs the Line Between Government Endorsement of Religion and Private Religious Expression' (2023) 35 *Regent University Law Review* 295–337

Schiavone, Ann L. 'Mere Shadow of a Conflict: Obscuring the Establishment Clause in Kennedy v. Bremerton' (2023) 61 *Duquesne Law Review* 40–48

103 See e.g., John Dayton, *Legal Research, Analysis, and Writing* (John Dayton 2020).

Solomon, Sheldon, Jeff Greenberg and Tom Pyszczynski. 'A Terror Management Theory of Social Behavior' (1991) 24 *Advances in Experimental Social Psychology* 93–159

Tinker, Mary Beth. 'Foreword: Special Issue of the Education Law & Policy Review Free Speech in Public Educational Institutions' (2015) 2 *Education Law & Policy Review* 10–20

4 Clinical Legal Education, Just Not as You Know It

Innocence Work and Its Pedagogical Benefits and Challenges

Louise Hewitt

Introduction

The work of an innocence organisation in England and Wales starts after the criminal appeals process where an individual is maintaining their innocence. A person convicted at Crown Court has 28 days in which to make an appeal, starting the process with leave to appeal.[1] If leave to appeal is granted, but a full appeal is dismissed, then the only body left to consider the claim of innocence is the Criminal Cases Review Commission (CCRC).[2]

The CCRC is an independent body that has the power to return criminal cases back to the Court of Appeal Criminal Division (Court of Appeal). It was established in March 1997 by virtue of s.8 Criminal Appeal Act 1995. Applicants must show either fresh evidence or a new legal argument not used at trial or on appeal, to which the CCRC applies the statutory real possibility test identified in s.13 of the Criminal Appeal Act 1995:

> A reference of a conviction, verdict, finding or sentence shall not be made [...] unless the Commission consider that there is a real possibility that the conviction, verdict, finding or sentence would not be upheld were the reference to be made.

There is no statutory definition of 'real possibility' but Lord Bingham attempted to provide one in *R v Criminal Cases Review Commission (ex parte Pearson)*:

> The 'real possibility' test [...] denotes a contingency which, in the Commission's judgment, is more than an outside chance or a bare possibility, but which may be less than a probability or a likelihood or a racing

1 Appeal a Crown Court decision, available at: www.gov.uk/appeal-against-crown-court-verdict, accessed 3 January 2024.

2 ibid.

DOI: 10.4324/9781003457985-4

> certainty. The Commission must judge that there is at least a reasonable prospect of a conviction, if referred, not being upheld.[3]

This limited explanation means that any application being put together by an innocence organisation, or indeed any legal representative needs to focus on showing that the fresh evidence and/or new legal argument undermines the safety of the conviction. The English Criminal Appeal Act 1995 provides the Court of Appeal with the power to quash a conviction if it is found to be 'unsafe.'[4] The CCRC's statutory real possibility test is intrinsically linked to the Court of Appeal's test of safety, in that a review of any application has to consider whether there is a real possibility that the Court of Appeal will find the conviction unsafe. The process of investigating a claim of innocence to meet the requirements for an application to the CCRC presents a unique learning opportunity for students working for an innocence organisation, one which is rooted in clinical legal education. When students deconstruct a claim they have to research all aspects of the case to inform their learning, which ultimately informs their ability to make an application to the CCRC on behalf of their client.

The innocence project model of learning started in America in 1992,[5] and was introduced in England and Wales in 2004 when the Innocence Network UK (INUK) was established.[6] At its peak, the INUK was supporting over 30 innocence organisations across the country, before it folded in 2015.[7] Research has demonstrated a steep decline in innocence organisations in England and Wales.[8] The reasons for are three-fold. First there is significant time commitment involved in administering an innocence organisation.[9] From personal experience, it takes time to manage the cases, in terms of the number of students working on each one, arranging casework meetings where everyone can attend, managing the writing of letters to the client, managing the minutes of each meeting (although they are written by a student in each group they need to be checked to ensure they can be understood), and managing the workload on a week-by-week basis.

Second, the case intake process is ongoing and requires careful organisation,[10] not only to ensure that individuals are receiving application packs but also

3 [1999] 3 All ER 498.
4 Section 2 (1)(a) Criminal Appeal Act 1995.
5 Keith A Findley, 'The Pedagogy of Innocence: Reflections on the Role of Innocence Projects in Clinical Legal Education' (2006) 13(1) *Clinical L Rev* 1101.
6 Michael Naughton & Carole McCartney, 'The Innocence Network UK The Innocence Network UK' (2004) 7(2) *Legal Ethics* 150.
7 Louise Hewitt & Claire McGourlay, 'Still Standing: Innocence work in England and Wales' (2021) 2(3) *The Wrongful Conviction Law Review* 226.
8 ibid, 236.
9 ibid.
10 ibid.

to manage the ongoing communication with applicants to help them obtain the necessary paperwork for the case assessment process. All applications are assessed to determine the possibility of fresh evidence or a new legal argument, either of which are necessary for an application to the CCRC. It is made clear to each applicant that the case assessment is not a judgment as to the validity of their claim to innocence. The documents required for the case assessment are the completed Innocence Project London (IPL) preliminary questionnaire; a copy of the trial Judges summing up and a copy of any appeal documents, for example the grounds of appeal, decision for leave to appeal or the decision of the Court of Appeal. Where evidence and legal arguments used at trial and for an appeal are considered exhausted, they cannot be reused for an application to the CCRC. So, these documents help the IPL understand what evidence and legal arguments were presented at trial, and what evidence and/or legal arguments were used for an appeal. The case intake process can include the straightforward copying of documents such as the trial judges' summing-up and returning them by recorded post, to the more complicated task of trying to obtain these documents from the lawyers that represented the applicant at trial and/or on appeal. Third, there is a limited number of cases where there is the opportunity to find fresh evidence or show a new legal argument to meet the CCRC's requirements.[11] This makes case assessment very important, which means that obtaining the relevant documents is a fundamental part of that process. As will be discussed below, obtaining case documents can be difficult, but without access to documents such as the trial judges summing up, which provides an understanding as to what evidence was used in court, it is almost impossible to assess a case to determine the potential for a new legal argument or fresh evidence.

Innocence work is unlike the traditional form of clinical legal education because the learning is driven by the decided case as opposed to preparation for a case to be heard. Students work in an innocence organisation is based on deconstructing claims of innocence, making critical judgments based on what happened when the case was decided in court.[12] Students working for an innocence organisation are able to get an understanding of the whole of the criminal justice process starting with the police investigation, how and what evidence was presented at trial, the grounds of appeal and the client's claim to innocence. They are also exposed to issues surrounding the CCRC's statutory real possibility test, the criminal appeals process and accessing client paperwork. This chapter considers the pedagogical challenges and benefits presented by innocence work through the lens of the authors own experience as Director of the Innocence Project London and that of the students who

11 ibid.

12 Stephanie Roberts & Lynne Weathered, 'Assisting the factually innocent: the contradictions and computability of innocence projects and the Criminal Cases Review Commission' (2009) 29(1) *Oxford J Leg Stud* 43.

have worked for the organisation. At times, to provide examples, the stories of IPL clients are used, but they are sufficiently anonymised, so as not to reveal who they are. Some aspects of this chapter refer to existing research whilst other aspects use the lens of personal narrative to show how innocence work is clinical legal education, just not as you know it.

A Brief History of Post-Conviction Innocence Work

The Innocence Project London (IPL) is based at the University of Greenwich in the School of Law and Criminology. Initially created in 2010 under the umbrella of the INUK,[13] it became a member of the global Innocence Network in 2016, the first English organisation to do so. Manchester Innocence Project followed a year later.[14] The Cardiff Law School Innocence Project uses the title 'Innocence Project' under licence from the Innocence Network. As a member of the Innocence Network, the IPL has to adhere to a set of ethics and best practice requirements which include having policies on case management and confidentiality.

The first innocence project was created in 1992 by Barry Scheck and Peter Neufeld.[15] Based in Cardozo Law School, New York their work initially focused on new advances in DNA, which has resulted in 196 exonerations.[16] The innocence model of clinical legal education spread throughout America in the 1990's where it inspired projects created in law schools in Arizona,[17] California[18] and Washington,[19] amongst others. The movement reached the United Kingdom in 2004 when the INUK was set up.[20] When it folded in 2015, the 30 innocence projects it successfully set-up had to decide whether to continue their work alone. The IPL was one of those organisations, and is now thought to be one of only 11 still in existence.[21] The IPL works to make an application to the CCRC on behalf of its clients. It is not able to work on cases where the individual requires an out of time appeal to the Court of

13 Naughton & McCartney (n 6).

14 Hewitt & McGourlay (n 7).

15 Innocence Project: History of Impact, available at: https://history.innocenceproject.org/ accessed 1 January 2024.

16 The Innocence Project, available at: https://innocenceproject.org/exonerations-data/ accessed 1 January 2024.

17 University of Arizona Innocence Project, available at: https://law.arizona.edu/academics/clinics/university-arizona-innocence-project accessed 1 January 2024.

18 California Innocence Project, available at: https://californiainnocenceproject.org/?gclid=CjwKCAjw-7OlBhB8EiwAnoOEk20l_2OVwzFgdiRjepzO4UG6-KyReBi5e7tPGACKHwRDjMdATVe54xoCNRQQAvD_BwE accessed 1 January 2024.

19 Washington Innocence Project, available at: https://wainnocenceproject.org/ accessed 1 January 2024.

20 Holly Greenwood, 'Rethinking Innocence Projects in England and Wales: Lessons for the future' (2021) *How J Crim Justice* 1, 26.

21 Hewitt & McGourlay (n 7), 227.

Appeal Criminal Division because it does not have the capacity to support a live case.[22]

Being based in higher education and providing students with a learning experience that translates classroom learning into practice, meant there was a need to be able to articulate to students how they learn on the IPL. The nature of innocence work means that any pedagogy is underpinned by the experiential learning model from clinical legal education[23] that is rooted in David Kolb's cyclical learning model for reflective practice.[24] Experiential learning in the context of the IPL pedagogy is emphasised through the importance of facts and attention to detail.[25] The value of this process lies in students learning how to be thorough, learning how to keep going when one area of investigation reaches a dead-end and learning how to creatively approach complex problems arising from the cases.[26] These are skills which can only be developed by learning through experience.[27] The four stages of Kolb's learning model; concrete experience, reflective observations, abstract conceptualisation and active experimentation are, for students working for the IPL, all part of analysing and problem solving.[28]

The IPL has incorporated aspects of work based learning (WBL) into its pedagogy,[29] the purpose of which has been to stimulate an environment where learning develops in response to workplace issues.[30] The combination of experiential learning and elements of WBL has produced a positive employer/

22 *R v Conaghan* [2017] EWCA Crim 597 reminded students and supervisors alike as the timeliness of making appeals, but also to comply with the relevant procedures particularly where there is criticism of trial counsel (*R v McCook* [2014] EWCA Crim 734). Other Innocence Projects in England and Wales do work on appeal cases, see for example the Cardiff Innocence Project.

23 For a full outline of what Clinical Legal Education is see Richard J Wilson, 'Training for Justice: The Global Research of Clinical Legal Education' (2004) 22(3) *Penn State International Law Review* 421.

24 David Kolb, *Experiential Learning: Experience as the Source of Learning and Development* (2nd ed) (Pearson Education 2014).

25 Findley (n 5), 1111.

26 ibid, 1109.

27 RJ Sternberg and LF Zhang (eds), *Perspectives in cognitive, learning and thinking styles, in Experiential Learning Theory: Previous Research and New Directions* (Lawrence Erlbaum, 2000).

28 Kolb (n 24) 1106 fn16.

29 J Flanagan, S Baldwin and D Clarke, 'Works-based learning as a means of developing and assessing nursing competence' (2000) 9(3) *Journal of Clinical Nursing* 360. See also Brian Stanley Lester and Carol Costley who state, 'all and any learning that is situated in the workplace and arises directly out of workplace concerns.' (Brian Stanley Lester and Carol Costley, 'Work-based learning at higher education level: value, practice and critique' (2010) 35(5) *Studies in Higher Education* 561.

30 J Gear, A McIntosh, & G Squires, *Informal learning In the professions* (University of Hull Department of Adult Education 1994); M Eraut, S Steadman, F Maillardet, C Miller, A Ali, C Blackman, J Furner & C Caballero, *Learning during the first three years of postgraduate employment* (Economic and Social Research Council 2005) (Project LINEA); M Eraut, & W Hirsh,

employee environment.[31] This pedagogy started to develop after the IPL was set up in 2010, but it wasn't until the IPL became part of the global innocence network that the author recognised an emerging framework for three core areas of activity; clinical legal education, developing a critical perspective of the criminal justice system and access to justice.

Clinical Legal Education: Learning through the Innocence Experience

The term clinical legal education is used to mean any form of experiential learning where students are required to apply legal knowledge to real legal problems and to reflect on that process.[32] A significant part of the pedagogy on the IPL, therefore, is that students learning is as a result of the direct involvement with a case. Bringing this together with elements of work-based learning creates what has become known as the employer/employee environment.[33] The concept of students being employees of the IPL supports the development of professional skills that last beyond the life of their degree.[34] These include, but are not limited to, developing professional skills including time management, critical thinking, working to deadlines and attention to detail;[35] self-directed learning leading to a sense of responsibility, a skill essential to developing professional ethics; and academic writing including referencing and the detail required for research.[36]

The employment process starts with a two-stage application, where students submit a researched report which is then assessed in order for them to progress to interview. Every application receives feedback on their report, and the process places emphasis on presenting research concisely and accurately. Students that are successful at interview start working for the IPL in September each year, at the beginning of the academic year. These are normally highly-motivated students, on the basis they have to put effort into the application process to get a place in an organisation that requires them to volunteer their time.

An initial six-week training programme is undertaken by all new student caseworkers. A series of two-hour workshops introduces the history of

---

The Significance of Workplace Learning for Individuals, Groups and Organisations (University of Oxford 2007) (SKOPE Monograph 6).

31 Louise Hewitt, 'Learning by Experience on the Innocence Project in London: The Employer/Employee Environment' (2018) 25(1) *Int J Clin Leg Educ* 73.

32 Lucy Yeatman & Louise Hewitt, 'Feedback: a reflection on the use of Nicol and Macfarlane-Dick's feedback principles to engage learners' (2021) 55(2) *The Law Teacher* 227.

33 Hewitt (n 31).

34 LB Stephanie & MA Cavanaugh, 'Learning Through Injustice: Student Experiences of the Innocence Project London,' Research Evaluation Report, April 2023, available at: www.IPLondon.org, accessed on 1 January 2024.

35 ibid, 11.

36 JB Biggs & K Collis, *Evaluating the Quality of Learning. The SOLO Taxonomy* (Academic Press 1982).

innocence work, the IPL, the English criminal appeals process and the CCRC. Guest speakers provide additional insight into the process of police investigations and introduce the concept of bias, examining what it is and how students can be aware of it in their work for the IPL. After the training is completed students are then allocated the case they will be working on. Cases accepted by the IPL have already been appealed so the starting point for all students is to understand how and why their client was convicted. The problem-solving aspect of learning is developed in the context of critical judgement based on what happened in court.[37] Once students have been allocated a case, they are asked to create two timelines, one for the defence and one for the prosecution to pull together not only the chain of events that led up to the offence, but to identify the evidence and legal arguments that have already been used at trial and on appeal. In order to complete these timelines, students have to read the trial judgment and associated paperwork including, but not limited to, witness statements, defence statement, rulings on legal arguments, jury bundles and the grounds for appeal, decision for leave to appeal and any appeal documents if relevant. Attention to detail underpins innocence work globally[38] and can be directly applied to the reading of these documents. Students have to know the details of their client's case and what evidence was presented that led to their conviction in order to determine what can be used as new evidence or a new legal argument. Their learning is driven by the subject matter of each case, which makes the teaching environment unique but also unstructured.[39] This is one of the pedagogical challenges. The unpredictability of each case makes it difficult to design and apply a consistent case management strategy.[40] The only consistent aspect of case work is putting together timelines for the prosecution and defence, thereafter, finding the all-important new evidence or developing a new legal argument will depend on the offence and the evidence used to get the conviction.

The clinic experience is unique, in that students working for the IPL are required to produce documents to a professional standard, this includes writing letters to the client or engaging with members of the legal profession and experts in particular areas. The feedback that students receive on their work is to get it up to a standard that is acceptable for the client and the professionals that use it.[41] Students develop the ability to self-regulate their learning[42] because they want to do the best for their client. When the focus moves away from marking criteria and the need to achieve a certain grade, the learning environment becomes discursive and is based on positive relationships

37 Daniel S Medwed, 'Actual Innocents: Considerations in Selecting Cases for a New Innocence Project' (2003) 81 *Neb L Rev* 1097.

38 Findley (n 5), 1111.

39 Medwed (n 37).

40 ibid.

41 Yeatman & Hewitt (n 32).

42 ibid.

between members of the casework group.[43] The conversations during casework meetings, where both the case and ideas are discussed, generates a type of learning based on social relationships, where emotions are recognised as contributing to not only students' motivation, but also their self-esteem. The findings of a research evaluation report into the IPL published in April 2023 emphasised this point.[44] One student described the IPL experience as:

> Promising, because it just shows you that the work I'm doing and the people I'm working with in IPL are good, there are still good people working in the justice system. There are still good people that want to see justice again.[45]

Another student said:

> I am hopeful that things will change, and things will improve because more and more people, like this year, will apply to work in the IPL. I think more organisations can be built and we will get somewhere eventually. It's just going to take time that's all.[46]

Where students feel motivated to effect change, it helps them feel that the work they are doing for the IPL is valuable. In the same report students said, "I feel like [my] job has meaning and value. That's a big one for me, that's why I applied here," and "What we do has purpose."[47] These feelings also tied into the IPL generating a sense of community for students.[48] Comments from students include, "I've made friends and built really strong friendships with other people," and "I've made friends that I hope will last forever I suppose. The IPL has given me a place to find people and make friends with like-minded people."[49]

Developing a Critical Perspective of the Criminal Justice System

The Criminal Cases Review Commission and the Real Possibility Test

Innocence work means that students have to learn about the form and function of the CCRC. Students are exposed to the issues concerning the CCRC's statutory test as to whether there 'is a real possibility that the conviction, verdict,

43 ibid.
44 Stephanie & Cavanaugh (n 34).
45 ibid, 16.
46 ibid, 16.
47 ibid, 13.
48 ibid, 13.
49 ibid, 13.

finding or sentence would not be upheld were the reference to be made.'[50] The language of the test has been criticised on the basis that it makes the CCRC subservient to the Court of Appeal.[51] Subsequently this has created an unequal relationship because the CCRC has to 'second-guess' what the Court of Appeal may think about cases that are received following a referral.[52] These criticisms were included in the Justice Select Committee's 2015 inquiry into the work of the CCRC.[53] They were echoed and added to by the Westminster Commission on Miscarriages of Justice in 2021. Michael Birnbaum QC (now KC) expressed concern about the predictive nature of the test, on the basis that the Court of Appeal was inconsistent in the way it assessed the safety of convictions making it difficult for the CCRC to predict the cases for referral.[54] Dr Michael Naughton said that the current test prevents the CCRC referring cases where there is a potential miscarriage of justice if it is thought that the Court of Appeal may conclude the case lacks legal merit.[55]

Students working in an innocence organisation learn about these issues first-hand and develop a critical perspective on the effect the test has on their work when they are putting together an application for their client. The threshold of what amounts to a real possibility has been described as 'more than an outside chance or a bare possibility, but which may be less than a probability or a likelihood or a racing certainty.[56] The flexibility attached to the current real possibility test enables the CCRC to apply it on a case-by-case basis, however the exercise of its judgment has been said to be overly cautious[57] and thereby limiting its ability to reach an independent judgment. The Justice Select Committee in 2015[58] recommended that the CCRC should 'be less cautious' when referring cases to the Court of Appeal,[59] and the Westminster Commission in 2021 recommended that the CCRC should 'be bolder in interpreting it: determining in each case whether there is more than a fanciful chance of the verdict being quashed, even if quashing is less likely than not.'[60]

The benefit of students being aware of these issues means that they think about evidence and how it is used in criminal cases in a more meaningful way. For example, investigations in one IPL case indicated the potential for the

50 Section13 of the Criminal Appeal Act 1995.
51 Commons Select Committee, Justice 12th report Criminal Cases Review Commission (17 March 2015), [11].
52 ibid.
53 ibid.
54 Westminster Commission on Miscarriages of Justice, *In the Interest of Justice: an inquiry into the Criminal Cases Review Commission* (5 March 2021) 33.
55 ibid.
56 *R v Criminal Cases Review Commission, ex parte Pearson* [1999] 3 All ER 498, [2000] 1 Cr App R 141 at 149F-150A.
57 Westminster Commission on Miscarriages of Justice (n 54).
58 Commons Select Committee (n 51).
59 ibid, 27.
60 Westminster Commission on Miscarriages of Justice (n 54) 64.

diagnosis of a medical condition (that no one was aware of at the time of the trial or the appeal) which would mean that the client could not have committed the crime for which they had been convicted. The students had to research the condition which is a type of parasomnia and then speak to the consultant that provided the initial report into the condition. From there they identified a world-leading expert in this specific type of parasomnia and contacted them to see if they would assist in assessing their client. The expert agreed and a study was subsequently undertaken, and a report written. The diagnosis made sense of the clients claim to innocence and how they understood what had happened. The students are now in a position to determine how they best use the report and the associated case law in an application to the CCRC on their clients' behalf.

The Criminal Appeals Process

The process of deconstructing a case to identify a new legal argument or fresh evidence for a CCRC application enables students to learn about the function of the Court of Appeal and the difficulties appellants face in persuading the court to quash a conviction.[61] The Court of Appeal made clear its role during the third appeal by the Birmingham Six[62] and in doing so set out the limited nature of the appeal process. The first point the Court made is that its role is to 'hear criminal appeals' and that it does not have the 'power to conduct an open-ended investigation into an alleged miscarriage of justice.'[63] The second point, is that the Court of Appeal is solely concerned with the questions of whether the verdict of the jury can stand and that there is nothing in statute that obliges the court to state whether an appellant is innocent.[64] The Court of Appeal accepted it is a court of review, highlighting the primacy of the jury on the basis that 'justice is as much concerned with the conviction of the guilty as the acquittal of the innocent, and the task of convicting the guilty belongs constitutionally to the jury.'[65] It is at this point that students begin to realise that the CCRC's real possibility test can be described as protecting the Court of Appeal, ensuring it remains the final decision-maker as to whether a conviction should be quashed or upheld.

There is no precise definition as to the meaning of unsafe for the Court of Appeal. [66] It has been characterised as a lurking doubt or unease as to whether injustice has been done.[67] In *Davis, Rowe and Johnson*, the court held that:

61 Kevin Kerrigan, *Real Possibility or Fat Chance? In The Criminal Cases Review Commission: hope for the innocent* (Palgrave Macmillan 2010) 166–177.

62 *R v McIlkenny and others* [1991] 93 Cr.App.R.287 at 310–312

63 ibid.

64 ibid.

65 ibid.

66 Section 2 (1)(a) Criminal Appeal Act 1995

67 *R v Criminal Cases Review Commission, exp Pearson* [2000] 1 Cr App R 141 at 146.

> A conviction can never be safe if there is doubt about guilt. However, the converse is not true. A conviction may be unsafe even where there is no doubt about guilt but the trial process has been vitiated by serious unfairness or significant legal misdirection.[68]

The safety test is used because it provides a safeguard for not only individuals who are claiming innocence, but for individuals who have been convicted where there were irregularities in the arrest, investigation or trial procedure.[69] This means that a person could be guilty of the crime but their conviction found to be unsafe because of a procedural irregularity. It has been noted that appeals based on procedural irregularities have succeeded far more in the Court of Appeal than those based on fresh evidence.[70] One reason for this is 28-day time limit to lodge an application for leave to appeal, on the basis it is difficult to find fresh evidence within 28 days so grounds of appeal tend to focus on procedural issues.[71] Roberts and Weathered have suggested that this means fresh evidence is often used for an application to the CCRC placing innocence organisations in the best position to be able to assist clients who are claiming factual innocence,[72] on the basis they can dedicate time to uncovering this type of evidence. For students, understanding the relationship between the CCRC and the Court of Appeal helps them understand the realities of the English criminal justice system;[73] that funding cuts in legal aid lead to people not being able to access justice[74] and in the words of one student 'Justice is not what everyone gets.'[75]

It would be a measure as to the effectiveness of the English criminal justice system if innocence organisations were not needed in England and Wales, however from the author's professional experience, it is clear they are. As far back as 2008, studies have found that there is limited legal representation available for individuals who want help making an application to the CCRC. Professor Jacqueline Hodgson and Juliet Horne identified that from 2248 applications made between 2001 and 2007 that were rejected as ineligible or having no reviewable grounds of appeal, only 29% of them were legally represented.[76] A more recent 3-year study published in 2021 from the University of

68 [2001] 1 Cr App R 115, 131-132 per Mantell L J.

69 Hannah Quirk, 'Identifying Miscarriages of Justice: Why Innocence in the UK Is Not the Answer' (2007) 70(5) *The Modern Law Review* 759, 769.

70 Stephanie Roberts, 'Fresh Evidence and Factual Innocence in the Criminal Division of the Court of Appeal' (2017) 81(4) *Journal of Criminal Law* 303, 305.

71 ibid.

72 Roberts & Weathered (n 12).

73 Stephanie & Cavanaugh (n 34) 20.

74 ibid.

75 ibid.

76 JS Hodgson and J Horne, 'The Extent and Impact of Legal Representation on Applications to the Criminal Cases Review Commission (CCRC)', 6 October 2009.

Sussex[77] identified that 42% of lawyers who participated in the research were no longer willing to accept publicly funded CCRC cases,[78] a position caused by low remuneration rates for what is a demanding area of work. The study suggests that the lack of funding has led law firms to select cases where the issues are straight forward and reject those that are time consuming or where there is considerable evidence to consider.[79] Innocence organisations should not need to exist in any country, but they do because individuals are being convicted and sent to prison for crimes they did not commit.

Access to Justice: Obtaining Case Documents

From direct experience one of the most prevalent issues surrounding case work in an innocence organisation is accessing legal documents. A number of applicants do not have documents from their trial or their appeal, mainly because they did not know they could ask for them. Clients and applicants often move between prisons and their documents get lost. Clients and applicants send documents to various organisations attempting to secure assistance, and unfortunately during this process documents do not get returned or they get lost in the post. Innocence organisations often investigate cases that have incomplete paperwork which requires time to contact previous lawyers and/or organisations that have supported the individual to see if they have originals or copies of files. Losing case files can be costly, for example replacing a copy of the Judges summing-up requires paying a transcription service, and many clients and applicants do not have the funds to do so. The IPL has in the past, found case files for a client which were in the possession of another organisation, where they had been sitting in a cupboard for seven years. During a legal visit, a client brought a number of letters to the meeting and one of them indicated this particular organisation had received the entire case file. After a brief email exchange, the file was sent to the IPL, but the client had no idea that they had sent the majority of their documents to this organisation. The organisation had ceased working on the case, it said they had communicated this to the client. This is not the only example and sadly it won't be the last time the IPL has to find case files.

There is very limited information for convicted individuals about how they can access their legal documents after the court process. There is an assumption that the relevant information will be provided by a defendant's legal representative however the experience from the IPL suggests this is often not the case. There is very limited academic commentary about prisoners understanding of

77 R Vogler, L Welsh, A Clarke, S Wiedlitzka and L McDonnell, 'The Criminal Cases Review Commission: Legal Aid and Legal Representatives', Final Report, University of Sussex 2021.

78 See also A Clarke and L Welsh, '"F** k this game… I'm off": financial and emotional factors in declining legal representation in miscarriage of justice cases' (2022) *Journal of Law and Society* 527.

79 Vogler et al. (n 77) 18.

the law as it relates to their criminal case files. Existing literature examines the issues with prisoners accessing legal advice when they are on remand,[80] and access to legal aid and legal representation.[81]

For IPL students, when they start working on a case, they start to understand how important their client's case file is. Firstly, in terms of their work in understanding the evidence that was used and not used at trial which helps to determine what may be possible to use for an application to the CCRC. Secondly, from their clients' perspective paperwork is a form of currency, it means they can provide relevant and necessary information to innocence organisations or other representatives that they reach out to. From the point of view of an innocence organisation deconstructing a claim of innocence is increasingly more difficult without the necessary case files and it is even more difficult to assess a case to determine whether it is eligible for the IPL to work on it without having the trial judges summing up and the appeal documents at the very least. These documents show what evidence has already been used at trial and what was argued on appeal, which helps identify what could potentially be fresh evidence or a new legal argument for the CCRC.

Conclusion

The learning on the Innocence Project London is unique, in that it is driven by the subject matter of each case. Whilst this makes the learning environment unstructured and challenging, the work of finding new evidence and/or a new legal argument both of which underpin an application to the CCRC, it provides a consistent approach. Case work meetings enable the opportunity for not only innovative ideas, but also discussions that motivate students, helping them to understand the value of their efforts.

The IPL pedagogy provides a foundation for students to examine the English criminal justice system in a way that they would otherwise not be exposed to. Understanding the CCRC's role and its relationship with the Court of Appeal, as well as examining concerns over the statutory real possibility test, helps students develop a critical perspective of the criminal justice process. Being exposed to how evidence has been used in trials, and the difficulty in obtaining leave to appeal helps students think about their client's case in a meaningful way. They know their client has come to the IPL because they are unable to access justice elsewhere, and normally that is because they are unable to afford to pay for a lawyer to help them make an application to the CCRC. Whilst obtaining all the relevant documents to a client's case file

80 F Brookman & H Pierpoint, 'Access to legal advice for young suspects and remand prisoners' (2003) 42(5) *The Howard Journal of Criminal Justice* 452.

81 A Flynn, J Hodgson, J McCulloch and B Naylor, 'Legal aid and access to legal representation: redefining the right to a fair trial' (2016) 40 *Melb. UL Rev* 207; V Kemp, 'Transforming legal aid: Access to criminal defence services', Ministry of Justice 2010; Brookman & Pierpoint (n 8).

can be time consuming and frustrating, students recognise how important this paperwork is. Not only for the client to keep, but in terms of being useful to determine what is potentially new evidence not used at trial or for an appeal and, therefore, able to be used for a CCRC application.

The sense of community built from innocence work is enriching, for the students but also to those who work with them. As Director of the IPL, I find their enthusiasm and willingness to learn inspiring. This is not easy work, but it is important work, both for the clients and the students who become advocates for what they have learnt. This is clinical legal education, just not as you know it.

Bibliography

Biggs, J.B. & Collis, K. *Evaluating the Quality of Learning. The SOLO Taxonomy* (Academic Press 1982)

Brookman, F. & Pierpoint, H. 'Access to legal advice for young suspects and remand prisoners' (2003) 42(5) *The Howard Journal of Criminal Justice* 452

Clarke, A. & Welsh, L. '"F**k this game… I'm off": Financial and emotional factors in declining legal representation in miscarriage of justice cases' (2022) 49(3) *Journal of Law and Society* 518–541

Eraut, M. & Hirsh, W. *The Significance of Workplace Learning for Individuals, Groups and Organisations* (University of Oxford 2007) (SKOPE Monograph 6)

Eraut, M., Steadman, S., Maillardet, F., Miller, C., Ali, A., Blackman, C., Furner, J., & Caballero, C. *Learning During the First Three Years of Postgraduate Employment* (Economic and Social Research Council 2005) (Project LINEA)

Findley, K.A. 'The pedagogy of innocence: Reflections on the role of innocence projects in clinical legal education' (2006) 13(1) *Clinical Law Review* 1101

Flanagan, J., Baldwin, S., & Clarke, D. 'Works-based learning as a means of developing and assessing nursing competence' (2000) 9(3) *Journal of Clinical Nursing* 360

Flynn, A., Hodgson, J., McCulloch J., & Naylor, B. 'Legal aid and access to legal representation: Redefining the right to a fair trial' (2016) 40 *Melbourne University Law Review* 207

Gear, J., McIntosh, A., & Squires, G. *Informal Learning in the Professions* (University of Hull Department of Adult Education 1994)

Greenwood, Holly. 'Rethinking innocence projects in England and Wales: Lessons for the future' (2021) 60(4) *The Howard Journal of Crime and Justice* 1

Hewitt, L. 'Learning by experience on the innocence project in London: The employer/employee environment' (2018) 25(1) *International Journal of Clinical Legal Education* 73

Hewitt, L. & McGourlay, C. 'Still standing: Innocence work in England and Wales' (2021) 2(3) *The Wrongful Conviction Law Review* 226

Hodgson, J.S. & Horne, J. 'The extent and impact of legal representation on applications to the criminal cases review commission (CCRC)' (6 October 2009)

Kemp, V. *Transforming Legal Aid: Access to Criminal Defence Services* (Ministry of Justice 2010)

Kerrigan, K. *Real Possibility or Fat Chance? In The Criminal Cases Review Commission: Hope for the Innocent* (Palgrave Macmillan 2010) 166–177

Kolb, D. *Experiential Learning: Experience as the Source of Learning and Development* (2nd ed., Pearson Education 2014)

Lester, B.S. & Costley, C. 'Work-based learning at higher education level: Value, practice and critique' (2010) 35(5) *Studies in Higher Education* 561

Medwed, D.S. 'Actual innocents: Considerations in selecting cases for a new innocence project' (2003) 81 *Nebraska Law Review* 1097

Naughton, M. & McCartney, C. 'The innocence network UK the innocence network UK' (2004) 7(2) *Legal Ethics* 150

Quirk, H. 'Identifying miscarriages of justice: Why innocence in the UK is not the answer' (2007) 70(5) *The Modern Law Review* 759

Roberts, S. 'Fresh evidence and factual innocence in the criminal division of the court of appeal' (2017) 81(4) *Journal of Criminal Law* 303

Roberts, S. & Weathered, L. 'Assisting the factually innocent: The contradictions and computability of innocence projects and the criminal cases review commission' (2009) 29(1) *Oxford Journal of Legal Studies* 43

Stephanie, L.B. & Cavanaugh, M.A. 'Learning through injustice: Student experiences of the innocence project London', *Research Evaluation Report*, April 2023

Sternberg, R.J. & Zhang, L.F. (eds). *Perspectives in Cognitive, Learning and Thinking Styles, in Experiential Learning Theory: Previous Research and New Directions* (Lawrence Erlbaum 2000)

Vogler, R., Welsh, L., Clarke, A., Wiedlitzka, S., & McDonnell, L. 'The criminal cases review commission: Legal aid and legal representatives', Final Report, University of Sussex 2021

Westminster Commission on Miscarriages of Justice. *In the Interest of Justice: An inquiry into the Criminal Cases Review Commission* (Westminster Commission on Miscarriages of Justice, 5 March 2021)

Wilson, R.J. 'Training for justice: The global research of clinical legal education' (2004) 22(3) *Penn State International Law Review* 421

Yeatman, L. & Hewitt, L. 'Feedback: A reflection on the use of Nicol and Macfarlane-Dick's feedback principles to engage learners' (2021) 55(2) *The Law Teacher* 227

5 Teaching (In)Justice

Navigating the Fault Lines in Criminal Procedure

Lissa Griffin and Anne-Alexa Stanica

Introduction

Justice and injustice are difficult subjects to teach. The terms are laden with normative judgments, provoke emotional reactions and can only be understood fully by examining them in the context of an entire judicial system and culture. What may be unjust in one society may not seem unjust in another, given that a justice system reflects its own society's history, values, politics, economics, demography and even geography. Despite its difficulties, teaching law students to identify and analyze issues of justice and injustice is important. Among other things, it develops their critical thinking skills and strengthens their intellectual creativity. And teaching injustice from a comparative perspective can make an understanding of its dimensions even more rich by teaching students to think critically beyond accepting the familiar.

In the United States, law schools offer a course that analyzes the criminal adjudication process, the so-called 'Bail to Jail' stages of the criminal process. In addition to analyzing the steps and the roles of the players, the course can also focus on issues that have resulted in wrongful convictions or miscarriages of justice. This chapter will explore teaching criminal procedure by focusing on the fault lines in the US process, that is, the steps in the criminal process that are most vulnerable to and are most frequently the cause of injustice. Once having identified those steps, we identify them in other criminal justice systems, compare them and consider solutions. Albeit somewhat generalized, through this comparative analysis, the students learn that each part of the process is a choice reflecting many factors such as history, culture, socioeconomics, demography, politics, sources of law and even geography. By identifying, contextualizing and comparing the fault lines in this way, students can bring a deeper and more objective perspective to the debate on rights and justice in criminal procedure.

Teaching Criminal Procedure

Criminal procedure is the process by which a society brings its penal law to bear on its citizens. The rules governing this process can be found in constitutional

DOI: 10.4324/9781003457985-5

provisions, statutes, court rules and judicial decisions. While criminal justice systems differ, most of them are characterized by a series of steps beginning with investigation by law enforcement and ending with the appellate process and post-conviction collateral attack. In any US criminal procedure course, analysis of those steps proceeds as follows: arrest, detention, charging, discovery, plea bargaining and alternatives to trial, right to jury trial, defendant as a source of evidence, trial rights, sentencing, appeal, post-conviction review. Some, like me, emphasize the roles of the players: the prosecutor, defense counsel, the court and the jury. In some schools, the investigation process is a one-semester Criminal Procedure course and the adjudication process ('Bail to Jail') is its own semester-long course.

Several challenges exist in teaching criminal procedure. Students, like others, often have an emotional reaction to the question of what to do with people suspected of breaking the law: they may have themselves been a victim of crime or may know others who have been victimized. The subject of crime invariably involves some sense of personal fear or vulnerability. They may have an emotional reaction to policing or police. In the United States, this is exacerbated by the historical and continuing use of crime as a political campaign tool, which not only emphasizes danger – real or not[1] – but which also labels a person as either pro- or anti-public safety, which can intimidate a student trying in good faith to understand the pros and cons of various aspects of the process. Finally, but importantly, crime sells newspapers, and there is an almost constant diet of crime drama, real or imagined, on TV, in movies, in the press and on social media.[2]

Additional pitfalls exist because criminal procedure is usually taught in the context of the students' domestic criminal justice system so that the dangers associated with studying the familiar are real. First, students may suffer from the recognized psychological phenomenon of mistaking the familiar with the good: our system is the right system. This mindset may also manifest itself in the rigid belief that how we do it is the only way to do it, just or not. As psychologists have documented, familiarity with one's own system (exacerbated by the media's portrayals of crime drama) can rigidify someone's thinking (our way is the only way) or mistake familiar with the good (our way is the best way). American exceptionalism, a doctrine that refuses to die, further narrows

1 See, e.g., Melissa Segura, 'Crime Researchers Say Political Candidates Are Ignoring Evidence As The Midterm Campaigns Heat Up' (*BuzzFeed.News*, 2022), available at: < https://www.buzzfeednews.com/article/melissasegura/crime-ads-midterms-misinformation> ('tough on crime' political campaign doesn't match reality); Jiawei Liu, et al., 'Campaign Advertising and the Cultivation of Crime Worry: Testing Relationships With Two Large Datasets From the 2016 U.S. Election Cycle' (2023) *The International Journal of Press/Politics* 70, available at: <https://www.cbsnews.com/video/how-crime-data-is-used-by-election-campaigns/>

2 See, e.g., John Alldredge, 'The CSI Effect and Its Impact on Juror Decisions' (2015) 3(1) *Themis* 114, available at: <https://scholarworks.sjsu.edu/themis/vol3/iss1/6/> accessed 19 February 2024.

one's critical thinking by insisting that because the United States is different it can learn nothing from examining other systems. Finally, focusing on precedent alone, as may be the case in some classes devoted to constitutional criminal procedure, runs the risk that a student will analyze the criminal process as abstract doctrine: with criminal procedure a real understanding requires understanding what happens 'on the ground.'

Methodology

In Criminal Procedure – Adjudication, we go through the process chronologically from charge through appeal and collateral attack by examining constitutional and statutory sources and case law interpreting them. We often use media reports of real, current cases for discussion. In addition to the steps, there is also a focus on the adversary system and the players in the process: the prosecutors defense counsel, the court and the jury. We describe their constitutional, statutory and ethical roles. As we focus on the players and the process we identify and analyze the fault lines in the process: to what extent is the topic we're discussing one that leads to injustice or wrongful conviction? Which areas are most vulnerable to unfairness and resulting injustice. Those include: the role of the prosecutor/prosecutorial discretion; the inadequacy of discovery and disclosure; ineffective defense counsel; and the pressures placed on the system by the broad right to trial by jury.[3]

Comparative analysis comes next: having identified these fault lines, are there other, existing ways to operate the criminal justice system to avoid injustice or at least improve the odds against injustice? The first issue is, of course, what to compare, that is, what comparisons will give the student the best perspective and understanding. There are many different criminal justice systems categorized generally along a continuum from adversarial to inquisitorial and based on common law or civil law. There are of course systems based on religion, like Sharia law. One basis for choosing is to identify a system similar to the US system like the UK criminal justice system. Both are western democracies with adversarial systems based on common law. By comparing them, whatever differences there are, for example, in the requirements of prosecutorial disclosure to the defense – become not only significant but present

3 Significantly, these are not necessarily the same as the recognized causes of factually erroneous, wrongful convictions: false confessions, misapplication of scientific expertise, eyewitness misidentification, inadequate defense, unreliable and unregulated informants, prosecutorial misconduct, harmful surveillance and investigative techniques and coerced pleas. University of Colorado Boulder, 'Why Do Wrongful Convictions Happen?' (*Korey Wise Innocence Project*, 2023) available at: <https://www.colorado.edu/outreach/korey-wise-innocence-project/our-work/why-do-wrongful-convictions-happen>; Innocence Project, 'The Issues' (2023) available at: <https://innocenceproject.org/the-issues/> accessed 19 February 2024. As will be seen, these four aspects of the criminal process lead to the admission of the kinds of unreliable evidence identified by the Innocence Project.

alternatives. Comparing disparate systems, like the United States and Spain, which is an example of an inquisitorial system based on civil law, can reinforce the point that any country's domestic criminal justice process reflects its history, demographics, politics and culture.

My introduction to comparative analysis begins with the seminal work by Herbert L. Packer, *Two Models of the Criminal Process*.[4] In that law review article, Prof. Packer identifies the *universal* value choices underlying criminal procedure and suggests a single continuum that unites all criminal justice systems, with the Due Process Model at one end (most rights, least efficient) and the Crime Control Model at the other (fewer rights, greater efficiency).[5] A system based on crime control values considers suppression of criminal conduct to be the most important function of the criminal process and thus is characterized by high numbers, low resources, speed, informality and finality. It resembles an 'assembly line.'[6] Systems based on these values tend to trust early determinations of probable innocence or guilt based on expertise, i.e., probable cause, and have confidence in the reliability of informal administrative factfinding activities at early stages, that is, in the ability of police and prosecutors to construct a tolerably accurate account of what took place. What follows after is perfunctory.[7] On the other hand, a system based on due process values resembles an 'obstacle course.'[8] It is characterized by a distrust of informal and early factfinding processes, requires a high degree of reliability tested by an adversarial proceeding and stresses the primacy of the individual, fairness, equality and thus limitations on official power.[9] Packer makes no judgments about which system is better, but he makes the point that these values are in tension in *any* society's criminal process.[10] By starting here, students can understand that all criminal justice systems face the same normative challenges. The next analytical step is to identify why a society makes the choices it does. Factors include the goals of the system (crime control v. due process), politics, history, sources or law, socioeconomic considerations, geography and demographics.

An Example: Prosecution Suppression of Exculpatory Evidence

In this section, we focus on one of the fault lines in US criminal procedure: prosecutorial suppression of exculpatory evidence.

4 HL Packer, 'Two Models of the Criminal Process' (1964) 113 U. Penn. L. Rev. 1.
5 ibid, 9.
6 ibid, 13.
7 ibid, 10–13.
8 ibid.
9 ibid, 14–15.
10 ibid, 5.

The Problem

In class, we use a film clip from the limited TV series 'The Night Of' to help illustrate the issue. In the series, Naz Khan (Riz Ahmed), the defendant, is accused of murder. He spent the night with a young woman at her apartment in New York City, did drugs with her, passed out and woke up to find her murdered. He left the apartment and was stopped for a traffic infraction; when searched, the police find a bloody knife from the apartment. He is connected to the murder scene and charged. Khan is a student, has no prior record and lives with his family in Queens. He did not know the victim until that night and had no motive to harm her.

Helen Weiss (Jeannie Berlin) is a New York district attorney. She is prosecuting Khan for the murder. Dennis Box (Bill Camp) is an NYPD homicide detective. In the film clip, Box presents Weiss with the evidence he has uncovered suggesting another suspect in the crime – someone the victim knew well as a family friend and who may have stolen $300,000 from her – a theft she only recently discovered – who drove later that night in what might have been an attempt not to be detected and who then appeared to dump a large garbage bag surreptitiously. In response to the evidence presented, Weiss says to Box, 'We have more on the kid.'

In the second scene, Weiss argues in summation to the jury that Naz was the only suspect and recounts the evidence against him. Camp, present at the trial, leaves in disgust. The information about the other suspect has not been disclosed to the defense at any time, so that the defense does not know about the other suspect.

The United States

Among the lessons learned from this dramatization is the incredibly broad power of the prosecutor to decide who and what to charge. As many scholars have observed, the US prosecutor has more power and discretion than any other player in the US system.[11] Separation of powers, among other things, has resulted in tremendous deference by the judiciary, manifested in a refusal by the judiciary to prescribe the conduct of the executive branch beyond the requirements of due process.[12] The standard governing prosecutorial conduct is the constitutional due process standard. That standard has been used to

11 See, e.g., Angela Davis, 'The Power and Discretion of the American Prosecutor' (2023) 85(1) *Droit et Cultures* available at: <https://journals.openedition.org/droitcultures/1580?lang=en> accessed 19 February 2024; Bennett L. Gershman, *Prosecutorial Misconduct* (2d Ed. Clark, Boardman and Callaghan 1999) (noting that the prosecutor decides whether or not to bring criminal charges who to charge; what charges to bring; whether a defendant will stand trial, plead guilty, or enter a correctional program in lieu of criminal charges; and whether to confer immunity from prosecution).

12 See, *United States v. Armstrong*, 517 US 456 (1996) (relating to charging); *United States v. Bagley*, 473 US 667 (1985) (relating to disclosure of exculpatory evidence).

regulate prosecutorial conduct only on a case-by-case basis and only when the result is fundamentally unfair (that is, not only improper but prejudicial).[13] This deferential, high standard is also the result of the adversarial US criminal justice system, which requires for its success that each side do its best to present its best case. Such a system implicitly sanctions each side to do everything legally and ethically possible to succeed. While the prosecutor wears two hats as an advocate and a 'minister of justice,'[14] the justice role is less dominant than the role of adversary. In reality, US prosecutors 'frequently exist in a culture of extreme adversariness, a win-at-all-costs approach to lawyering.'[15]

It is important to focus on the fact that the existence of the other suspect and the evidence against him are never disclosed to the defense.

In the United States, the prosecution has a constitutional due process duty to disclose to the defendant exculpatory evidence that is material to guilt or punishment.[16] In *Brady v. Maryland*,[17] the US Supreme Court held that 'the suppression by the prosecution of evidence favourable to an accused upon request violates due process where the evidence is material either to guilt or punishment.'[18] Violation of this duty has been described as 'epidemic.'[19] Part of the reason may be the materiality requirement: a prosecutor deciding whether to disclose may conclude that the proof against the defendant is so strong that disclosure would not impact the verdict.[20]

Categories of undisclosed evidence that are represented in the case law include exculpatory eyewitness evidence, impeachment evidence, such as

13 ibid.

14 *Berger v. United States*, 295 US 78 (1935) ('[prosecutor's] interest, therefore, in a criminal prosecution is not that it shall win a case, but that justice shall be done.'); see, ABA Model Rules of Professional Conduct Rule 3.8, Cmt. (1) (1983) (noting that 'a prosecutor has the responsibility of a minister of justice and not simply that of an advocate.'); ABA Standards for Criminal Justice, Standard 3-1.2 (c) (1993) ('the duty of the prosecutor is to seek justice, not merely to convict.').

15 Lissa Griffin, 'The Correction of Wrongful Convictions: A Comparative Perspective' (2001) 16(5) Am. U. Intl L. Rev 1241, 1265, and cases cited therein. See also, Mark Baker, *DA: Prosecutors in Their Own Words* (Simon & Schuster1999) (noting one prosecutor's description as a 'constant pressure to win cases, to keep the office statistics of "guilty as charged" climbing from one political season to the next').

16 *Brady v. Maryland*, 373 U.S. 83, 87 (1963).

17 ibid.

18 ibid, 87. *United States v. Bagley*, 473 US 667 (1985), the Court held that the due process disclosure obligation applied to impeachment evidence (there, evidence of deals made by prosecution witnesses) and reversed the conviction finding that the non-disclosure was material.

19 *United States v. Olsen*, 737 F.3d 625, 626 (9th Cir. 2013) (Kozinski, C.J., dissenting from denial of rehearing en banc). Other sources of a duty to disclose may be found in *Giglio v. United States*, 405 U.S. 150, 154 (1972) (prior statements of witnesses); 18 USC 3500 (same); F. R. Cr. P 16 (specific prosecution evidence required to be disclosed: defendant's statements, record, objects, tests, experts).

20 See, e.g., *United States v. Agurs*, 427 US 97 (1976) (conviction affirmed where prosecution failed to disclose victim's criminal record, which would have supported the defendant's claim of self-defense, further clarifying the materiality standard).

incentive deals made with prosecution witnesses in exchange for testimony, prior inconsistent statements, bolstered identifications as well as the existence of other suspects.[21] For example, in *Strickler v. Greene*,[22] significant changes in an eyewitness's testimony from uncertainty to certainty that was memorialized in a series of statements made in continuing interviews by the police were not disclosed.[23] The conviction was affirmed because the non-disclosure was held not to be material.[24] Moreover, in *Kyles v. Whitley*,[25] the US Supreme Court held that the prosecutor's duty to disclose extends to material held by law enforcement even if the prosecution is unaware of the material.[26] That decision assumed that there were ways for the prosecution to secure exculpatory information from the police.[27] Yet, despite this duty, in fact, there are no protocols or standards for ensuring that law enforcement turns over exculpatory evidence to the prosecutor. If the police do not turn it over, it will never be part of the adjudication process. However, unlike prosecutors in the United Kingdom, aside from the Department of Justice's manual,[28] state prosecutors do not have published guidelines, checklists or any other systematic method for ensuring they receive exculpatory evidence held by the police by which they may be held accountable.

The United Kingdom

In the United Kingdom, the prosecutorial role is less adversarial and the duty to disclose is broader and more transparent, with greater accountability. The dual system of barristers and solicitors serves several purposes, including creating a distance between the barrister and the client that is absent in the United States, and, through the system of inns of court, creating a small, elite professional community.[29] Moreover, barristers may represent both the defense and the prosecution at different times. For this and for reputational reasons, they are less likely to be motivated to push the boundaries of proper conduct to win than their US counterparts. Thus, while the UK prosecutor is part of an

21 See, Innocence Project, 'Undisclosed Evidence May Be a Turning Point in Ivan Henry's Wrongful Conviction Lawsuit' (2015) available at: <https://innocenceproject.org/undisclosed-evidence-may-be-a-turning-point-in-ivan-henrys-wrongful-conviction-lawsuit/> accessed 19 February 2024.

22 527 U.S. 263 (1999).

23 ibid, 282.

24 ibid, 296.

25 514 US 419 (1995).

26 ibid, 437.

27 ibid, 43. There is no 'serious doubt that 'procedures and regulations can be established to carry [the prosecutor's] burden and to ensure communication of all relevant information on each case to every lawyer who deals with it. *Giglio v. United States*, 405 U. S. 150, 154 (1972).

28 US Department of Justice Manual, available at: <https://www.justice.gov/jm/justice-manual.>

29 James Holland and Julian Webb, *Learning Legal Rules* (10th edn, OUP 2019).

adversary system, it plays a less partisan role than that in the United States, with an emphasis on independence. There is less of an institutional history in the United Kingdom as well, since there was no institutional prosecutor until 1986, when the Crown Prosecution Service (CPS) created by statute began operation.[30] Moreover, the CPS is more transparent and more accountable than the US prosecutor, who, arguably is considered accountable by way of election. The CPS is governed by its own published codes of practice, detailed statutes and codes of practice and greater transparency.[31]

This less partisan approach applies to all stages of the prosecution and includes a broader duty to disclose exculpatory material than in the United States. In the United Kingdom, by statute, the prosecutor must turn over any 'material which might reasonably be considered capable of undermining its case or assisting the case for the accused' of which they are aware.[32] The prosecution makes the disclosure determination based on two schedules that must be provided to the prosecution by the police: a schedule of sensitive unused material and a schedule of nonsensitive unused material. Moreover, the Code for Crown Prosecutors contains a description of the prosecution's duty and is publicly available on its website as are several other documents.[33] In addition, the police have clear procedures that must be carried out by a hierarchy of police officers and disclosure officers who work on turning 'unused materials' over to the prosecution[34] and schedules to be filled out and given to prosecutors of 'Unused Materials.'[35] The items listed on the schedule are exactly those types of facts that have led to erroneous convictions in the United States.[36]

30 Prosecution of Offences Act 1986.

31 CPS, 'The Code for Crown Prosecutors' (CPS GOV, 26 October 2018) available at: < https://www.cps.gov.uk/publication/code-crown-prosecutors> accessed 19 February 2024; 2.1 The independence of the prosecutor is central to the criminal justice system of a democratic society. Prosecutors are independent from persons or agencies that are not part of the prosecution decision-making process. CPS prosecutors are also independent from the police and other investigators. Prosecutors must be free to carry out their professional duties without political interference and must not be affected by improper or undue pressure or influence from any source. 2.8 Prosecutors must be even-handed in their approach to every case and have a duty to protect the rights of suspects and defendants, while providing the best possible service to victims.

32 Criminal Procedure and Investigations Act 1996 c. 25 s 3(1)(a). The CPIAs disclosure provisions were supplemented by the Criminal Justice Act, 2003 c. 44, which eliminated the distinction between a prosecutor's primary and secondary disclosure duties in favor of a continuing duty to disclose.

33 CPS, 'Disclosure Manual: Chapter 1 – Introduction' (*CPS GOV*, 14 July 2022) available at: <https://www.cps.gov.uk/legal-guidance/disclosure-manual-chapter-1-introduction#:~:text=Disclosure%20refers%20to%20providing%20the,has%20not%20previously%20been%20disclosed> accessed 19 February 2024; Crown Prosecution Service, Attorney General's Guidelines on Disclosure (2005); Judiciary of England and Wales, Disclosure: A Protocol for the Control and Management of Unused Material in the Crown Court.

34 ibid, ch 3.

35 ibid, ch 3, 4, 6.

36 One of the police schedules is attached as Appendix A. For example, the police must indicate other suspects, informants, prior statements or identifications, all of which are recognized

Despite the broader duty and structured procedural protections, failure to disclose exculpatory evidence continues to be a source of miscarriages of justice.[37] One particularly notorious case was *R. v. Liam Allan*.[38] In that case, the defendant was charged with rape and his defense was consent. The case was dismissed during trial when it was discovered that the prosecution had not disclosed extensive messages from the victim's phone in which she asked the defendant for sex, related her sexual fantasies, and spoke of a desire for violent sex and of her rape fantasies.[39] In other messages to friends she said that no crime had been committed by him. The messages also included some between the alleged victim and friends saying the defendant was a kind person, how much she loved him and that her experience with him had been 'great.'[40] A subsequent investigation concluded that the officer in charge of the case failed to find that evidence among 57,000 messages on the alleged victim's mobile phone.[41] The disc containing the messages had not been disclosed to the defence because the officer in the case said there was 'nothing relevant on it,' the review said, and the prosecution had not sufficiently challenged the police about the evidence.[42] After the case was dismissed, a systemic review of 306 rape or sexual assault cases was conducted by the CPS and the Met.[43]

---

causes of wrongful convictions in the United States. See Innocence Project <https://innocenceproject.org>.

37 CCRC Report on Phase 2 of the CCRC Disclosure Review 1 (2021) available at: <https://ccrc.gov.uk/news/commission-publishes-report-from-its-review-of-disclosure-in-ccrc-case-sample/> ('The CCRC's own experience of reviewing cases demonstrates that the most common underlying feature of unsafe convictions generally – and not just rape and serious sexual offence cases – nondisclosure coupled with failure to pursue lines of enquiry which should have been pursued by investigations and prosecutors but which were let undone.). See, e.g., *Malkinson v The King*, [2023] EWCA Crim 954 (conviction quashed on the basis of newly available DNA testing, but l material disclosure violations also rendered conviction unsafe); *R v. Balasubramanian*, available at: <https://ccrc.gov.uk/news/conviction-overturned-following-ccrc-referral-due-to-concerns-about-witness/> *Hamilton v Post Office Limited*, [2021] EWCA Crim 577 (failure to disclose bugs in Horizon computer system).

38 Emily Allbon & Sanmeet Kaur Dua, *Elliot' & Quinn's English Legal System* (21st ed., Pearson 2020) 528. See also 'Liam Allan: What Happens When the Justice System Fails,' Berkley Square Solicitors, available at: <https://www.bsblaw.co.uk/blog/y1ki1cx5jzxoaiwp48kegwc04ukcct> accessed 19 February 2024.

39 Allbon & Dua (n 40) 529.

40 ibid.

41 ibid.

42 Crown Prosecution Service, 'A joint review of the disclosure process in the case of R v Allan' (*Metropolitan Police,* January 2018) available at: <https://www.cps.gov.uk/sites/default/files/documents/publications/joint-review-disclosure-Allan.pdf> accessed 5 December 2023.

43 CJJI, 'Making it Fair: A Joint Inspection of the Disclosure of Unused Material in Volume Crown Court Cases' (18 July 2017) available at: < https://www.justiceinspectorates.gov.uk/cjji/wp-content/uploads/sites/2/2017/07/CJJI_DSC_thm_July17_rpt.pdf>accessed 19 February 2024.

Spain

The situation is quite different in Spain, where the impartial judge supervises the investigation of criminal cases, the so-called 'Examining Magistrate.'[44] The examining magistrate has a duty to investigate evidence that is both 'adverse and favourable' to the accused.[45] Obviously, unlike the adversarial system, that goal cannot be left to the activities of the parties.[46] Also consistent with this goal is the role of the Public Prosecutor to be an impartial agent of the State required to enforce the law.[47] The Spanish prosecutor is a civil servant, following a training regimen similar to that for judges.[48] The role of the prosecutor during investigation is to assist the investigating judge and enforce the law (the principle of legality).[49] Unlike the US prosecutor who is both a minister of justice and an adversary, at least until the trial, the Spanish prosecutor is not an adversary.

The Public Prosecutor works with the court in a supervisory capacity, but both the defense and prosecution may request investigative measures.[50] That is, the judge will take such measures 'proposed by the Public Prosecution Service or any of the parties if they do not consider them to be futile or prejudicial.'[51] While the judge may refuse to disclose evidence to the defence for security reasons, generally speaking, all results – inculpatory or exculpatory – are recorded in a court file called a dossier, which is then available to both parties.[52]

Contextualizing

The United States

The United States of course was born of rebellion a mere 250 years ago. It is a rights-based society, originally focused on protecting the people against the King and his colonial judges. It is a common-law system and is based on and bound by constitutional text. Separation of powers provisions attempt to ensure that no part of the government has too much power.[53] While the colonists transported the common law adversary system from England, the

44 LE Crim art 303; De Lucchi Lopez-Tapia et al, *The Criminal Justice System in Spain* (Atelier 2022) (hereafter, 'De Lucchi') 41.

45 LE Crim art. 2; De Lucchi (n 46) 43 (the goal is a search for objective truth).

46 De Lucchi (n 46) 43.

47 Spanish Const art 124(1); Organic Statute of the Prosecution, Preamble, art 2, 7.

48 Organic Statute art 42, 47.

49 Spanish Const art 124.2; Organic Statute art 2. Unlike in the United States, Spanish prosecutors also have very limited discretion in deciding whether to bring a charge, against whom, and for what crime: the legality principle requires that they prosecute.

50 LECrim 306.

51 LECrim 311, 312.

52 LECrim 315.

53 See, The Federalist 47 (James Madison) (liberty requires that 'three great departments of power should be separate and distinct'). While the term does not appear in the Constitution,

Bill of Rights added major protections for the 'accused.'[54] This focus on individual rights and rugged individualism is also a cultural norm,[55] at least partly influenced by the geography of the country: resolution of conflict that might be required in a densely populated island, like the United Kingdom, was not necessary since there was always room to move west, and move west people did.[56] Indeed, it was considered the United States's 'manifest destiny' to conquer the west and thus the entire territory.[57] Importantly, the United States suffers from an historic politicization of crime and criminals; with their prosecutors being elected officials, the issue of 'law and order' generally governs elections.[58] Facing a real problem of violent crime, and with racist overtones, the prosecutor has come to be viewed as a white knight, armed with whatever was required to protect society. Demographically, the United States has a powerful history of race-based slavery so the fear of crime merged with the fear of people of color. In the Constitution, and until after the Civil War, African-Americans were explicitly not considered full citizens.[59] It is difficult to overstate the extent to which the legacy of slavery continues to result in a disproportionate impact on people of color in the criminal justice system and in US prisons.[60]

---

government powers are vested in the executive (the president) (Art. 1 § 1), legislative (Congress) (Art. II § 1), and judicial (Supreme Court)(Article III §1) branches.

54 See US Const., amend VI., 'In all criminal prosecutions, the accused shall enjoy the right to a speedy and public trial, by an impartial jury of the state and district wherein the crime shall have been committed, which district shall have been previously ascertained by law, and to be informed of the nature and cause of the accusation; to be confronted with the witnesses against him; to have compulsory process for obtaining witnesses in his favor, and to have the assistance of counsel for his defense.'

55 Samuel Bazzi, Martin Fiszbein, Mesay Gebresilasse, 'Frontier Culture: The Roots and Persistence of "Rugged Individualism" in the United States' (2020) 88(6) *Econometrica* 2329.

56 ibid.

57 SAAM, 'America's Manifest Destiny' (2023) available at: <https://americanexperience.si.edu/historical-eras/expansion/pair-westward-apotheosis/> accessed 19 February 2024.

58 Supra (n 60).

59 US Const., art 1 s 2, 'Representatives and direct Taxes shall be apportioned among the several States which may be included within this Union, according to their respective Numbers, which shall be determined by adding to the whole Number of free Persons, including those bound to Service for a Term of Years, and excluding Indians not taxed, three fifths of all other Persons.' The Fourteenth Amendment repudiated this inequality. US Const. amend XIV ('All persons born or naturalized in the United States, and subject to the jurisdiction thereof, are citizens of the United States and of the State wherein they reside. No State shall make or enforce any law which shall abridge the privileges or immunities of citizens of the United States; nor shall any State deprive any person of life, liberty, or property, without due process of law; nor deny to any person within its jurisdiction the equal protection of the laws.).

60 For a small sample of the literature documenting this phenomenon, see Michelle Alexander, *The New Jim Crow* (The New Press: 2010); Aaron Gottlieb and Kalen Flynn, 'The Legacy of Slavery and Mass Incarceration: Evidence from Felony Case Outcomes' (2021) *Social Service Review* 3; Kica Matos and Jamila Hodge, 'The Chains of Slavery Still Exist in Mass Incarceration' (*Vera Institute of Justice*, 17 June 2021) available at: <https://www.vera.org/news/the

The United Kingdom

The United Kingdom, of course, is a centuries-old, mature society. Rather than historically accentuating individual rights, it is a monarchy, where everyone is a subject and everyone has an allegiance to the king or queen. Although historically it ruled an empire, it is also an island nation with limited space for expansion. Although it is a common-law system based on precedent, parliament is supreme with the result that there are detailed statutes and accompanying codes of practice that govern each stage of the criminal process. As a parliamentary system with an unwritten constitution, it is not bound by constitutional text. As of 2000, of course, it is subject to the European Convention on Human Rights which includes the right to a fair trial under Article 6. While there is a history of rebellion against the king, as represented by the Magna Carta, it was the landed classes who sought protection of their rights against the king. The history of rigid class discrimination is very old. And the guild system for barristers reinforced elitism while creating a small and select professional body, where reputation is extremely important. Finally, while the United Kingdom is certainly multi-racial, it does not have the same long legacy of enslaving minorities domestically, slavery having been declared illegal in the late 1770s.

Spain

Ironically, Spain is also a very young criminal justice system. Its Constitution was enacted only about 50 years ago, after the end of the Franco dictatorship. Like the United States, its constitution was drafted to prevent the abuses that preceded it. As such it contains many protections of fundamental rights. It is also subject to the European Convention on Human Rights and the decisions of the European Court of Human Rights. As a civil law system, it relies on a detailed criminal procedure code.

Comparison

While the context and comparison among the systems may indeed be superficial from a true comparativist's analytical perspective, in a domestic Criminal Procedure course, this added insight yields rich results. First, with a comparative perspective, students should be able to appreciate that prosecution disclosure of evidence that would be helpful to the defense falls neatly into a continuum from the limited disclosure in the United States, to the broader disclosure

-chains-of-slavery-still-exist-in-mass-incarceration>; Bryan Stevenson, 'Slavery gave America a fear of black people and a taste for violent punishment. Both still define our criminal-justice system' (*NY Times*, 14 August 2019) available at: <https://www.nytimes.com/interactive/2019/08/14/magazine/prison-industrial-complex-slavery-racism.html>accessed 19 February 2024.

in the UK, to the even broader disclosure in Spain. Students will come to understand this and will also see that, despite their different approaches to disclosure, all three countries are western democracies that grapple with the challenges of Packer's due process/crime control values. In law school we do not ask whose choices are better. But we do inquire why those different procedures were chosen and what can be learned, if anything, about addressing injustice in the United States. When viewed in context, what is unjust and what is just and what, if anything, can the United States learn? Should the existence of evidence against a different suspect have been revealed to avoid injustice?

Returning to our hypothetical, in the United States the defense could very likely never learn of the existence of an alternative suspect or the evidence against him. To the prosecutor, pre-trial, the evidence against the defendant is stronger so that the existence of the other suspect is not material. Without any written record, the information given to the prosecutor by the detective will not be available anywhere. In the United Kingdom this information will almost certainly need to be revealed on the police schedule, which will be turned over to the prosecution and, ultimately, to the defense. In Spain, investigation of the other suspect would likely be included in the dossier.

Students should be able to discuss whether changes could be made to the US disclosure system through increased judicial participation, changing the standard, internal police and prosecution protocols or legislation. They should come to realize that given US history, the text of the US Constitution and the US adversary system's reliance on an uninformed judge and party presentation of proof, it is unlikely that, as in Spain, a judge would be in charge of an investigation or of disclosure to the defense. Courts simply don't know enough about a case and are unwilling to supervise the prosecution. On the other hand, one could argue that there might be more meaningful disclosure if a US judge took a more active role in mediating the process, perhaps through discovery conferences. Some US courts already do that. Another alternative that could be raised would be to make a discovery violation a contempt of court. Various forms of judicial supervision could be discussed, anywhere from the essentially hands-off US policy to Spain's participation of the examining magistrate.

Students should also be able to discuss whether, as in the United Kingdom, the scope of the duty to disclose could be made broader. Could the US 'materiality' dimension of the standard be omitted so that the United Kingdom's 'reasonably helpful' standard would control? That is already the ethical standard in most US jurisdictions. But the duty to disclose is rooted in the text of the Fifth and 14th amendment due process clauses of the US Constitution. To the extent that we, unlike other countries, are bound by constitutional text, that language mandates fundamental fairness, meaning that, as the Supreme Court has held, non-disclosure would result in an appellate reversal only where it had an impact on the verdict. It is possible that the legislature could prescribe specific items that need to be disclosed as on the UK's checklists, as has been done, for example, in New York State's recent legislation.[61] However, the problem remains in the US and UK systems that the prosecutor is still in charge.

Students should be able to discuss the significance of adopting some variety of the UK's protocols for disclosure by the police. Requiring the police to fill out schedules of specific categories of unused materials would not prevent the police from hiding helpful evidence, but, combined with the hierarchy of responsibility within the department and the requirement that those schedules be disclosed to the prosecution and then the defense, would make meaningful the Supreme Court's holding in *Kyles* that the prosecution is responsible for ensuring that the police disclose exculpatory evidence.

Conclusion

By understanding the criminal process, identifying injustices, looking at other choices and contextualizing them, students learn 1) that the normative struggle is the same in most systems, but the solutions are different; 2) that there are other ways to do things; 3) that the familiar is not necessarily the good; and 4) to think creatively about possible improvements.

Bibliography

ABA Model Rules of Professional Conduct Rule 3.8, Cmt. (1) (1983).

ABA Standards for Criminal Justice, Standard 3-1.2 (c) (1993).

Alexander, Michelle, *The New Jim Crow* (The New Press 2010) .

Allbon, Emily and Dua, Sanmeet Kaur, *Elliot' & Quinn's English Legal System* (21st ed., Pearson 2020).

Alldredge, John, 'The CSI Effect and its Impact on Juror Decisions' (2015) 3(1) *Themis* 114, available at: <https://scholarworks.sjsu.edu/themis/vol3/iss1/6/>.

Baker, Mark, *DA: Prosecutors in Their Own Words* (Simon & Schuster 1999).

Bazzi, Samuel, Fisbein, Martin, and Gebresilasse, Mesay, 'Frontier Culture: The Roots and Persistence of "Rugged Individualism" in the United States' (2020) 88(6) *Econometrica* 2329.

Berkeley Square Solicitors, 'Liam Allan: What Happens When the Justice System Fails' (2021) available at: <https://www.bsblaw.co.uk/blog/y1ki1cx5jzxoaiwp48kegwc04ukcct>.

CCRC, 'Report on Phase 2 of the CCRC Disclosure Review 1' (2021) available at: <https://ccrc.gov.uk/news/commission-publishes-report-from-its-review-of-disclosure-in-ccrc-case-sample/>.

CJJI, 'Making it Fair: A Joint Inspection of the Disclosure of Unused Material in Volume Crown Court Cases' (18 July 2017) available at: <https://www.justiceinspectorates.gov.uk/cjji/wp-content/uploads/sites/2/2017/07/CJJI_DSC_thm_July17_rpt.pdf>.

61 NY Criminal Procedure Law Article 245 Discovery s 245.20(a-u).

Crown Prosecution Service, 'A Joint Review of the Disclosure Process in the Case of R v Allan' (*Metropolitan Police*, January 2018) available at: <https://www.cps.gov.uk/sites/default/files/documents/publications/joint-review-disclosure-Allan.pdf>.

Davis, Angela, 'The Power and Discretion of the American Prosecutor' (2023) 85(1) *Droit et Cultures* 55, available at: <https://journals.openedition.org/droitcultures/1580?lang=en>.

De Lucchi Lopez-Tapia et al., *The Criminal Justice System in Spain* (Atelier 2022).

Gershman, Bennett L., *Prosecutorial Misconduct* (2nd ed., Clark, Boardman and Callaghan 1999).

Gottlieb, Aaron and Flynn, Kalen, 'The Legacy of Slavery and Mass Incarceration: Evidence from Felony Case Outcomes' (2021) 95(1) *Social Service Review* 3.

Griffin, Lissa, 'The Correction of Wrongful Convictions: A Comparative Perspective' (2001) 16 *American University International Law Review* 1241.

Holland, James and Webb, *Learning Legal Rules* (10th ed., OUP 2019).

Innocence Project, 'The Issues' (2023) available at: <https://innocenceproject.org/the-issues/>.

Innocence Project, 'Undisclosed Evidence May be a Turning Point in Ivan Henry's Wrongful Conviction Lawsuit' (2015) available at: <https://innocenceproject.org/undisclosed-evidence-may-be-a-turning-point-in-ivan-henrys-wrongful-conviction-lawsuit/>.

Liu, Jiawei et al., 'Campaign Advertising and the Cultivation of Crime Worry: Testing Relationships With Two Large Datasets From the 2016 U.S. Election Cycle' (2023) 28(1) *The International Journal of Press/Politics* 70, available at: https://www.cbsnews.com/video/how-crime-data-is-used-by-election-campaigns/.

Matos, Kica and Hodge, Jamila, 'The Chains of Slavery Still Exist in Mass Incarceration' (*Vera Institute of Justice*, 17 June 2021) available at: <https://www.vera.org/news/the-chains-of-slavery-still-exist-in-mass-incarceration>.

SAAM, 'America's Manifest Destiny' (2023) available at: <https://americanexperience.si.edu/historical-eras/expansion/pair-westward-apotheosis/>.

Segura, Melissa, 'Crime Researchers Say Political Candidates Are Ignoring Evidence As The Midterm Campaigns Heat Up' (*BuzzFeed.News*, 2022) available at: <https://www.buzzfeednews.com/article/melissasegura/crime-ads-midterms-misinformation>.

Stevenson, Bryan, 'Slavery Gave America a Fear of Black People and a Taste for Violent Punishment. Both Still Define our Criminal-justice System' (*New York Times*, 14 August 2019) available at: <https://www.nytimes.com/interactive/2019/08/14/magazine/prison-industrial-complex-slavery-racism.html>.

University of Colorado Boulder, 'Why Do Wrongful Convictions Happen?' (*Korey Wise Innocence Project*, 2023) available at: <https://www.colorado.edu/outreach/korey-wise-innocence-project/our-work/why-do-wrongful-convictions-happen>.

US Department of Justice Manual, available at: <https://www.justice.gov/jm/justice-manual>.

6 Teaching Law Students to Advocate for Human Rights and Global Justice through the UPR Project at BCU

Alice Storey[1]

Introduction

Today, the need for clinical human rights teaching and advocacy within higher education institutions is vital for law students (and their teachers and wider communities). Students often leave university to enter the workplace and do so in an increasingly internationalised context. Clinical legal education (CLE) provides the ideal space to support students in navigating a globalised world, whilst providing them with transferrable employability skills. This chapter focuses on using extra-curricular opportunities as a vehicle to provide such opportunities, specifically to teach our law students to advocate for human rights and global social justice, through the Universal Periodic Review (UPR) Project at Birmingham City University (BCU).

Under the auspice of the United Nations' Human Rights Council, the Universal Periodic Review (UPR) is an intergovernmental process providing a review of the human rights record of all United Nations (UN) Member States. Crucially, it involves the participation of civil society organisations (CSOs) of all shapes and sizes acting as 'stakeholders'. The UPR Project at BCU engages with the UPR mechanism through three intersecting streams: (1) research, (2) education, and (3) practice, providing CLE opportunities through extra-curricular activities.

In 2012, Jocelyn Getgen Kestenbaum, Esteban Hoyos-Ceballos, and Melissa C. Del Aguila Talvadkar published their article, 'Catalysts for Change: A Proposed Framework for Human Rights Clinical Teaching and Advocacy' ('*Catalysts for Change*').[2] They provide six distinct components to this framework, arguing that 'rethinking roles and adopting certain models for clinical

1 Thank you to attendees at the Workshop in June 2023 for their helpful comments on the themes of this chapter and thank you to Stella Mguli for their research assistance. Any errors remain my own.

2 Jocelyn Getgen Kestenbaum, Esteban Hoyos-Ceballos, and Melissa C. Del Aguila Talvadkar, 'Catalysts for Change: A Proposed Framework for Human Rights Clinical Teaching and Advocacy' (2012) 18 Clinical L Rev 459.

DOI: 10.4324/9781003457985-6

legal education and advocacy can successfully realize both the pedagogical and advocacy goals of [human rights clinics]'.[3]

This chapter applies the six framework components to the UPR Project at BCU in terms of its ability to teach law students to advocate for human rights and global justice. The following section introduces the UPR Project at BCU, its aims and work to date. The third section situates the UPR Project within the existing literature on CLE. The section proceeding that then analyses the UPR Project at BCU's operation through the framework set out in *Catalysts for Change*, identifying the positives and challenges, along with providing suggestions for further developing clinical human rights teaching in relation to advocating for human rights and global justice. The final section concludes with broader proposals for engaging, supporting, and celebrating law students in international human rights CLE.

The UPR Project at BCU

The UPR Project at BCU is a stream of work within the Centre for Human Rights, which is part of Birmingham City University's College of Law, Social and Criminal Justice.[4] It was created in 2018 and engages with the UN's human rights mechanism, the Universal Periodic Review, through three streams: (1) research, (2) education, and (3) practice, led by Dr Alice Storey, Dr Amna Nazir, and Professor Jon Yorke.

We engage in traditional academic research, contributing to the growing body of scholarship on the UPR mechanism.[5] The UPR Project also participates in practice with the UPR as a stakeholder, through submitting stakeholder reports to selected countries' UPRs and taking part in UPR Pre-sessions, which involves direct engagement with UN government delegations from across the globe and other civil society organisations. This allows our

3 ibid 462.

4 See: https://www.bcu.ac.uk/law/research/centre-for-human-rights/consultancy/upr-project-at-bcu. Professor Jon Yorke created the Centre for Human Rights in 2014 and leads it as the Director, alongside Dr Amna Nazir and Dr Alice Storey as Associate Directors. It will celebrate its 10th anniversary in 2024.

5 See e.g., Alice Storey, 'Challenges and Opportunities for the UN Universal Periodic Review: A Case Study on Capital Punishment in the USA' (2021) 90 UMKC L Rev 129; Amna Nazir, 'The Universal Periodic Review and the Death Penalty: A Case Study of Pakistan' (2020) 4(1) RSIL Law Review 126; Amna Nazir, Alice Storey, and Jon Yorke, 'The Universal Periodic Review as Utopia' in Damian Etone, Amna Nazir and Alice Storey (eds), *Human Rights and the UN Universal Periodic Review Mechanism: A Research Companion* (2024); Alice Storey, 'Improving Recommendations from the UN's Universal Periodic Review: A Case Study on Domestic Abuse in the UK' (2023) 35 *Pace International Law Review* 193; Alice Storey and Mark Eccleston-Turner, 'Transparency, Accountability, and Legitimacy in the United Nations' Human Rights Council's Universal Periodic Review', in, Salvador Santino Regilme Jr and Irene Hadiprayitno (eds), *Human Rights at Risk: Rethinking International Institutions, American Power, and the Future of Dignity* (Rutgers University Press 2022).

academic research to be translated into practical change. As of 31 December 2023, we have submitted 34 reports to 32 UN Member States' UPRs and engaged in three UPR Pre-sessions, fostering multiple global partnerships. The UPR Project engages with many thematic areas of human rights in countries across the globe, although thematic decisions are made with the expertise of BCU's academics and partners in mind. This work feeds into the education stream, which has multiple strands, including dedicated LLB modules. Most important for this chapter is the clinical legal education we engage in, to provide students with employability and transferrable skills opportunities. While it is the education stream of work that this chapter is broadly focused upon, all three streams purposely intersect, with each aspect informing the others.

Currently, students predominantly engage in CLE through research assistance on our UPR stakeholder reports, and this includes BCU undergraduate and postgraduate students, as well as externs from other universities across the world. At the time of writing, we have engaged 47 BCU law students and 26 externs from universities across the world, including Brazil, Pakistan, and the United States. To facilitate the students' engagement in this CLE, we use law's Student Research Collaborations (SRC) programme.[6] The SRC provides a framework for students to work directly with academic staff on live research projects, offering them a unique opportunity to improve their CV and gain valuable research and wider employability skills.[7] I am a vocal supporter of the SRC, having supervised 60 + students through the SRC since 2018. Less frequently, but equally as valuable, students also engage in CLE with the UPR Project through externally funded projects, where we can use the funding to recruit student research assistance and involve students in the related activities.

Clinical Legal Education

There is an ever-growing corpus of literature on CLE, particularly from a human rights perspective, and predominantly from a practical lens.[8] Scholarship spans the globe, with examples including how to set up a CLE programme in New Zealand,[9] the successes of clinical legal education on human rights in the Maldives,[10] how CLE can 'increase human rights knowledge in the

6 See: https://www.bcu.ac.uk/law/research/student-research-collaborations.

7 Sharon Milner, Wendy Cousins, and Iain McGowan, 'Does All Work and No Play Make a Dull Graduate? Perceptions of Extra-curricular Activities and Employability' (2016) Vol 4(1) *Journal of Perspectives in Applied Academic Practice* 13–18.

8 For a theoretical approach to clinical legal education, see Omar Madhloom, Hugh McFaul (eds), *Thinking About Clinical Legal Education: Philosophical and Theoretical Perspectives* (Taylor and Francis 2021).

9 Kris Gledhill, 'Establishing an International Human Rights Clinic in the New Zealand Context' (2013) *International Journal of Clinical Legal Education* 19, 295.

10 Marium Jabyn, 'Advancing Justice Interests and Human Rights of Vulnerable Groups through Clinical Legal Education' (2020) 11(2) *Jindal Global Law Review* 271–288.

community' more so than traditional teaching through lectures in Iran,[11] and how law schools can house legal aid clinics in Kenya.[12]

Traditionally, CLE has been considered as a credit-bearing exercise for students that supports the local community. From a US perspective, Arturo Carrillo defines a human rights clinic to be:

> a law school-based, credit-bearing course or program that combines clinical methodology around skills and values training with live case-project work, all or most of which takes place in the human rights context ... [where] the students receive some degree of in-house skills and values training in addition to faculty supervision and feedback on live case-project work.[13]

Robert Collinson et al. provide a practical example of this from the United Kingdom, through Edge Hill University's Department of Law and Criminology's CLE. They note that 'by providing pro bono legal advice to members of the public, LLB students are contributing to the alleviation of poverty and discrimination, and raising local awareness of human rights principles'.[14] Moreover, led by Samantha Gargaro, BCU has its own Law Clinic, providing students with practical work experience to enhance their legal skills and employability, whilst also supporting the local community.[15]

While these examples showcase incredibly impactful opportunities both for students and the local community, the UPR Project does not fit within this mould of credit-bearing, local advocacy, as its core focus for students is international research through an extra-curricular activity. Literature supports this approach, identifying a wider scope for CLE opportunities. For example, Evan Hamman et al. found that, in Australia, 'CLE programs have embraced non-casework activities such as assisting with law reform and community legal education initiatives'.[16] Kestenbaum et al. also noted that 'many clinicians have embraced an increasingly internationalized curriculum, as well as the global

11 Mohammed Mahdi Meghdadi & Ahmad Erfani Nasab, 'The Role of Legal Clinics of Law Schools in Human Rights Education; Mofid University Legal Clinic Experience' (2011) 15 *Procedia Social and Behavioral Sciences* 3014–3017, 3017.

12 Asha Mikinyango & Judith Nguru, 'Law Schools as Legal Aid Providers in Kenya: Challenges and Lessons Learnt from Practice' (2021) 28(2) *International Journal of Clinical Legal Education* 117–48.

13 Arturo J. Carrillo, 'Bringing International Law Home: The Innovative Role of Human Rights Clinics in the Transnational Legal Process' (2004) Columbia Human Rights Law Review 35(3) 527, 533-4.

14 Robert Collinson et al., 'Clients, Clinics and Social Justice: Reducing Inequality (and Embedding Legal Ethics) via an LLB Portfolio Pathway' (2018) Higher Education, Skills and Work-Based Learning, 8(3), pp. 323–36, 334.

15 See: https://www.bcu.ac.uk/law/student-experience-and-employability/law-clinic.

16 Evan Hamman et al., 'Pro Bono Partnerships in Environmental Law: Enhancing Outcomes for Universities and CLCs' (2014) Alternative Law Journal, 39(2), pp. 115–19, 115.

human rights movement, by establishing clinics that focus on international human rights efforts'.[17] Tamar Ezer et al. considered the work conducted by collaborations between clinical legal educators across Thailand, South Africa, and Ukraine, in the context of improving healthcare provisions.[18] In particular:

> at the University of Pretoria, Master of Laws students drafted a submission to the African Commission on Human and People's Rights requesting both recognition of access to medicines as an essential component of the right to health and a process to ensure implementation.[19]

This is similar to the UPR Project's work, particularly in relation to stakeholder reports.

The definition that fits most neatly with the UPR Project at BCU's CLE is provided by Lucy Yeatman and Louise Hewitt, who state that:

> We use the term clinical legal education to mean any form of experiential learning where students are required to apply legal knowledge to real legal problems and to reflect on that process. This can be as part of a credit-bearing module, or as an extracurricular activity. Clinical legal education can take many different forms and those who work in the field can wax lyrical about the transformational nature of their work and the positive impact on the student experience, learning and employability.[20]

This definition of CLE allows students to find their identity in a broader scope of CLE, even when engaging in extra-curricular activities such as with the UPR Project at BCU. It is also important to recall the employability emphasis of CLE. Margaret Thornton and Lucinda Shannon reflect upon the surge of Australian Law Schools and the how experiential learning and CLE is used to 'market' law programmes, specifically focusing on how CLE improves employability and provides a positive learning experience.[21] Across higher education in the United Kingdom in particular, there has been a 'sustained drive to develop employability skills' wherein 'universities, student unions, and

17 Kestenbaum et al. (n 2) 461.

18 Tamar Ezer, Ludmylla Deshko, Nicola Gunn Leark, Enga Kameni, and Bruce A. Lasky, 'Promoting Public Health through Clinical Legal Education: Initiatives in South Africa, Thailand, and Ukraine' Human Rights Brief Vol 17(2) 27–33.

19 ibid 27.

20 Lucy Yeatman and Louise Hewitt, 'Feedback: A Reflection on the use of Nicol and Macfarlane-Dick's Feedback Principles to Engage Learners' (2021) The Law Teacher, Vol 55, No 2, 227–240, 230.

21 Margaret Thornton & Lucinda Shannon, 'Selling the Dream: Law School Branding and the Illusion of Choice' (2013) 23 Legal Educ Rev 249.

employers often encourage students' engagement in [extra-curricular activities] as a mechanism for developing such skills'.[22]

The overarching aim of the UPR Project's human rights-focused CLE is summed up by Vananthi's definition, that '[c]linical legal education is a pedagogical tool aimed at making legal education socially relevant and oriented towards social justice'.[23]

Kestenbaum et al.'s Framework: Analysis of the UPR Project at BCU

Kestenbaum et al. provide a framework for clinical human rights teaching and advocacy through the example of the Cornell Law School International Human Rights Clinic:

> The framework consists of six general steps: (1) determine broad clinical legal education goals; (2) determine general project purpose and goals; (3) form and strengthen strategic alliances among local clinic partners; (4) develop local human rights legal and advocacy strategies; (5) implement local legal strategy and human rights advocacy; and (6) reflect and process with partners and students.[24]

This section takes each element of the framework in turn, analysing the CLE opportunity created through the UPR Project at BCU in terms of its ability to teach law students to advocate for human rights and global justice. As the UPR Project has been operating for five years as of October 2023, this has provided an opportune moment to reflect upon its practice. As such, positives and challenges are identified, along with suggestions for further developing clinical human rights education.

Determine Broad Clinical Legal Education Goals

As a first step, Kestenbaum et al. suggest that broad goals should be set, relating to the work of the clinical human rights teaching and advocacy. They propose that this could include goals to advance human rights and social justice, provide practical employability skills to students, or empower vulnerable or marginalised groups.[25] While the UPR Project takes a less traditional approach to CLE, setting goals is still a fundamental part of its viability.

22 Jill Dickinson, Teri-Lisa Griffiths, and Alex Bredice, '"It's Just Another Thing to Think About": Encouraging Students' Engagement in Extracurricular Activities' (2019) 45(6) *Journal of Further and Higher Education* 744–757, 744.

23 Nimushakavi Vasanthi, 'Strengthening Clinical Legal Education in India' (2012) 42(4) *Social Change* 443.

24 Kestenbaum et al. (n 2) 481.

25 ibid.

The UPR Project at BCU's mission statement sets out its broad clinical legal education goals:

The UPR Project at BCU serves three key functions, through its research, education, and practice streams of work:

1. Advance human rights protections through the UN's Universal Periodic Review (UPR) mechanism, to support vulnerable populations and ensure social justice, through our academic **research** on substantive human rights issues.
2. **Educate** people about the UPR, through (1) providing students with opportunities to develop their employability and transferrable skills, and (2) training programmes on the modalities of the UPR mechanism.
3. Engage in **practice** with the UPR, through submitting stakeholder reports to selected sessions, engaging in advocacy through pre-sessions and dialogues with Member States and civil society, and working with selected partners.[26]

The UPR's overarching goals align with the suggestions in *Catalysts for Change*. In particular, goal 2 has a specific aim to educate students on the UPR, whilst also providing students with employability and transferrable skills (as expanded upon later in this chapter). This puts into practice Carrillo's understanding that CLE specifically from a human rights perspective is a 'fortunate fusion of pedagogy and practice in international law; as such, they draw constantly from one to improve the function of the other'.[27] A key task for the team will be to regularly review and reflect upon the broad goals of the UPR Project at BCU, to ensure we are delivering the best experience for all stakeholders, and especially our students.[28]

Moreover, there must be a consideration of the impact on inclusivity, given that this is an extra-curricular activity that is usually unpaid. While research has found that voluntary extra-curricular activities 'help to distinguish graduates in the job market',[29] Mary Stuart et al.'s study found that '[s]tudents classified as working class, mature and/or minority ethnic (with the exception of Asian students) are generally engaging less in university-linked' extra-curricular activities, preferring 'community' or 'solitary' activities often owing to 'time constraints, and feelings of non-inclusion'.[30] This is confirmed by Jill

26 The UPR Project at BCU, 'Strategy and Mission Statement' (June 2023) on file with the author.

27 Carrillo (n 13) 586.

28 See section 4(vi).

29 Mary Stuart, Catherine Lido, Jessica Morgan, Lucy Soloman, and Steve May, 'The Impact of Engagement with Extracurricular Activities on the Student Experience and Graduate Outcomes for Widening Participation Populations' (2011) 12(3) *Active Learning in Higher Education* 203–215.

30 ibid.

Dickinson et al.'s research on students from a post-92 university, which found that there are multiple barriers to such students engaging in extra-curricular activities, including time, money, carer commitments, cultural expectations, and a lack of confidence.[31]

BCU is a post-92 university, where my own experience of our students is that many must work part-time, or even full-time hours, alongside their full-time studies, and others go home from university to caring or familial responsibilities, making it challenging for them to engage in extra-curricular activities. Dickinson et al. suggest that universities 'could encourage the development of student-centred approaches to the development and communication of their extracurricular activities (ECA)-programmes through meaningful consultation with their student bodies'.[32] This is a point of action for the UPR Project at BCU, to identify from the students themselves how we can improve the inclusivity of our extra-curricular CLE offering.

Determine General Project Purpose and Goals

During the second stage of the *Catalysts for Change* framework, staff and students should 'enumerate the specific short-term teaching and project goals, ideally broken down semester by semester, given the realities and limitations of the law school academic calendar'.[33] This is a vital step when planning CLE opportunities within the UPR Project at BCU.

In terms of UPR stakeholder reports, the leadership team (Storey, Nazir, and Yorke) collectively make plans for submissions around one year in advance, prior to student involvement. We consider which UN Member States have their UPR scheduled in the Human Rights Council's sessions and then narrow the list down to which ones we will submit reports to and on which human rights themes. In terms of making these decisions, we consider things such as our own expertise, as well as that of our partner organisations and other colleagues at BCU.[34] Other factors include the availability and reliability of data, as well as our own workloads around the time leading up to submission. Kestenbaum et al. advised that noting the 'realities and limitations of the law school academic calendar' is important for both staff and students, and we make sure this is a core factor when planning stakeholder submissions. Particularly because the CLE with the UPR Project is an extra-curricular activity for the students we are conscious of students' other commitments across the year, including assessment deadlines and other factors noted in the section above. It is important to ensure that we are offering students extra-curricular

31 Dickinson et al. (n 22) 750–752.

32 ibid 755.

33 Kestenbaum et al. (n 2) 486.

34 See, Jeff Giddings, 'Contemplating the Future of Clinical Legal Education' (2014) *Clinical Legal Education Symposium* 1–26, 22, noting that CLE teachers must have the relevant 'skills and expertise'.

CLE opportunities without causing 'burnout'.[35] We must also consider our own staff workloads and annual leave, making sure that we have the time not only to complete the task, but to support the students effectively.[36]

Once we have a clear schedule of reports, around six months in advance of each deadline, we turn to recruiting the students. This is done either through the Student Research Collaborations,[37] and/or through our externship programmes, and we try to offer opportunities to as many students as is feasible, usually one per human rights theme. In the first instance, the students will be invited to a meeting with the supervising staff member, who will provide them with written and verbal guidance on their tasks. The tasks are usually legal research-related but can be quite complex for a first attempt, particularly when collating UPR recommendations and identifying their implementation status domestically. This requires students not only to be able to identify, analyse, and apply international human rights law, but to do the same for domestic law often in jurisdictions they are unfamiliar with. Template documents are provided for the students, along with dates for check-ins and the final deadline. This package of documents that is sent to students is a particular strength of the model,[38] as it provides clarity for the students, but also allows the staff member to plan their diary accordingly.

A further example of how the UPR Project determines project goals is through externally funded projects. I am currently working on a British Academy and Leverhulme Trust-funded project related to strengthening civil society organisations' engagement with the UPR, which has allowed me to recruit a current PhD student to work as a research assistant.[39] The project has links to the students' own research and involves mixed methods research using a survey and participant interviews to collect data. Owing to the amount of time it takes to prepare, submit, and receive a decision on a funding bid, plans for the student's time, work, and goals started around 18 months in advance of the project commencing in September 2022, particularly as the funding bid had to provide a rationale for recruiting a research assistant and what the benefits of doing so would be, not only for the project itself, but importantly for the research assistant. This included benefits for their personal development and enhancement of their employability skills. The plans and goals have been

35 Kestenbaum et al. (n 2) 496.

36 For an overview of the importance of the supervisory role in CLE, see Gemma Smyth & Marion Overholt, 'Framing Supervisory Relationships in Clinical Law: The Role of Critical Pedagogy' (2014) 23 JL & Soc Pol'y; Michael John McNamara, 'Supervision in Clinical Legal Education' in Michael John McNamara (ed), *Supervision in the Legal Profession* (Palgrave Macmillan 2020).

37 See section 2.

38 Kestenbaum et al. (n 2) 486.

39 See: https://www.bcu.ac.uk/law/research/centre-for-human-rights/consultancy/upr-project-at-bcu/implementing-recommendations-from-the-uns-upr.

refined as time has gone on and have been tailored to the individual research assistant.

Form and Strengthen Strategic Alliances among Local Clinic Partners

The third part of the framework is 'building and strengthening strategic alliances between the clinic and local partners'.[40] The need for creating strong alliances is important and the UPR Project has eight ongoing global partnerships, all of which have co-authored joint stakeholder report submissions with the UPR Project.

Kestenbaum et al. note that 'building and maintaining relationships with local clinic partners in developing countries, especially with limited resources for travel, can be challenging'.[41] However, for the UPR Project, particularly following the pandemic and the subsequent lockdowns imposed, the increased use of technology for communication has been helpful in creating and strengthening partnerships.[42] In particular, the availability of video calling has meant that we can easily engage with partners across the globe. For example, when working on the externally-funded CSO project, my research assistant sent 200 + individual personalised emails to CSOs that have engaged with the UPR across the world to invite them to engage with the survey and interview. This not only improved participant numbers on the CSO project but has had the initially unexpected but positive consequence of CSOs reaching out directly to the UPR Project regarding future partnerships. Moreover, when the UPR Project has spoken as a panellist at the UPR Pre-sessions, UPR Info created WhatsApp group chats to co-ordinate the panel. This has had another positive outcome, as it puts CSOs in touch with each other, allowing further dialogues to take place and partnerships to be created.

In terms of our stakeholder reports, another positive example is that we are more frequently partnering with other academic institutions, including LUMS University in Pakistan, Arizona State University in the Unites States, and Universidade Federal Fluminense and Universidade Estacio De Sa in Brazil, with other partnerships currently in development. This allows more human

40 Kestenbaum et al. (n 2) 487.

41 ibid 487.

42 While most of the literature refers to the pandemic's increase in the use of technology to bolster partnerships in the field of global health (see: Nik Norma Nik Hasan and Aswati Hamzah, 'Global Partnership Under a New Normal: Challenges and Response to COVID-19' in W. Leal Filho et al. (eds.), *Partnerships for the Goals, Encyclopedia of the UN Sustainable Development Goals* (Springer 2020); Theresa Bernado et al., 'Collaborating in the Time of COVID-19: The Scope and Scale of Innovative Responses to a Global Pandemic' (2021) 7(2), this is also true for other areas, including human rights.

rights academic research to be translated into practice, being viewed by UN bodies, Member State delegations, civil society, and lay people.[43]

A particular area that the UPR Project could strengthen in terms of this step of the framework is creating local partnerships in *all* countries that we submit stakeholder reports on. Kestenbaum et al. did note the issue of 'the time constraints within which the clinic must operate',[44] and we are also working to the UN's timeframe, meaning that there is not always time to find a local partner when writing stakeholder reports. However, we know that local human rights defenders' expertise is required. As Natalie Baird found in her study, in some instances international CSOs can 'distort … [the] authentic local voice' when submitting UPR stakeholder reports without local expertise and support.[45] The UPR Project team has already noted that this 'is a point of action for us to strengthen'[46] and the aim is to start by mapping out potential local partners earlier in the process when we make decisions on which Member States' UPRs we will submit to.

Kestenbaum et al. suggest that there is another way to alleviate this issue, by 'leveraging the intellectual capital available' in the current student body.[47] BCU has a diverse student community and, in particular, our LLM International Human Rights and LLM International Law students, as well as our PhD community, would be ideal candidates to support a local perspective on our reports while gaining CLE experience. There are examples of this working well in other CLE programmes, see the example previously from the University of Pretoria's Centre for Human Rights, where two African students (from Somaliland and Malawi) were part of a team that researched and wrote its submission to the African Commission regarding access to medicines and human rights.[48] Actioning this within the UPR Project's CLE offering would involve diversifying how we currently operate, with the students being further involved in the write-up phase of the report. This is a clear way of strengthening the CLE programme and we plan to trial this through inviting a current PhD student to lead on the research and drafting a stakeholder report in 2024.

Another way we currently leverage existing domestic expertise, is by utilising our diverse staff backgrounds to support a local viewpoint on submissions. For example, our reports to Nigeria and Mexico were co-written by

43 Alice Storey, 'Engaging with the UN Human Rights Council's Universal Periodic Review as an Academic' (2020) 23 (32) *Juris Poiesis* 662–664.

44 Kestenbaum et al. (n 2) 497.

45 Natalie Baird, 'The Role of International Non-Governmental Organisations in the Universal Periodic Review of Pacific Island States: Can 'Doing Good' Be Done Better?' (2015) *Melbourne Journal of International Law* 18.

46 Nazir, Storey and Yorke (n 5).

47 Kestenbaum et al. (n 2) 497.

48 Ezer et al. (n 18) 30–32.

Law colleagues with experience of living and working in the legal profession in those countries.

Develop Local Human Rights Legal and Advocacy Strategies

The fourth stage is to develop legal and advocacy strategies in order to meet the goals set out in previous stages. Kestenbaum et al. make clear that 'human rights legal strategy development is a process that involves identifying the legal problem(s), pinpointing and analyzing strategies to solve the problem(s), and weighing the pros and cons of each human rights litigation or advocacy strategy'.[49] While the UPR Project's advocacy starts at the international level (through the UPR), working our way back down to the domestic level via implementation of UPR recommendations, we still must consider the local, domestic human rights situation in order to prepare our strategy. For instance, in each country we report on, we must consider what the significant human rights issues are that require addressing at the UPR.

In terms of stakeholder reports, while the lead staff member decides upon the overarching human rights theme to focus on, the students are given the autonomy to lead on developing the detail. The students identify international and domestic laws, along with the relevant UPR recommendations from the previous cycle and whether there has been any implementation of those recommendations. The students will highlight significant issues that they believe should be included in the report and, from there, the supervising staff member (usually the lead author) will start to strategise in terms of which sub-themes should be included in the report.

A recent development has been to show the students examples of how we use the data that they produce. This includes showing them the method of how we divide their data into themes and do our data quality checks, and how this ultimately supports us in deciding which themes to include in the final report. We also provide clear feedback on their work (which Victor Goode suggests should 'meaningfully advance students' learning process')[50] and sometimes they are asked to revisit a task if it is incomplete. This allows students to 'learn from their experiences'[51] but in a 'supportive environment'.[52]

The subsequent stages, in terms of planning post-submission advocacy, including what takes place pre- and post-review, usually takes place outside of the students' involvement. This is another key point of reflection for the

49 Kestenbaum et al. (n 2) 489.

50 Victor M. Goode, 'There is a Method(ology) to This Madness: A Review and Analysis of Feedback in the Clinical Process' (2000) 53 Okla L Rev 223, 224.

51 Adrian Evans et al., 'Best Practices: Australian Clinical Legal Education' (September 2012) <https://cald.asn.au/wp-content/uploads/2012/11/Item_12.3_Best_Practices_Australian_Clinical_Legal_Education_Sept_2012.pdf> 4

52 ibid 17.

UPR Project team to consider whether there is a further, more in-depth role students could play.

Implement Local Legal Strategy and Human Rights Advocacy

This stage is when the strategies decided upon in step four are implemented in practice.[53] At this point, Kestenbaum et al. suggest that 'it is important to revisit the original goals and assigned tasks and revise and supplement them if necessary'.[54] Taking the UPR Project's recent engagement with the UPR of the United Kingdom of Great Britain and Northern Ireland provides an example of how we have implemented strategy and revised our goals and tasks as the advocacy developed. The United Kingdoms's Fourth Cycle UPR took place in 2022, for which we submitted two joint reports, harnessing two of our external partners, and inviting two BCU students and one extern to provide research assistance. Furthermore, two of our BCU PhD students co-authored on one of the submissions. This provided a multi-pronged opportunity for students across multiple levels of study to engage in CLE.

Our advocacy strategy continued after submission of the reports as Yorke, on behalf of the UPR Project at BCU, was selected as a panellist at the United Kingdom's UPR Pre-session. Created by leading non-government ogaisation (NGO), UPR Info, the Pre-sessions were created to provide 'civil society [with] an international platform to directly advocate to State delegations ahead of the UPR session' and also 'to facilitate diplomatic delegations to ascertain information on countries' human rights landscapes'.[55] While not a formal part of the UPR cycle itself, they are viewed as being vital to the UPR process and are well-attended by UN Member States delegations and CSOs alike.

Speaking at the United Kingdom's Pre-session involved drafting a short statement to deliver on the day, but also required the team to revisit the original goals of this specific stream of work, particularly because the human rights landscape in the United Kingdom had developed since we submitted our reports, and we wanted to discuss current, pressing issues such as the then-proposed Bill of Rights Bill.[56] This was a continuing CLE opportunity, as a PhD student who co-authored one of the reports was able to travel to Geneva to attend the Pre-session and engage in discussions with Member States, providing invaluable networking opportunities. Following this, the UPR Project at BCU and its partner organisation 4 King's Bench Walk were awarded funding from the Equality and Human Rights Commission to bring together human

53 Kestenbaum et al. (n 2) 492.

54 ibid 492.

55 UPR Info Pre-sessions: Empowering Human Rights Voices from the Ground, UPR Info (2016) www.upr-info.org/sites/default/files/generaldocument/pdf/2016_pre-sessionsempoweringhuman_rightsvoices from the ground.pdf 5–6.

56 See: https://bcuassets.blob.core.windows.net/docs/the-upr-project-at-bcu-pre-session-statement-on-the-uk-133126348239673018.pdf.

rights CSOs across England and Wales to engage with the United Kingdom's UPR. This included a broad range of events and publications[57] and led to the UPR Project being invited to give expert evidence to the UK Parliament's Joint Committee on Human Rights in May 2023, to inform its response to the United Kingdom's most recent UPR. By this time, said PhD student was nearing completion of their doctorate and was a full-time academic, but this had provided a level-appropriate CLE opportunity that the student could see through from start to finish.

This idea of ensuring students can see projects through to the end encourages 'a high level of student ownership of the work'.[58] A further example of this can be seen in relation to my funded CSO project. While the project was designed by me, my PhD-level research assistant was recruited at the very start. This has allowed the student to engage in mixed methods research for the first time, provided networking opportunities with CSOs, and has given them ideas for post-doctoral research. Owing to the excellent standard of work conducted, this has led to us continuing to work together on the project, analysing the dataset together, and we will co-author and launch all the outputs as a joint effort.

The employability and transferrable skills opportunities afforded by the UPR Project's CLE programme are not just open to PhD students. In 2019, I obtained an internal funding grant to recruit five undergraduate LLB students as paid research assistants, working on how the UPR engages with the right to health in the context of accessing HIV medication in five African countries. Their role was to collect data, then analyse and present that data both informally and formally. Their work informed multiple UPR Project stakeholder reports, as well as a book chapter on transparency within the UPR.[59] One student, reflecting on their experience of working on this project, said:

> I have gained and developed many valuable skills. For example, collecting and critically analysing United Nations data, which is an opportunity not many LLB students have. Also being able to collate and present my findings, not only to my supervisors, but at a staff research seminar and at a student conference enhanced my professional skills.[60]

57 See: https://www.bcu.ac.uk/law/research/centre-for-human-rights/consultancy/upr-project-at-bcu/universal-periodic-review-2022-uk-civil-society-engagement.

58 Anna E. Carpenter, 'The Project Model of Clinical Education: Eight Principles to Maximize Student Learning and Social Justice Impact' (2013) 20 *Clinical Law Review* 39–94, 44.

59 Storey and Eccleston-Turner (n 5).

60 Forward Thinking (2019) Vol 1 https://bcuassets.blob.core.windows.net/docs/Forward%20Thinking%20Vol%201%20Issue%201.pdf 18.

Reflect and Process with Partners and Students

The final stage of the framework is a reflective period, as Kestenbaum at al. find that engaging in reflections upon the work conducted, with both partners and students, is vital to the success of a clinical legal education programme.[61] There are various points of reflection that should be carried out by the UPR Project at BCU.

Firstly, consideration must be given to reflecting with the students and a suggestion from Hamman et al is to collect student feedback on their experiences.[62] Thornton and Shannon also believe that there should be a specific reflection on how the CLE has contributed to employability and a positive student learning experience.[63] To some extent, the UPR Project does this through the SRCs, as I, alongside my co-lead Laura Smillie, created the journal *Forward Thinking* in 2019 as an opportunity to promote the successes of the students and the SRC programme.[64] This was the first of its kind at BCU and is something that other departments are now keen to replicate. This also provided a further employability opportunity to students by being published in *Forward Thinking*, asking them to provide written reflections on their experiences (one such example is provided at the end of the previous section).

However, this reflective step is something that could be improved on. Particularly as the UPR Project's mission statement specifically aims to provide employability and transferrable skills for students, we must design a way of capturing this information and reflecting upon it regularly. A suggestion would be at the end of each UPR submission period, asking all students to complete a survey, as well as attend an informal discussion about their experiences. It is important that this is not just an exercise for us as the Project leads, but also for the students, as Kestenbaum et al found that teaching 'students the challenges, rewards, and skills needed for successful local, long-term, collaborative international human rights projects is essential for their future as human rights attorneys'[65] or indeed in any related field of work.

Secondly, and equally important, Katie Spillane cautions against 'a narrow focus on student outcomes'[66] instead there should be a broadening of 'the evaluative lens and embrace the perspectives and participation of all stakeholders'.[67] Spillane suggests that '[o]ne way of doing this is to use the signature pedagogy model that asks us to evaluate not only our surface actions and objectives but also the implicit values that the structures of our programs

61 Kestenbaum et al. (n 2) 493.

62 Hamman et al. (n 16) 118.

63 Thornton & Shannon (n 21).

64 See: https://www.bcu.ac.uk/law/research/student-research-collaborations.

65 Kestenbaum et al. (n 2) 493.

66 Katie Spillane, 'Being the Change: Social Justice in Externship Program Evaluation' (2016) 33(2) *The Windsor Yearbook of Access to Justice* 45–67, 47.

67 ibid 67.

embody and communicate'.[68] In some ways, the UPR Project at BCU does this quite well, as we monitor the impact of our work at the UPR, including how our work influences recommendations and their implementation domestically. However, we could incorporate a clearer reflective practice with our partner organisations into the UPR Project's operation.

I would add a third point of reflection to this stage of the framework, which is to check in with colleagues who work on the UPR Project. Student burnout was mentioned above, but this is also relevant for staff members, especially when we are consistently working on real-life human rights abuses, whilst supervising students in relation to this.[69]

Conclusion

By engaging in this reflective exercise, it has allowed me to identify the strengths of the operation of the UPR Project at BCU, and ways it could be improved as an extra-curricular CLE activity. Moreover, I have identified broader proposals for engaging law students in more non-traditional clinical legal education opportunities in the human rights field and I conclude by setting them out here.

First, it is advantageous to utilise existing expertise for CLE, for example, how the UPR Project at BCU has harnessed our existing expertise on the UPR mechanism and specific thematic human rights issues in different countries. Using the expertise of colleagues, students, and partner organisations is a way of expanding CLE opportunities. CLE directors should also be encouraged to think outside of the box, in that it does not have to be a traditional credit-bearing live case-work clinic. While there are inclusivity factors to be considered, extra-curricular, non-traditional CLE holds much value for students and their employability skills.

Second, formal opportunities for reflection upon multiple aspects of the CLE must be created, reflecting upon the student experience and the impact upon their employability skills as well as partner organisations' experiences. Ideally, a first iteration of this reflective model should be in place prior to the CLE opportunity beginning, to ensure reflection is a core concept, with regular reflections being built into the structure of the programme.

Finally, consider creating a dedicated publication to celebrate students' successes in the CLE, such as *Forward Thinking*.[70] This not only celebrates the achievements of the students but encourages them to think reflectively and identify how the CLE has benefited their personal development.

68 ibid.

69 Sarah Knuckey, Margaret Satterthwaite, and Adam Brown, 'Trauma, Depression, and Burnout in the Human Rights Field: Identifying Barriers and Pathways to Resilient Advocacy' (2018) 49 Colum Hum Rts L Rev 267.

70 Forward Thinking (n 60).

The UPR Project at BCU is just one example of a CLE programme that seeks to teach students to advocate for human rights and global justice. What is clear is that clinical legal education, in all of its forms, provides significant opportunities for students that I argue all law students should be given the chance to experience.

Bibliography

Baird, Natalie, 'The Role of International Non-Governmental Organisations in the Universal Periodic Review of Pacific Island States: Can "Doing Good" Be Done Better?' (2015) 16(2) *Melbourne Journal of International Law* 18.

Bernado, Theresa, et al., 'Collaborating in the Time of COVID-19: The Scope and Scale of Innovative Responses to a Global Pandemic' (2021) 7(2) *JMIR Public Health Surveill.*

BCU Centre for Human Rights, 'Implementing Recommendations from the UN's UPR: Strengthening the Role of Civil Society' <https://www.bcu.ac.uk/law/research/centre-for-human-rights/consultancy/upr-project-at-bcu/implementing-recommendations-from-the-uns-upr> accessed 18 December 2023.

BCU Centre for Human Rights, 'The UPR Project at BCU' <https://www.bcu.ac.uk/law/research/centre-for-human-rights/consultancy/upr-project-at-bcu> accessed 18 December 2023.

BCU Centre for Human Rights, 'Universal Periodic Review 2022 – UK Civil Society Engagement' <https://www.bcu.ac.uk/law/research/centre-for-human-rights/consultancy/upr-project-at-bcu/universal-periodic-review-2022-uk-civil-society-engagement> accessed 18 December 2023.

BCU, Forward Thinking (2019) Vol. 1 <https://bcuassets.blob.core.windows.net/docs/Forward%20Thinking%20Vol%201%20Issue%201.pdf.

BCU, 'Law Clinic' <https://www.bcu.ac.uk/law/student-experience-and-employability/law-clinic> accessed 18 December 2023.

BCU, 'Student Research Collaborations' <https://www.bcu.ac.uk/law/research/student-research-collaborations> accessed 18 December 2023.

Carpenter, Anna E., 'The Project Model of Clinical Education: Eight Principles to Maximize Student Learning and Social Justice Impact' (2013) 20 *Clinical Law Review* 39–94.

Carrillo, Arturo J., 'Bringing International Law Home: The Innovative Role of Human Rights Clinics in the Transnational Legal Process' (2004) 35(3) *Columbia Human Rights Law Review* 527.

Collinson, Robert, et al., 'Clients, Clinics and Social Justice: Reducing Inequality (and Embedding Legal Ethics) via an LLB Portfolio Pathway' (2018) 8(3) *Higher Education, Skills and Work-Based Learning* 323–336.

Dickinson, Jill, Griffiths, Teri-Lisa, and Bredice, Alex, '"It's Just Another Thing to Think About": Encouraging Students' Engagement in Extracurricular Activities' (2019) 45(6) *Journal of Further and Higher Education* 744–757.

Ezer, Tamar, Deshko, Ludmylla, Gunn Leark, Nicola, Kameni, Enga, and Lasky, Bruce A., 'Promoting Public Health through Clinical Legal Education: Initiatives in South Africa, Thailand, and Ukraine' (2020) 17(2) *Human Rights Brief* 27–33.

Giddings, Jeff, 'Contemplating the Future of Clinical Legal Education' (2014) 17(1) *Clinical Legal Education Symposium* 1–26.

Gledhill, Kris, 'Establishing an International Human Rights Clinic in the New Zealand Context' (2013) 19 *International Journal of Clinical Legal Education* 295–310.

Goode, Victor M., 'There is a Method(ology) to This Madness: A Review and Analysis of Feedback in the Clinical Process' (2000) 53 *Oklahoma Law Review* 223.

Hamman, Evan, et al., 'Pro Bono Partnerships in Environmental Law: Enhancing Outcomes for Universities and CLCs' (2014) 39(2) *Alternative Law Journal* 115–119.

Hasan, Nik Norma Nik, and Hamzah, Aswati, 'Global Partnership Under a New Normal: Challenges and Response to COVID-19' in W. Leal Filho et al. (eds.), *Partnerships for the Goals, Encyclopedia of the UN Sustainable Development Goals* (Springer 2020).

Jabyn, Marium, 'Advancing Justice Interests and Human Rights of Vulnerable Groups through Clinical Legal Education' (2020) 11(2) *Jindal Global Law Review* 271–288.

Kestenbaum, Jocelyn Getgen, Hoyos-Ceballos, Esteban, and Talvadkar, Melissa C. Del Aguila, 'Catalysts for Change: A Proposed Framework for Human Rights Clinical Teaching and Advocacy' (2012) 18 *Clinical Law Review* 459.

Knuckey, Sarah, Satterthwaite, Margaret, and Brown, Adam, 'Trauma, Depression, and Burnout in the Human Rights Field: Identifying Barriers and Pathways to Resilient Advocacy' (2018) 49 *Columbia Human Rights Law Review* 267.

Madhloom, Omar, and McFaul, Hugh. (eds), *Thinking About Clinical Legal Education: Philosophical and Theoretical Perspectives* (Taylor and Francis 2021).

McNamara, Michael John, 'Supervision in Clinical Legal Education' in Michael John McNamara (ed.), *Supervision in the Legal Profession* (Palgrave Macmillan 2020).

Meghdadi, Mohammed Mahdi, and Nasab, Ahmad Erfani, 'The Role of Legal Clinics of Law Schools in Human Rights Education; Mofid University Legal Clinic Experience' (2011) 15 *Procedia Social and Behavioral Sciences* 3014–3017.

Mikinyango, Asha and Nguru, Judith, 'Law Schools as Legal Aid Providers in Kenya: Challenges and Lessons Learnt from Practice' (2021) 28(2) *International Journal of Clinical Legal Education* 117–48.

Milner, Sharon, Cousins, Wendy, and McGowan, Iain, 'Does All Work and No Play Make a Dull Graduate? Perceptions of Extra-curricular Activities and Employability' (2016) 4(1) *Journal of Perspectives in Applied Academic Practice* 13–18.

Nazir, Amna, 'The Universal Periodic Review and the Death Penalty: A Case Study of Pakistan' (2020) 4(1) *RSIL Law Review* 126.

Nazir, Amna, Storey, Alice, and Yorke, Jon, 'The Universal Periodic Review as Utopia' in Damian Etone, Amna Nazir and Alice Storey (eds.), *Human Rights and the UN Universal Periodic Review Mechanism: A Research Companion* (Routledge2024).

Smyth, Gemma, and Overholt, Marion, 'Framing Supervisory Relationships in Clinical Law: The Role of Critical Pedagogy' (2014) 23(1) *Journal of Law and Social Policy* 62–82.

Spillane, Katie, 'Being the Change: Social Justice in Externship Program Evaluation' (2016) 33(2) *The Windsor Yearbook of Access to Justice* 45–67.

Storey, Alice, 'Challenges and Opportunities for the UN Universal Periodic Review: A Case Study on Capital Punishment in the USA' (2021) 90 *University of Missouri-Kansas City School of Law* 129.

Storey, Alice, 'Engaging with the UN Human Rights Council's Universal Periodic Review as an Academic' (2020) 23(32) *Juris Poiesis* 662–664.

Storey, Alice, 'Improving Recommendations from the UN's Universal Periodic Review: A Case Study on Domestic Abuse in the UK' (2023) 35 *Pace International Law Review* 193.

Storey, Alice, and Eccleston-Turner, Mark, 'Transparency, Accountability, and Legitimacy in the United Nations' Human Rights Council's Universal Periodic Review' in Salvador Santino Regilme Jr and Irene Hadiprayitno (eds.), *Human Rights at Risk: Rethinking International Institutions, American Power, and the Future of Dignity* (Rutgers University Press 2022).

Stuart, Mary, Lido, Catherine, Morgan, Jessica, Soloman, Lucy, and May, Steve, 'The Impact of Engagement with Extracurricular Activities on the Student Experience and Graduate Outcomes for Widening Participation Populations' (2011) 12(3) *Active Learning in Higher Education* 203–215.

The UPR Project at BCU, 'Pre-session Statement: The United Kingdom of Great Britain and Northern Ireland' <https://bcuassets.blob.core.windows.net/docs/the-upr-project-at-bcu-pre-session-statement-on-the-uk-133126348239673018.pdf> accessed 18 December 2023.

The UPR Project at BCU, 'Strategy and Mission Statement' (June 2023).

Thornton, Margaret, and Shannon, Lucinda, 'Selling the Dream: Law School Branding and the Illusion of Choice' (2013) 23 *Legal Education Review* 249.

UPR Info Pre-sessions: Empowering Human Rights Voices from the Ground, UPR Info (2016) <www.upr-info.org/sites/default/files/generaldocument/pdf/2016_pre-sessionsempoweringhuman_rightsvoices from the ground.pdf>.

Vasanthi, Nimushakavi, 'Strengthening Clinical Legal Education in India' (2012) 42(4) *Social Change* 443.

Yeatman, Lucy, and Hewitt, Louise, 'Feedback: A Reflection on the use of Nicol and Macfarlane-Dick's Feedback Principles to Engage Learners' (2021) 55(2) *The Law Teacher* 227–240.

7 The Changing Experience of Teaching Public Law Since 2010

New Labour, a Novel Coalition Government, the Scottish Referendum, Brexit and the Trampling of Constitutional Norms

Chris Monaghan

Introduction

In this chapter I will draw upon my experiences of teaching Public Law since 2010. I have taught Public Law at a number of different universities which reflect the changing nature of higher education within England and Wales. These were two private universities and four public universities which all received university status at different times since the 1980s. I will consider the impact of the last twelve years, which can be properly described as a constitutional and political rollercoaster, on teaching Public Law and the context in which those who teach Public Law have had to confront the changing educational, financial and political landscape as part of their teaching. As Alan McGuinness of Sky News declared, '[w]hen it comes to upheaval and drama, you would be hard-pressed to find a more jam-packed decade in British politics than the 2010s.'[1] This is not hyperbole, as readers may find themselves having to struggle to remember the precise order of prime ministers since 2019, or a time when politics was not caught up with bitter controversy over Brexit. The 2010s presented the rollercoaster of a decade.

This rollercoaster began with the demise of New Labour and a resurgent Conservative party led by David Cameron.

A Farewell to New Labour

New Labour promised so much and delivered a lot during its 13 years in government. However by 2010 Labour was tainted by the 2003 invasion of Iraq and questions of the accuracy of the information told to Parliament, the bitter

This chapter is based on a paper that was originally presented at the Reimagining Public Law: Teaching the Constitution in a Permacrisis workshop, organised by Dr Alex Latham at the University of Birmingham.

1 Alan McGuinness, 'The 2010s: A decade that shook the foundations of British politics,' Sky News, 7 January 2000, available at: https://news.sky.com/story/the-2010s-a-decade-that-shook-the-foundations-of-british-politics-11894896, accessed on 11 June 2024.

DOI: 10.4324/9781003457985-7

rivalry between Tony Blair and Gordon Brown, the departure of Blair and his replacement by Brown in 2007.[2] The former Labour Cabinet Minister Lord Andrew Adonis noted that, 'Tory governments are the norm in England; Labour governments the exception. That was the rule before Blair. It has been the rule since Blair. In the electoral sphere, New Labour's achievement was highly personal and much of it transient.'[3] For the success of the Blair government, 'The obvious points are that New Labour barely outlived Tony Blair, and proved unable to win an election even under his decade-long chancellor, Gordon Brown.'[4] The New Labour experiment was over in 2010 and the Labour party would struggle in opposition as it faced a repeat of the 1980s, where different factions within the party fought a civil war for the soul of the party.

But New Labour had changed the face of the constitution. Starting from 1997 and right up until 2010 Labour had been bold, perhaps not as bold as some people may have wanted, but bold never the less so that today its reforms are viewed with outright hostility by some sections of the political right.[5]

In terms of Public Law the government's constitutional reform agenda saw the creation of a Supreme Court, the exclusion of the majority of hereditary peers from the House of Lords, a devolution settlement for Wales and Scotland, the return of self-rule to Northern Ireland and the Good Friday Agreement, the reform of the office of the Lord Chancellor, the enactment of the Human Rights Act 1998, the Equality Act 2010, the harmonisation of the age of consent between heterosexual and homosexual relationships, the Constitutional Reform and Governance Act 2010 which saw the civil service placed on a statutory footing and the Ponsonby convention (which governed foreign treaties) being placed on a statutory footing.[6] However, it is vital to consider just how significant this constitutional reform was.

The former New Labour Lord Chancellor, Lord Falconer of Thoroton, held that, 'Between 1997 and 2010, the Labour government overhauled our

2 For example see Rabbil Sikdar, 'The middle class will never understand how much Tony Blair's policies improved the lives of families like mine,' *Independent*, 28 January 2018, available at: https://www.independent.co.uk/voices/new-labour-tony-blair-socialism-working-class-families-a8182031.html, accessed on 11 June 2024. For a lukewarm assessment see Polly Toynbee and David Walker, 'The Labour years: Could have done better,' *The Guardian*, 25 September 2010, available at: https://www.theguardian.com/politics/2010/sep/25/labour-years-term-report, accessed on 11 June 2024.

3 Andrew Adonis, 'What did New Labour achieve?,' *Prospect*, 4 May 2022, available at: https://www.prospectmagazine.co.uk/politics/38600/what-did-new-labour-achieve, accessed on 11 June 2024.

4 ibid.

5 See for example, Jemma Slingo, 'Abolish Supreme Court – think tank,' *The Law Society Gazette*, 31 July 2020, available at: https://www.lawgazette.co.uk/news/abolish-supreme-court-think-tank-/5105245.article, accessed on 11 June 2024.

6 For a review of what Labour achieved in government see Michael Gordon and Adam Tucker (eds), *The New Labour Constitution: Twenty Years On* (Hart Publishing 2022).

constitution to bring it closer to the people – to increase the people's control over those who governed them. Those changes have served the country well.'[7] Commenting in 2005 Matthew Flinders offered a cautious assessment, 'although significant, the actual degree of reform in Britain is less radical than is commonly assumed: although New Labour is committed to far-reaching constitutional reform in *principle* it has been far less committed in *practice*.'[8]

The May 2010 General Election resulted in no overall winner within the traditional Westminster expectations of 'the winner takes it all.' David Cameron's Conservatives had 307 Members of Parliament (MPs), Gordon Brown's Labour had 257 MPs and Nick Clegg's Liberal Democrats had 58 MPs. No one was remotely close to having a majority in the House of Commons. The situation necessitated a coalition government to be formed. But between which political parties? There had been talk of a Labour-Liberal Democrat coalition government before Labour's resounding success in the 1997 General Election. But 2010 was not 1997, and Gordon Brown was not a fresh-faced Tony Blair who promised change after almost 18 years of Conservative governments, rather he was serious and reportedly hot-tempered former Chancellor of the Exchequer who had been second only to Tony Blair during Blair's time as Prime Minister.[9]

Prime Minister Gordon Brown's perceived squatting in 10 Downing Street, whilst he waited (perfectly constitutionally appropriately) for the emergence of a Coalition government, was heavily criticised in some sections of the media.[10] What was Brown to do? Resign as Prime Minister and advise the late Queen Elizabeth II to appoint a caretaker Prime Minister from amongst his frontbench

7 Lord Falconer of Thoroton, '*Labour's Constitutional Changes 1997–2010: Time for More*' in Michael Gordon and Adam Tucker (eds), *The New Labour Constitution: Twenty Years On* (Hart Publishing 2022) 24.

8 Matthew Flinders, 'Majoritarian democracy in Britain: New Labour and the Constitution' (2005) 28(1) *West European Politics* 61–93.

9 See for example, Patrick Wintour, 'How Gordon Brown's tantrums caused a storm over Downing St,' *The Guardian*, 21 February 2010, available at: https://www.theguardian.com/politics/2010/feb/21/gordon-brown-tantrums-downing-street, accessed on 11 June 2024.

10 For context (from a Labour perspective) see Andrew Adonis, *5 Days in May: The Coalition and Beyond* (Biteback Publishing 2013).

In Jackie Ashley's opinion, 'Gordon Brown has not been "squatting" in Downing Street for the last few days – he has had to stay on as prime minister until a new prime minister emerged.' (See 'Gordon Brown's resignation statement: verdict', *The Guardian*, 10 May 2010, available at: https://www.theguardian.com/commentisfree/2010/may/10/gordon-brown-statement, accessed on 11 June 2024. However, see *The Daily Mail's* view: 'Mr Brown, who has effectively been a 'squatter' at Number Ten since the election delivered Labour's worst result in decades and ended in a hung parliament, at last gave in to the inevitable.' (Nicola Boden, 'From green-eyed Chancellor to the "squatter of No10", Gordon Brown finally admits he can't hang on to job he coveted for so long,' Daily Mail, 10 May 2010, available at: https://www.dailymail.co.uk/news/election/article-1272278/From-green-eyed-Chancellor-squatter-No10-Gordon-Brown-finally-admits-hang-job-coveted-long.html, last accessed on 11 June 2024.

cabinet ministers, or to advise the Queen to invite David Cameron to form the new government (even if it was far from clear that Cameron would, without a coalition with the Liberal Democrats, enjoy the confidence of the House of Commons).

'England Does Not Love Coalitions' and Brexit

The Coalition that formed between the Conservatives and Liberal Democrats parties was novel, as the United Kingdom never really does peacetime coalitions[11] (the last one being in the 1930s), and the Fox-North of Coalition is just one example of how these can be perceived.[12] Hence the rollercoaster of the past 13 years has taken us through constitutional reform, the introduction of the Cabinet Manual, a nationwide referendum on changing the method of voting at a General Election, stalled reforms to the House of Lords, the rise and (fall) of the war power convention and a referendum on Scottish independence. The 2015 emergence of a sole Conservative government resulted in the Brexit referendum, the *Miller* litigation,[13] the Daily Mail's 'Enemies of the people' labelling of the judiciary[14] and a spectacular succession of Conservative prime ministers including one who was outlasted by a lettuce.[15] By 2023 the plan to

11 As Disraeli observed in 1852, 'England does not love coalitions' (see JP Parry, 'Disraeli and England' (2000) 43(3) *The Historical Journal* 699, 708. See also Vernon Bogdanor, *The Coalition and the Constitution* (Hart Publishing 2011).

12 The Fox-North Coalition between Lord North and Charles James Fox was viewed with hostility by George III which led to the King's intervention over India Bill of 1783 (known as Fox's East India Bill). As CH Philips observed, 'It caused the fall of the Fox-North coalition, gave George III the opportunity to make a daring use of his influence, doomed Fox to be "a voice crying in the wilderness" for almost the rest of his life, and put Pitt in office practically for his lifetime.' (CH Philips, 'The East India Company "Interest" and the English Government, 1783–4' (1937) 20 *Transactions of the Royal Historical Society* 83). For context see John Cannon, *The Fox-North Coalition: Crisis of the Constitution, 1782–4* (Cambridge University Press 1970) and Chris Monaghan, 'In defence of intrinsic human rights: Edmund Burke's controversial prosecution of Warren Hastings, Governor-General of Bengal' (2011) 1(2) *Law, Crime and History* 58. See also Thomas Rowlandson, 'Brittannia roused or the coalition monsters destroyed' (3 February 1784) for a caricature depicting the fall of the Fox-North Coalition.

13 *R (on the application of Miller) v Secretary of State for Exiting the European Union* (Miller no. 1) [2017] UKSC 5 and *R (on the application of Miller) v The Prime Minister* (Miller no. 2) [2019] UKSC 41.

14 See James Slack, 'Enemies of the people: Fury over "out of touch" judges who have "declared war on democracy" by defying 17.4m Brexit voters and who could trigger a constitutional crisis,' *The Daily Mail*, 3 November 2016, available at: https://www.dailymail.co.uk/news/article-3903436/Enemies-people-Fury-touch-judges-defied-17-4m-Brexit-voters-trigger-constitutional-crisis.html, accessed on 11 June 2024. For expert commentary see Joshua Rozenberg, *Enemies of the People? How Judges Shape Society* (Bristol University Press 2020).

15 Matthew Weaver, 'Iceberg lettuce in blonde wig outlasts Liz Truss,' *The Guardian*, 20 October 2022, available at: https://www.theguardian.com/politics/2022/oct/20/iceberg-lettuce-in-blonde-wig-outlasts-liz-truss, accessed on 11 June 2024.

repeal the Human Rights Act 1998 and replace it with a British Bill of Rights had been abandoned, former Prime Minister Boris Johnson, who was ousted from office by an exodus of his senior ministers, finally faced parliamentary accountability for lying to Parliament over party-gate and as a consequence left the House of Commons in order avoid a formal suspension. Early 2024 saw a resurgent Labour Party is promising wholesale constitutional reform in the event that it won the next general election (which it did win in July 2024).[16]

The Problem for Teachers of Public Law

Thus, the problem presented by this brief and far from comprehensive account is namely, how do we as teachers of Public Law teach our subject to (typically) first year law students. Although colleagues teaching students who are coming to law as graduates of another academic discipline will teach Public Law as part of a graduate diploma or equivalent.

Yes, the inevitable photo of the lettuce will surely get a laugh, party-gate may trigger memories of the national lockdown and family bereavement, but is this enough to show relevancy? From the outset we need to teach Public Law in a way that explains the significance of these events and decisions, as they have shaped the constitutional landscape and must be taught. It is very easy to reduce the period of time since 2010 to a series of caricatures, memes and horror stories (depending on one's interpretation of the political situation), but to do so risks simplifying this period into one where we can pick goodies and baddies and in doing so bring in our own implicit moral and political judgement.

If we are lucky to have a 30-credit module[17] dedicated to this material in Public Law, then how do we teach this to a students who may, or may not, be aware of this rollercoaster ride. It might often be the temptation to presume that people living and growing up during the period in which this rollercoaster ride took place would for the most part be fully aware of what happened, if not perhaps its significance. Their belies the problem, as even if the events only occurred just a few years previously, how can we presume that people (including those who might have been young children when the Brexit referendum occurred) would somehow have the same level of awareness (and interest) as someone in their thirties or forties who had voted or at least followed the events on the television, print media, online websites or through social media.

This cannot be helped given the rollercoaster ride. By way of example, most students beginning their law studies in 2002 would have known at that point just three Prime Ministers during their lifetimes. Today's new law students

16 See Robert Greally, 'The Brown Report: Political legitimacy and the power of the assembly,' U.K. Const. L. Blog (26 January 2023) (available at https://ukconstitutionallaw.org/), accessed on 11 June 2024 and Tarun Khaitan, 'A Fourth Branch of the State? On Constitutional Guarantors in the UK', U.K. Const. L. Blog (30 March 2023) (available at https://ukconstitutionallaw.org/), accessed on 11 June 2024.

17 In England and Wales an undergraduate degree is constituted of 360 credits.

might have known four Prime Ministers just since starting High School, and find the intricate minutiose fine detail of the Brexit saga difficult to follow.

Presumption of knowledge cannot always be a given, and there is a balance needed when setting the pace and style of teaching. Across my teaching career to date I have taught Public Law at six different universities and teaching Public Law effectively has required me to adapt how and what I teach, in terms of scope, presumption of contextual knowledge and what material engages with, and is of relevance to, the students.

Higher education has changed since 2010. For starters in England and Wales we have increased competition within the university sector with more providers willing to claim a share of the undergraduate market, the end of the Qualifying Law Degree (in terms of the SRA), the introduction of the Teaching Excellence Framework, the increase in tuition fees and the treatment of higher education as a commodity, the societal and economic impact of Covid, the financial crisis and the on-going cost of living crisis.[18]

Times are tough, students expect more from universities at a time when universities themselves are struggling amid a shortage of public funding, and from a student perspective there is an understandable need for us as teachers to justify why we teach what we do and how we teach it.

We as teachers of Public Law face another challenge. More often than not students enrolling on a law degree will initially think of law as being Criminal Law (a perception reinforced by the glut of crime dramas on television and the student favourite, *How to Get Away with Murder*,)[19] and Commercial Law

18 See Helena Gillespie, 'Higher education funding shake-up: what it means for students and universities,' The Conversation, 25 February 2022, available at: https://theconversation.com/higher-education-funding-shake-up-what-it-means-for-students-and-universities-177778, accessed on 11 June 2024. Commenting on the restriction to higher education and the limitation student finance loans to perceived weaker students, Gillespie states, '[n]ow, the proposals under consultation – limiting loans for students who do not achieve certain grades – aim to prevent students who might not be academically capable from getting government backed student finance for a degree. As currently billed, the bar is low enough that it may not exclude many students. But it still matters. Some of those likely not to have made the grade might be those most in need of an educational second chance – those who have suffered illness in their teens, or had a disrupted family background or educational history.' This is important, given the need to open up disciplines and professions, such as the legal profession, and the implications that the *defacto* exclusion of certain students may have on equality. See also, 'Despite some huge changes, the last 20 years of higher education policy have left some big questions unresolved,' HEPI, 12 July 2023, available at: https://www.hepi.ac.uk/2023/07/12/despite-some-huge-changes-the-last-20-years-of-higher-education-policy-have-left-some-big-questions-unresolved/, accessed on 11 June 2024. For the impact of the internalisation on higher education see David Law and Michael Hoey (eds). *Perspectives on the Internalisation of Higher Education* (Routledge 2018).

19 Adam Banner, '"How to Get Away with Murder" takes a somewhat realistic look at law school and legal employment,' *ABA Journal*, 15 October 2018, available at: https://www.abajournal.com/news/article/how_to_get_away_with_murder_takes_a_somewhat_realistic_look_at_law_schoo, accessed on 11 June 2024.

(think for example the television show *Suits*).[20] Perhaps the most famous law student of recent times (albeit in the United States), Kim Kardashian posted on *Instagram*, that 'I f[***]ing hate Constitutional Law!!! Anyone else feel me?.'[21] Therefore, studying Criminal Law and Contract Law may appear to make sense from a student's perspective – however, where does this leave Public Law?

As Public Law teachers we can make reference to the constitutional and political rollercoaster, but just how aware and comfortable our students may be with this will depend on the extent of their own prior knowledge, prior study (such as A level politics) and their background. Given that we *will* cover comparative political events, political history and constitutional history over the course of the Public Law module, students are correct in observing 'it is not like our other modules.'

My view is that since 2010 we have faced a number of challenges as teachers of Public Law. These challenges are not unique to now, and I am sure that these challenges were just as relevant to those teaching Public Law at the advent of the Callaghan, Thatcher, Major or Blair governments in the 1970s to 2000s.

Firstly, how do we engage students with often complex political, legal and constitutional events and disputes? Engagement is key – we cannot presume prior knowledge, even where we imagine that a large part of the cohort may have an interest in current affairs or politics. Therefore, how do we engage students (thus ensuring student success and a positive experience) and teach Public Law in a manner that is not superficial or conceals the complexities and nuances of our discipline?

Secondly, how do we achieve the first point, and manage to avoid student fatigue especially given the dominance of the issues in the press and media? We may presume that there has never been a more interesting time to study Public Law. That may be true of the opportunities for us to research, and the perception that we can illustrate our in-class examples with reference to current affairs and events. For example, since drafting my initial problem scenarios at the University of Worcester in 2016 I have seen elements of the purposely far-fetched situations become reality, or very close to reality (not least Prince Harry, the Duke of Sussex's judicial review over his security arrangements when he is in the United Kingdom,[22] or the rule of law issues associated with

20 Katie King, 'Too many students aspire to be Harvey Specter "rainmakers", says law school director,' *Legal Cheek*, 28 September 2017, available at: https://www.legalcheek.com/2017/09/too-many-students-aspire-to-be-harvey-specter-rainmakers-says-law-school-director/, accessed on 11 June 2024.

21 Emma Hinkley, '"I f****** hate Constitutional Law,' says Kim Kardashian,' *Legal Cheek*, 2 March 2023, available at: https://www.legalcheek.com/2023/03/i-f-hate-constitutional-law-says-kim-kardashian/, accessed on 11 June 2024.

22 *R (on the application of the Duke of Sussex) v The Secretary of State for the Home Department* [2024] EWHC 418 (Admin).

an incoming government's proposed constitutional reforms). The problem we face is fatigue – students have been bombarded in the news by Brexit, the foibles of politicians, bullying and criminality in politics etc. Sections of the media and some politicians have targeted experts, thus seemingly pitting the person on the Clapham Omnibus against those teaching the rationale for a judicial decision (despite political criticism and media hostility).[23] Few will have forgotten how a Conservative MP requested information from universities about the 'the names of professors... who are involved in the teaching of European affairs, with particular reference to Brexit' and seeking copies 'of the syllabus and links to the online lectures.'[24] As Anna Fazackerley in *The Guardian* observed that 'Neatly ignor[ed] the long tradition of academic freedom that universities consider crucial to their success.'

In response the Vice-Chancellor at my own institution refused and was reported in *The Guardian* as saying that, 'This letter just asking for information appears so innocent but is really so, so dangerous... Here is the first step to the thought police, the political censor and newspeak, naturally justified as 'the will of the British people.' Another academic, Professor Kevin Featherstone from the LSE was highly critical of the letter and the implications raised by Heaton-Harris' approach: 'The letter reflects a past of a McCarthyite nature. It smacks of asking: are you or have you ever been in favour of remain? There is clearly an implied threat that universities will somehow be challenged for their bias.'[25]

In terms of whether Heaton-Harris' approach had the support of the Prime Minister, Downing Street offered an implicit rebuke when questioned by journalists: '"Chris Heaton-Harris wrote to universities in his capacity as an MP, not as a representative of the government," the prime minister's spokesman said. "I think what the prime minister has always been very clear on is her

23 See Matt Motta, '"Had enough of experts?" Anti-intellectualism is linked to voters' support for movements that are skeptical of expertise,' LSE Blogs, 30 August 2017, available at: https://blogs.lse.ac.uk/usappblog/2017/08/30/had-enough-of-experts-anti-intellectualism-is-linked-to-voters-support-for-movements-that-are-skeptical-of-expertise/, accessed on 11 June 2024. As Motta wrote, 'In June 2016, outspoken Brexit advocate Michael Gove claimed that the United Kingdom has "had enough of experts." Gove was apparently "glad" that his campaign failed to win the support of European Union economists; echoing the catchphrase of America's most-prominent Brexit supporter in telling them, "*you're fired!*"' It is not just academics that come under attack, see Dominic Grieve, 'Blaming the Judges: What is our problem with politicians when it comes to the Law,' Talk to Judicial Institute, University College London, 6 December 2022, available at: https://www.ucl.ac.uk/judicial-institute/sites/judicial_institute/files/blaming_judges_final_53092.pdf, accessed on 11 June 2024.

24 Anna Fazackerley, 'Universities deplore "McCarthyism" as MP demands list of tutors lecturing on Brexit,' *The Guardian*, 24 October 2017, available at: https://www.theguardian.com/education/2017/oct/24/universities-mccarthyism-mp-demands-list-brexit-chris-heaton-harris#:~:text=Chris%20Heaton%2DHarris%2C%20Conservative%20MP,with%20particular%20reference%20to%20Brexit, accessed on 11 June 2024.

25 ibid.

respect for the freedom and independence of universities and the role they play in creating open and stimulating debate."'[26] Chris Heaton-Harris subsequently used Twitter to defend his actions, 'To be absolutely clear, I believe in free speech in our universities and in having an open and vigorous debate on Brexit.'[27] My concern with this both at the time, and now, is that whilst academics invite debate and accept that the public must feel that universities are to some extent accountable (and I use this term cautiously) for what they teach, this felt to many like a direct attempt to implicitly regulate how Brexit was being taught. Heaton-Harris' curiosity is perfectly fine, but given the broader context, the text of the letter, and his position, it was concerning.

Thirdly, as teachers of Public Law how do we approach controversial and divisive events in a way that does not alienate any section of the cohort, but with the aim of always maintaining the underlying importance of academic freedom? To put it another way how do we give time to discussing views that we (and the majority of our fellow Public Law colleagues) may disagree with, or find problematic? The answer is that where appropriate – we should critique, but we must be open about our position and invite our students to reach their own conclusions. Furthermore, how do we manage cohorts where there may differing opinions about Brexit, repealing the Human Rights Act 1998 or the conduct of politicians, in such a way to not alienate, silence or deter students from contributing?[28] The title for this chapter is deliberately provocative with the inclusion of the words, 'the trampling of constitutional norms'. This quite rightly implies that I take a view as to whether the constitution has been respected by those in power. My view is that the government of Boris Johnson was characterised by a lack of respect for constitutional norms. Therein lies the problem, how to teach Public Law and make an informed judgement, whilst avoiding political point-scoring and not alienating those students who may take a different view as to Johnson and his government. Thus, we need to reference a counter-view, and demonstrate why this conduct is concerning. As Lord Hennessy put it pithily, '[i]f the prime minister is the number one wrong 'un, you're in deep, deep trouble. It's shown us the fragility of our constitution.'[29]

26 Jessica Elgot et al., 'No 10 disowns Tory whip accused of "McCarthyite" behaviour,' *The Guardian*, 24 October 2017, available at: https://www.theguardian.com/education/2017/oct/24/no-10-disowns-tory-whip-accused-of-mccarthyite-behaviour-universities-brexit, accessed on 11 June 2024.

27 Twitter, 24 October 2017, available: https://twitter.com/chhcalling/status/922796314265571328?ref_src=twsrc%5Etfw%7Ctwcamp%5Etweetembed%7Ctwterm%5E922796314265571328%7Ctwgr%5Ed7df2ba618a1e4083f8516f40a49d71813e7d5ee%7Ctwcon%5Es1_&ref_url=https%3A%2F%2Fwww.theguardian.com%2Feducation%2F2017%2Foct%2F24%2Fno-10-disowns-tory-whip-accused-of-mccarthyite-behaviour-universities-brexit, accessed on 11 June 2024.

28 This is something that Josie Welsh and I discuss in Chapter 9.

29 Henry Mance, '"A bonfire of the decencies": Peter Hennessy on Boris Johnson's government,' *Financial Times*, 23 May 2022, available at: https://www.ft.com/content/37a5b18a-77d0-4f17-ae0a-99802396ff36, accessed on 11 June 2024.

Conclusion

This chapter was an attempt to outline the challenge as it stands, and one that will continue to be faced by teachers of Public Law in the years ahead. This is a challenge that welcomes research-led teaching as a way to ensure that as teachers we are informed, considered and able to evidence the material that we teach. Having our teaching underpinned by research ensures that we can take our students through the plethora of arguments that exist and critique in a way that explains when necessary the weakness of an argument or how it lacks an evidential basis.

References

Adonis, A. *5 Days in May: The Coalition and Beyond* (Biteback Publishing 2013).

Adonis, A. 'What did new labour achieve?', *Prospect*, 4 May 2022, available at: https://www.prospectmagazine.co.uk/politics/38600/what-did-new-labour-achieve, accessed on 11 June 2024.

Banner, A. '"How to get away with murder" takes a somewhat realistic look at law school and legal employment', *ABA Journal*, 15 October 2018, available at: https://www.abajournal.com/news/article/how_to_get_away_with_murder_takes_a_somewhat_realistic_look_at_law_schoo, accessed on 11 June 2024.

Boden, N. 'From green-eyed Chancellor to the "squatter of No10", gordon brown finally admits he can't hang on to job he coveted for so long', *Daily Mail*, 10 May 2010, available at: https://www.dailymail.co.uk/news/election/article-1272278/From-green-eyed-Chancellor-squatter-No10-Gordon-Brown-finally-admits-hang-job-coveted-long.html, accessed on 11 June 2024.

Bogdanor, V. *The Coalition and the Constitution* (Hart Publishing 2011).

Cannon, J. *The Fox-North Coalition: Crisis of the Constitution, 1782–1784* (Cambridge University Press 1970).

Elgot, J. et al, 'No 10 disowns Tory whip accused of "McCarthyite" behaviour', *The Guardian*, 24 October 2017, available at: https://www.theguardian.com/education/2017/oct/24/no-10-disowns-tory-whip-accused-of-mccarthyite-behaviour-universities-brexit, accessed on 11 June 2024.

Falconer, C. (Lord Falconer of Thoroton), 'Labour's constitutional changes 1997–2010: Time for more' in Michael Gordon and Adam Tucker (eds), *The New Labour Constitution: Twenty Years On* (Hart Publishing 2022).

Fazackerley, A. 'Universities deplore "McCarthyism" as MP demands list of tutors lecturing on brexit', *The Guardian*, 24 October 2017, available at: https://www.theguardian.com/education/2017/oct/24/universities-mccarthyism-mp-demands-list-brexit-chris-heaton-harris#:~:text=Chris%20Heaton%2DHarris%2C%20Conservative%20MP,with%20particular%20reference%20to%20Brexit, accessed on 11 June 2024.

Flinders, M. 'Majoritarian democracy in Britain: New labour and the constitution' (2005) 28(1) *West European Politics* 61.

Gillespie, H. 'Higher education funding shake-up: What it means for students and universities', *The Conversation*, 25 February 2022, available at: https://theconversation.com/higher-education-funding-shake-up-what-it-means-for-students-and-universities-177778, accessed on 11 June 2024.

Gordon, M. and Tucker, A. (eds), *The New Labour Constitution: Twenty Years On* (Hart Publishing 2022).

Greally, R. 'The brown report: Political legitimacy and the power of the assembly', *UK Constitutional Law Blog*, 26 January 2023 available at: https://ukconstitutionallaw.org/, accessed on 11 June 2024.

Grieve, D. 'Blaming the judges: What is our problem with politicians when it comes to the Law', *Talk to Judicial Institute, University College London*, 6 December 2022, available at: https://www.ucl.ac.uk/judicial-institute/sites/judicial_institute/files/blaming_judges_final_53092.pdf, accessed on 11 June 2024.

HEPI. 'Despite some huge changes, the last 20 years of higher education policy have left some big questions unresolved', 12 July 2023, available at: https://www.hepi.ac.uk/2023/07/12/despite-some-huge-changes-the-last-20-years-of-higher-education-policy-have-left-some-big-questions-unresolved/, accessed on 11 June 2024.

Hinkley, E. '"I f****** hate Constitutional Law", says Kim Kardashian', *Legal Cheek*, 2 March 2023, available at: https://www.legalcheek.com/2023/03/i-f-hate-constitutional-law-says-kim-kardashian/, accessed on 11 June 2024.

Khaitan, T 'A fourth branch of the state? On constitutional guarantors in the UK', *UK Constitutional Law Blog*, 30 March 2023, available at: https://ukconstitutionallaw.org/, accessed on 11 June 2024.

King, K. 'Too many students aspire to be Harvey Specter "rainmakers", says law school director', *Legal Cheek*, 28 September 2017, available at: https://www.legalcheek.com/2017/09/too-many-students-aspire-to-be-harvey-specter-rainmakers-says-law-school-director/, accessed on 11 June 2024.

Mance, H. '"A bonfire of the decencies": Peter Hennessy on Boris Johnson's government', *Financial Times*, 23 May 2022, available at: https://www.ft.com/content/37a5b18a-77d0-4f17-ae0a-99802396ff36, accessed on 11 June 2024.

McGuinness, A. 'The 2010s: A decade that shook the foundations of British politics', *Sky News*, 7 January 2000, available at: https://news.sky.com/story/the-2010s-a-decade-that-shook-the-foundations-of-british-politics-11894896, accessed on 11 June 2024.

Monaghan, C. 'In defence of intrinsic human rights: Edmund Burke's controversial prosecution of warren hastings, governor-general of Bengal' (2011) 1(2) *Law, Crime and History* 58.

Motta, M. '"Had enough of experts?" Anti-intellectualism is linked to voters' support for movements that are skeptical of expertise', *LSE Blogs*, 30 August 2017, available at: https://blogs.lse.ac.uk/usappblog/2017/08/30/had-enough-of-experts-anti-intellectualism-is-linked-to-voters-support-for-movements-that-are-skeptical-of-expertise/, accessed on 11 June 2024.

Parry, J.P. 'Disraeli and England' (2000) 43(3) *The Historical Journal* 699.

Philips, C.H. 'The East India Company "Interest" and the English Government, 1783–1784' (1937) 20 *Transactions of the Royal Historical Society* 83.

Rozenberg, J. *Enemies of the People? How Judges Shape Society* (Bristol University Press 2020).

Sikdar, R. 'The middle class will never understand how much Tony Blair's policies improved the lives of families like mine', *Independent*, 28 January 2018, available at: https://www.independent.co.uk/voices/new-labour-tony-blair-socialism-working-class-families-a8182031.html, accessed on 11 June 2024.

Slack, J. 'Enemies of the people: Fury over "out of touch" judges who have "declared war on democracy" by defying 17.4m Brexit voters and who could trigger a constitutional crisis', *The Daily Mail*, 3 November 2016, available at: https://www.dailymail.co.uk/news/article-3903436/Enemies-people-Fury-touch-judges-defied-17-4m-Brexit-voters-trigger-constitutional-crisis.html, accessed on 11 June 2024.

Slingo, J. 'Abolish supreme court – Think tank', *The Law Society Gazette*, 31 July 2020, available at: https://www.lawgazette.co.uk/news/abolish-supreme-court-think-tank-/5105245.article, accessed on 11 June 2024.

Toynbee, P. and Walker, D. 'The labour years: Could have done better', *The Guardian*, 25 September 2010, available at: https://www.theguardian.com/politics/2010/sep/25/labour-years-term-report, accessed on 11 June 2024.

Weaver, M. 'Iceberg lettuce in blonde wig outlasts Liz Truss', *The Guardian*, 20 October 2022, available at: https://www.theguardian.com/politics/2022/oct/20/iceberg-lettuce-in-blonde-wig-outlasts-liz-truss, accessed on 11 June 2024.

Wintour, P. 'How Gordon Brown's tantrums caused a storm over Downing St', *The Guardian*, 21 February 2010, available at: https://www.theguardian.com/politics/2010/feb/21/gordon-brown-tantrums-downing-street, accessed on 11 June 2024.

8 International Internships

Preparing Students for Rights and Justice in Action

Sarah L. Cooper[1]

Introduction

Birmingham City University (BCU) has offered an American legal studies provision since the 1990s, which has now advanced into a thriving portfolio. In 2012, the *Centre for American Legal Studies* was launched.[2] The centre scaffolds a team of local and international students, scholars, and practitioners, working in the areas of criminal justice, judicial process, intergovernmental relations, and human rights in the Americas.[3] BCU is also home to *Controversies in American Constitutional Law*[4] and the *British Journal of American Legal Studies* (*BJALS*), a peer review law journal that operates through the hands of faculty and law student editors, following typical law review practices in the United States.[5] In 2019, the *Judge Joseph A. Greenaway Jr Lecture Series on Law and Justice* was established to honour Judge Greenaway, a former judge of the US Third Circuit Court of Appeals and Chair of the *BJALS* Editorial Board. The lecture series has created connections with Birmingham Law

1 This chapter is based solely on my views and experiences. Many thanks to Dr Alice Storey for her thoughtful peer review and Hiren Chhiba for his excellent citation assistance and observations.

2 Birmingham City University, 'Centre of Excellence for study of US law officially launched' (*bcu.ac.uk*, 12 April 2012) https://www.bcu.ac.uk/news-events/news/centre-of-excellence-for-study-of-us-law-officially-launched> accessed 5 March 2004; Birmingham City University, 'Centre for American Legal Studies - School of Law' *(bcu.ac.uk)* https://www.bcu.ac.uk/law/research/centre-for-american-studies> accessed 5 March 2024.

3 Birmingham City University, 'Research streams – School of Law' *(bcu.ac.uk)* https://www.bcu.ac.uk/law/research/centre-for-american-studies/research-clusters> accessed 5 March 2024

4 Routledge & CRC Press, 'Controversies in American Constitutional Law: Controversies in American Constitutional Law – Book Series' (routledge.com) https://www.routledge.com/Controversies-in-American-Constitutional-Law/book-series/CONTROVERSIES> accessed 5 March 2024.

5 Birmingham City University, 'British Journal of American Legal Studies – School of Law' *(bcu.ac.uk)* https://www.bcu.ac.uk/law/research/centre-for-american-studies/british-journal-american-legal-studies> accessed 5 March 2024.

DOI: 10.4324/9781003457985-8

Society, the US London Embassy, and high schools and colleges nationwide.[6] Stitching together the entire portfolio is BCU's LL.B with American Legal Studies, which allows students to complement their English legal studies with US-centric modules,[7] including *American Legal Practice*, BCU's US internship programme, which I have delivered for nearly 15 years.

American Legal Practice[8] is a level six module open to law undergraduates for credit, and postgraduates to audit or use for other course credits. The module harnesses the expertise and partners of the *Centre for American Legal Studies* to prepare students for internships in the US, or with UK-based organisations focused on US legal matters. Hosts include private law firms, law libraries, innocence projects, public defenders, solo capital defence practitioners, law professors, and charities, who offer a range of experiences from prison and courtroom visits to coordinating social media campaigns and organising events. Most internships focus on criminal justice, span six-to-ten weeks, and are largely self-funded, although some students can benefit from bursaries through initiatives like the UK government's Turing Scheme.[9]

The module tends to welcome 10–20 students each academic year, but not all will go on to undertake internships. Some will end up not satisfying the module's academic requirements. Others will withdraw due to other responsibilities, like caring or employment, or because they do not have sufficient funds. Sometimes a surprise summer holiday or family celebration can get in the way. Some students will simply conclude an internship isn't for them. They might not feel ready to spend time away from family or travel alone, or realise they desire a different career path entirely. For those that do intern, though, it is my overwhelming experience that they have 'profound educational experiences'[10] that foster their 'empathy and sense of interconnectedness with people from other countries and cultures.'[11] As interns, students are exposed to 'real life situations'[12] – rights and justice in action – and they learn 'by doing.'[13]

6 Harvard Law School, 'Joseph Greenaway' (*hls.harvard.edu*) <https://hls.harvard.edu/faculty/joseph-greenaway/> accessed 5 March 2004; Hon. Joseph A. Greenaway, Jr., 'Joseph A. Greenaway Jr Lecture Series on Law and Justice: Speak at Your Own Peril' [2020] 9 Brit. J. Am. Legal Stud. 1.

7 Birmingham City University, 'Law with American Legal Studies – LLB (Hons) – 2024/25 Entry' (*bcu.ac.uk*) <https://www.bcu.ac.uk/courses/law-with-american-legal-studies-llb-2024-25> accessed 5 March 2024.

8 All relevant module materials are on file with the author.

9 Turing Scheme, 'Turing Scheme' (*turing-scheme.org.uk*) <https://www.turing-scheme.org.uk> accessed 5 March 2024.

10 Tim Connor et al.,'Becoming Global Citizens and Global Lawyers: Incorporating International Work and Study Experiences into the Australian Law School Curriculum' (2018) 25 Clinical L. Rev. 63, 93.

11 ibid 82.

12 William L. Berman, 'Why Not an International Clinical Legal Exchange Program? It Is Worth the Schlep' (2014) 21 Clinical L. Rev. 171, 172.

13 ibid.

These experiences can be 'disorienting'[14] for students and challenging to prepare for.

Each year, I deliberate over how to adjust the module to better prepare students. Beyond responding to feedback from students and hosts, the module must also be sensitive to political, economic, socio-cultural, and technological trends at home and abroad. In the last five years alone, the module has needed to respond to various happenings. The COVID-19 pandemic halted all in-person internships, and resulted in the US implementing, for a period, COVID-19 vaccination requirements for entry,[15] and, more long-term, many hosts shifting to hybrid and/or remote working patterns. Then there were the events of January 6, 2021, at the US Capitol, the so-called *Big Lie*,[16] and subsequent *January 6th Committee* proceedings and report.[17] In 2022, the US Supreme Court handed down its decision in *Dobbs v. Jackson Women's Health Organisation*.[18] The decision overturned *Roe v. Wade*[19] and triggered a wave of concern that other privacy-based rights, like access to contraception and marriage equality, might be under threat nationwide.[20] Later that year, ChatGPT was launched world-wide,[21] prompting discourse about how artificial intelligence (AI) will impact higher education,[22] legal services,[23] and international relations.[24] Closer to home, the United Kingdom has encountered particularly high inflation rates, energy prices, and food prices, which have

14 ibid 177.

15 United States Government, 'COVID-19 International Travel Advisories' (*usa.gov*) <https://www.usa.gov/covid-international-travel#> accessed 5 March 2004.

16 Edward D. Cavanagh, 'Countering the Big Lie: The Role of the Courts in the Post-Truth World' (2022) 107 Cornell L. Rev. Online 64 <https://live-cornell-law-review.pantheonsite.io/wp-content/uploads/2022/06/Cavanagh-online-essay-final-version-1.pdf> accessed 5 March 2024.

17 U.S. Government Publishing Office, 'Select January 6th Committee Final Report and Supporting Materials Collection' (*govinfo.gov*) <https://www.govinfo.gov/collection/january-6th-committee-final-report?path=/GPO/January%206th%20Committee%20Final%20Report%20and%20Supporting%20Materials%20Collection> accessed 5 March 2024.

18 *Dobbs v. Jackson Women's Health Org.*, (2022) 597 U.S. 215.

19 *Roe v. Wade*, (1973) 410 U.S. 113.

20 Amanda Hainsworth, 'Dobbs and the Post-Roe Landscape' (2022) Boston B.J. 9.

21 Samuel D. Hodge, Jr., 'Revolutionizing Justice: Unleashing the Power of Artificial Intelligence' (2023) 26 SMU Sci. & Tech. L. Rev. 217, 223.

22 Inside Higher Education, 'Benefits, Challenges, and Sample Use Cases of Artificial Intelligence in Higher Education' (2023) <https://www.insidehighered.com/sites/default/files/2023-10/Benefits%2C%20Challenges%2C%20and%20Sample%20Use%20Cases%20of%20AI%20in%20Higher%20Education.pdf>accessed 6 February.

23 Solicitors Regulation Authority, 'Risk Outlook Report: The Use of Artificial Intelligence in the Legal Market' (*sra.org.uk*) <https://www.sra.org.uk/sra/how-we-work/reports/risk-outlook/report-use-artificial-intelligence-legal-market.page> accessed 5 March 2024.

24 UK Parliament, 'The Governance of Artificial Intelligence: Interim Report' (*publications.parliament.uk*) https://committees.parliament.uk/publications/16471/governance-of-ai-interim-report> accessed 5 March 2024.

merged into a 'cost of living crisis,'[25] felt keenly by many, including university students.[26] *American Legal Practice* must recognise all this.

One way to effectively navigate this quagmire is to create an environment in the preparatory phase of the module, i.e., before internships take place, which fosters students' intercultural competency, namely their ability to 'relate to others comfortably, respectfully, and productively.'[27] In other words, their ability to empathise.[28] Equipping students with a strong sense of relatability in this way readies them for whatever might come their way on an internship, be that attending death row or a baseball game, witnessing a heated exchange about politics in the office or grocery store, or losing a laptop or passport.

Agreeing that intercultural competency is 'an increasingly critical skill set for law students,'[29] this chapter considers *American Legal Practice* in the context of existing research on development strategies. The first part summarises the *American Legal Practice* model, connecting the concepts of culture and intercultural competency with legal education in the following part. The third part then presents strategies for developing students' intercultural competency, organised into three categories, namely student-led, module design, and institutional strategies. Reflections on *American Legal Practice* are shared throughout with a view to sharing ideas for how this research might be applied in context. The chapter concludes that educators should feel empowered to explore this research base to co-create innovative approaches with students, colleagues, and partners.

The American Legal Practice Model

American Legal Practice is best described as a circle sliced into 12-week quarters that trace the traditional academic year, as per Figure 8.1. Quarter 1 introduces students to foundational knowledge, namely US legal and political infrastructures and skills transferable to all internships, specifically critical reflection (using the Situation-Task-Action-Result (STAR) method), fact

25 House of Commons Library, 'Cost of Living and Inflation' (*commonslibrary.parliament.uk*) https://commonslibrary.parliament.uk/cost-of-living-and-inflation/#:~:text=Further%20reading-,Overview,was%204.0%25%20in%20December%202023> accessed 6 February

26 Office for National Statistics, 'Student Voices: Experiences of the Rising Cost of Living' (*ons.gov.uk*) <https://www.ons.gov.uk/peoplepopulationandcommunity/educationandchildcare/articles/studentvoicesexperiencesoftherisingcostofliving/2023-09-06> accessed 5 March 2024.

27 Ritu Bhasin, 'Cultural Competence: An Essential Skill for Success in an Increasingly Diverse World' (2014) LAWPRO MAG. 9, 10.

28 Neil Hamilton, Jeff Maleska, 'Helping Students Develop Affirmative Evidence of Cross-Cultural Competency' (2017) 19 Scholar: St. Mary's L. Rev. & Soc. Just. 187, 190. ('[E]mpathy is at the heart of developing cross-cultural competency for students and lawyers.')

29 Shahrokh Falati, Ph.D., J.D., 'The Makings of A Culturally Savvy Lawyer: Novel Approaches for Teaching and Assessing Cross-Cultural Skills in Law School' (2020) 49 J.L. & Educ. 627, 628.

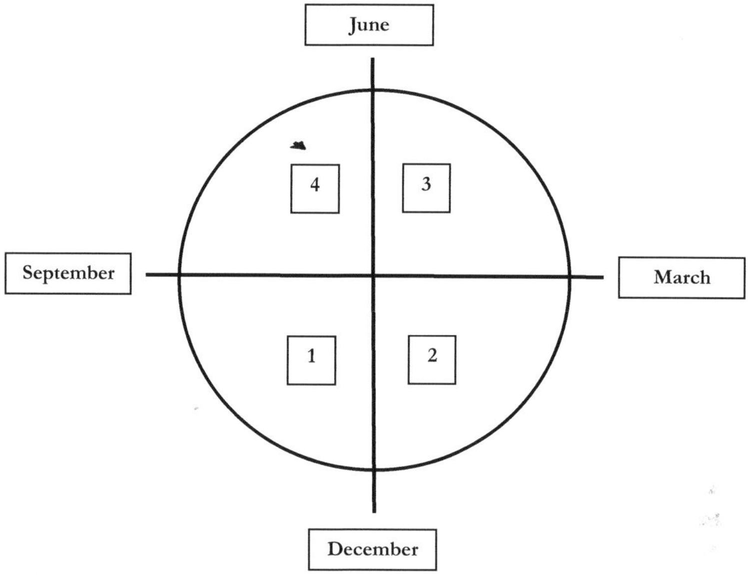

Figure 8.1 American Legal Practice.

investigation, legal research, and Bluebook citation. Quarter 2 supports students to apply their knowledge and skills in a series of simulations commonly encountered by interns, namely a social mixer, recruitment interview, client conference, and jury selection. Quarter 3 focuses on finalising internship applications and logistics. Internships take place in Quarter 4.

Programme of Teaching and Learning and Monitoring

During Quarters 1 and 2, the Programme of Learning and Teaching is organised into six, two-week themes. Centred around a topic (e.g., Client Contact) each theme generally comprises two in-person workshops, a series of asynchronous recorded lectures and corresponding quizzes, and a 'TEAMsTALK.' This final activity involves the class meeting on Microsoft Teams to engage with guest speakers. For each theme, students must complete the quizzes and workshop worksheet (one per theme) by a set deadline.

During this period, *American Legal Practice* also operates its own monitoring system. To generate a more detailed picture of a student's preparedness for an internship, this system tracks students' attendance, timeliness, quiz and class performance, and adherence to deadlines and instructions. A traffic light system is then applied, as demonstrated in Table 8.1. Consistent rules are applied for each traffic light colour. In terms of attendance at workshops and TEAMsTALKs, and the submission of the worksheets, green is applied if the student attends/submits on time; amber if they attend/submit late, and red if

Table 8.1 The American Legal Practice Monitoring System

Semester 1, Theme 1: Becoming/Being an Intern							
Student	Attendance Workshop 1	Attendance Workshop 2	Quiz 1	Quiz 2	Quiz 3	TEAMsTALK	Workshop Worksheet
X	(late, apologies) (amber)	(green)	60% (amber)	22% (red)	80% (green)	Non-attendance, no apologies. (red)	(late, no apologies) (amber)

the student did not attend/submit. Apologies are also noted. For quizzes, colours reflect certain score brackets, namely 0–50 (red), 51–60 (amber), 61–100 (green). Students receive updates on their record.

The thematic Programme of Teaching and Learning and enhanced monitoring concludes at the end of Quarter 2. Quarters 3 and 4 focus on, respectively, individual support for internship applications and logistics, and progress check-ins. Targeted assessment support is also provided.

Assessment

Given most students on *American Legal Practice* are undergraduates, this section focuses on that group's assessment diet. All students join the module as 'interning track' students i.e., aiming for an internship. Their position on this track is reviewed as part of the module's first summative assessment, which takes place at the end of Quarter 1. This assessment takes the form of a twenty-minute online interview, split into two parts. Part One simulates a meeting between a host (academic) and intern (student), where the intern has been requested to present their research regarding a client's case. Part Two requires the student to discuss and reflect on their preparedness for an internship, based on the information they provide in their *Internship Preparation Report.* This form requires students to reflect on their monitoring record; what type of internship they would like to undertake, where, and why; who, if anyone, they would like to travel with; what accommodation preferences they have; and any travel requirements they must consider, like visas and vaccinations. They must also provide an indicative budget.

Beyond a number grade, there are three outcomes from this assessment. One, a student can progress on the interning track with no concerns. Two, they can progress on the interning track with conditions (e.g., that their monitoring record improves). Three, they are transferred to the non-interning track. These outcomes are not necessarily dictated by grade, although a score of less than 60% does automatically transfer a student to the non-interning track. For example, a student can still score in the first-class bracket (70% +) and proceed on the interning track with conditions or shift to the non-interning track (e.g., because they do not desire an internship anymore). Indeed, some of the best assessment performances can come from students whose reflection has led them to reason the interning track is not for them.

As such, when students return for Quarter 2, *American Legal Practice* shifts to supporting two tracks: interning and non-interning, each with distinct assessment diets. Non-interning track students go on to complete the module through a coursework assessment that simulates an intern task, and interning-track students proceed to submit a Host Report and Reflective Diary post-internship. The Host Report requires hosts to comment on the student's overall performance, and the Reflective Diary requires students to record and critically reflect on notable achievements and disappointments, and to situate their experiences within relevant literature, for example on intercultural competency.

Intercultural Competency and Legal Education

The 'matter of culture'[30] is the subject of reams of writing. A 'deeply contested'[31] concept, it has been said 'culture' is used to explain 'everything and nothing.'[32] This can be a source of frustration for students and educators navigating intercultural issues,[33] including those in legal education. As Aldana says, 'law itself and lawyering are linked in complex and varied ways to culture.'[34] That said, Moran's advice that we should not 'become so mired in the theoretical debates over culture that the relevance of intercultural competency to resolving real-world dilemmas is lost,'[35] speaks strongly to this edited collection. As such, this chapter sets aside these debates.

Culture and Intercultural Competency

Research has adopted a broad definition of 'culture,' recognising that 'no two people have had the exact same experiences and thus, no two people will interpret or predict [culture] in precisely the same way.'[36] The dictionary describes culture as referring to the 'customary beliefs, social norms, and material traits of a racial, religious, or social group.'[37] This can extend to a 'person's age,

30 Dean Rachel Moran, 'When Intercultural Competency Comes to Class: Navigating Difference in the Modern American Law School' (2013) 26 Pac. McGeorge Global Bus. & Dev. L.J. 109.
31 ibid.
32 ibid.
33 ibid.
34 Raquel Aldana, 'Intercultural Legal Sensibility As Transformation' (2016) 25 S. Cal. Interdisc. L.J. 1, 8.
35 Moran (n 30) 110.
36 Neil Hamilton, Jeff Maleska, 'Helping Students Develop Affirmative Evidence of Cross-Cultural Competency' (2017) 19 Scholar: St. Mary's L. Rev. & Soc. Just. 187, 189.
37 Merriam-Webster Dictionary, 'Culture' (*merriamwebster.com*) <https://www.merriam-webster.com/dictionary/culture> accessed 5 March 2024.

gender, race, ethnicity, sexual orientation, physical ability, nationality, religion, or socio-economic group,'[38] as well as countries and organisations.[39] Applying this, everyone will likely belong to several cultures that can shape their 'understanding of the world.'[40] As Falati describes, we learn 'values and traditions'[41] from our 'families, friends, environment, communities and [in-person and online] social networks.'[42]

Learners taking an intercultural stance, though, not only look critically at their own culture, but that of the culture that is the focus of study.[43] For *American Legal Practice*, the culture in focus might broadly be considered American culture, or, specifically in the context of an internship with the Public Defender, let's say, how a defendant's race or socio-economic background might shape their experience of criminal justice in America. An intern's ability to navigate both types of cultural experiences, is 'premised upon the extent to which [they] understand [their] own and other peoples' cultures'[44] i.e., their intercultural competency. Taking one of my favourite practical examples to illustrate: dates. Let's say an intern needs to type March 1, 2024, in a numerical format. In the US, that date would generally be presented as 01/03/2024, whereas in the United Kingdom it would be 03/01/2024. If an intern gets this confused (i.e., thinks March 1, 2024, is January 3, 2024) while compiling a case chronology or arranging a meeting, it can reap havoc. Intercultural competency can help avoid this.

Legal Education

It is considered that law students, especially those that intend to practice law, will generally benefit from intercultural competency. As Ward and Miller describe, 'With an increasingly diverse potential client base, lawyers cannot ignore cultural competence...'[45] Lawyers need 'knowledge, skills, and values'[46] that will enable them to effectively represent and communicate with people from a range of cultures. For lawyers, being able to take account of cultural differences between themselves and other key stakeholders can help them to build trust and relationships, communicate clearly, and problem-solve,

38 Hamilton and Maleska (n 28) 188–189.
39 ibid 189.
40 Falati (n 29) 628.
41 ibid 629.
42 ibid.
43 Claire Kramsch, *Context and Culture in Language Teaching* (1st edn, Oxford University Press 1993) pg.223.
44 Falati (n 29) 629.
45 Cynthia M. Ward & Nelson P. Miller, 'The Role of Law Schools in Shaping Culturally Competent Lawyers' (2010) Mich. B.J. 16.
46 Hamilton and Maleska (n 28) 187–8 (citing Mary A. Lynch et al., 'Intercultural Effectiveness,' in Deborah Maranville et al., *Building on Best Practices: Transforming Legal Education in a Changing World* (eds., 2015) 338–39.)

particularly in terms of interpreting and applying the law 'in the context of applicable cultural norms,'[47] which may be 'very different from [a lawyer's] own.'[48] By contrast, intercultural *incompetence* can result in lawyers failing to signal they understand the needs and goals of their clients (and beyond), and therefore struggling to build trust. It can also mean they miss important information, and poorly execute key tasks like interviews, investigations, counselling, negotiations, litigation, and resolving conflict.[49] Effective legal representation is underpinned by intercultural competence, as Hamilton and Maleska say:

> For a lawyer to truly provide competent representation to his or her clients, the lawyer must not only understand the law, but also understand the culture of... the client, the groups with whom the lawyer works to advance the client's interests and... the adversaries and decisionmakers whom the lawyer seeks to influence.[50]

The contributions of guest speakers on *American Legal Practice* underscore the above. In terms of understanding clients, one guest, for example, shared feelings of limitation when describing their ability to represent a client who is deaf. In a particularly compelling example of the need to understand adversaries, Professor Gershman, a fellow author in this collection, shared his experiences of being a law student volunteer during Freedom Summer,[51] describing tactics used by the Ku Klux Klan to thwart the registration of African American voters.

Globalisation, an umbrella term used to 'encompass drastic changes in economic, political, and cultural phenomena'[52] has increased the need for law students to develop intercultural competency too. In the context of legal practice, globalisation is 'most often understood as a system that creates a smaller and increasingly interdependent world in which legal issues and transactions transcend national boundaries.'[53] This has transformed the law, legal problems, and lawyering, giving rise to new actors and organisations, legal challenges, and ideas about sovereignty.[54] Now, students who go on to practice law are

47 ibid 191 (citing E-mail from Laura Witte, Gen. Counsel, Corp. Sec'y, Corp. Vice President, Cargill, to Neil W. Hamilton, Professor of Law, Univ. of St. Thomas Sch. of Law (Sep. 29, 2015, 4:33 PM) (on file with authors)).

48 ibid.

49 ibid 192–194.

50 ibid 189.

51 King Institute, 'Freedom Summer' (*kinginstitute.stanford.edu*) <https://kinginstitute.stanford.edu/freedom-summer> accessed on 6 February 2024.

52 Farida Ali, 'Globalizing the U.S. Law School Curriculum: How Should Legal Educators Respond?' (2013) 41 Int'l J. Legal Info. 249, 250.

53 ibid.

54 Aldana (n 34) 8.

more likely to encounter 'global clients and issues'[55] that necessitate them to perform 'multicultural lawyering'[56] and to engage with 'foreign, international or global actors, laws, or legal systems.'[57]

American Legal Practice can be a student's first step into this space. The Programme of Teaching and Learning creates opportunities for students to recognise both points of cohesion and contrast, between the United States and the United Kingdom, in the global marketplace. For instance, workshops involve legal research and citation tasks that bring the international legal regime into focus, like the influence of international human rights law in the US Supreme Court. These sorts of tasks can prompt students to appreciate that whilst the United Kingdom and US are both members of international organisations, like the United Nations,[58] they can take different approaches in context. For example, the United Kingdom has ratified the Convention of the Rights of the Child, whereas the US has not.[59] Another example is when we are joined by guests who have both US and UK legal qualifications. These sessions often result in students gaining fresh perspectives on how their legal education *is* transferrable to other legal systems, but also that the options to practice law in the US are more limited for people only holding an undergraduate law degree from a UK university.[60] A final example is the discovery that takes place when we organise spaces for *American Legal Practice* students to engage with US law students. Here, students can realise they share some experiences with their US counterparts, for example feelings of low confidence and the impact of student debt. Equally, they can be humbled, for instance, when they learn about the scale of US law school tuition fees, when compared to the UK.[61]

Given the intellectual and practical richness intercultural competency offers, it is unsurprising that employers 'recognize the importance of building

55 ibid.

56 ibid.

57 ibid.

58 United Nations, 'United Nations: Peace, Dignity and Equality on a Healthy Planet' (youhttps://www.un.org/en/)< accessed 5 March 2024.

59 United Nations, 'Treaty Series – View Details' (*treaties.un.org*) <https://treaties.un.org/Pages/ViewDetails.aspx?src=TREATY&mtdsg_no=IV-11&chapter=4&clang=_en> accessed 6 February 2024.

60 American Bar Association, 'Bar Admissions' (*americanbar.org*) <https://www.americanbar.org/groups/legal_education/resources/bar_admissions/> accessed 5 March 2024.

61 To get a sense of fee structures in the US see, American Bar Association, 'Schedule of Law Fees' (*americanbar.org*) <https://www.americanbar.org/groups/legal_education/accreditation/schedule-of-law-school-fees/> accessed 6 February and for the UK see Law Careers. Net, 'Law Course Fees: A Guide for Students' (*lawcareers.net* 5 December 2023) <https://www.lawcareers.net/Explore/Features/05122023-Law-course-fees-a-guide-for-students#:~:text=You%27re%20likely%20to%20be,14%2C300%2C%20depending%20on%20the%20provider.accessed> accessed 6 February 2024.

cross-cultural skills'[62] and there is rising 'demand for inter-culturally effective professionals.'[63] That being so, it is also unsurprising that law students have been described as 'clamouring for international work experience.'[64] Considering that 'everyone has the capacity to become more proficient at cross-cultural interaction and communication skills,'[65] intercultural competency development strategies are key. Noting this, the next part outlines strategies for fostering the development of 'the law student as a multicultural being.'[66]

Development Strategies

Writing about a comparable model to *American Legal Practice* in the US, Blumberg references advice he received whilst volunteering in the Peace Corps, namely to 'sit by the well.'[67] This was an instruction to volunteers to listen, adapt, and embed culturally.[68] As an educator, Blumberg goes on to ask, in effect, how can we recreate this act, for students, before, during, and after international internships?[69] This resonates with me because, at the start of each *American Legal Practice* cycle, I will say something along the lines of, 'our job is to get you from here (the classroom) to there (the internship) and back again (being "better" than when you left).' To that end, this section offers strategies to help answer Blumberg's questions.

Developmental Models

There are various models for developing intercultural competency. In 1982, for instance, Howell offered a four-stage model,[70] which sees a person progress from a state of *unconscious incompetence* where they fail to recognise difference, to a state of *unconscious competence*, where they unconsciously incorporate intercultural skills and perspectives in their interactions.[71] In 1986, Bennett created the first iteration of the Developmental Model of Intercultural Sensitivity.[72] Built on observations from academic and corporate

62 Susan Bryant, 'The Five Habits: Building Cross-Cultural Competence in Lawyers' (2001) 8 Clinical L. Rev. 33, 38.
63 Falati (n 29) 650–651.
64 Jeffrey Blumberg, 'Sitting by the Well: The Case for Intercultural Competency Training in International Experiential Learning' (2014) 43 U. Balt. L. Rev. 395, 396.
65 Bryant (n 62) 38.
66 Aldana (n 34) 6.
67 Blumberg (n 64) 395.
68 ibid 395–396.
69 ibid 396.
70 Neil Hamilton and Jeff Maleska (n 28) 197–198.
71 ibid 198.
72 See IDRInstitute, 'The Developmental Model of Intercultural Sensitivity' (*idrinstitute.org*) <https://www.idrinstitute.org/dmis/> accessed 6 February.

settings, this framework is presented as an 'experience of difference' continuum, which extends 'from *ethnocentrisim* (the experience of one's own culture as "central to reality") to *ethnorelativism*, the experience of one's own and other cultures as "relative to context."'[73] The model intends to explain 'how people experience and engage cultural difference,'[74] and assumes that, as a person's perception of culture becomes more complex, their experience of culture becomes more sophisticated, and consequently their potential to exercise 'competence in intercultural relations'[75] increases. The American Board of Internal Medicine's Milestone Project includes relevant developmental stages for residents, for example in how they respond to the unique characteristics of each patient.[76] The tool scaffolds several progression points, including *not assessable* (no relevant learning experience), *critical deficiencies* (incompetent performance), and *aspirational* (expert and role model behaviours).[77]

Hamilton and Maleska adapted the medical model to the legal field, describing *critical deficiencies*, for example, as instances where a student/lawyer is insensitive to cultural differences and unwilling to modify their representation to take account of a client's unique characteristics and needs. *Aspirational* behaviours, they suggest, include role modelling interactions to negotiate difference based on a client's uniqueness and being consistently respectful.[78] They also synthesised their own model, which defines four stages of intercultural competency, namely (1) *lack of awareness* (a person is entirely unaware of their insensitivity to culture), (2) *recognition* (they recognise they lack cultural competence but are unsure how to develop), (3) *conscious implementation* (they take affirmative steps to develop their competence), and (4) *proficiency* (they regularly take affirmative steps and seek out diverse experiences).[79] Their model also offers insights for how 'a law student or practitioner could demonstrate affirmative evidence of the competency.'[80] To illustrate, positions associated with the *recognition* and *proficiency* stages, respectively, are 'I wish I could speak another language'[81] and 'It's important to look at the situation from someone else's shoes.'[82]

These models demonstrate intercultural competency is a phased and 'career-long endeavour.'[83] A synthesis of related literature reveals several strategies for

73 ibid.
74 ibid.
75 ibid.
76 American Board of Internal Medicine's, 'The Internal Medicine Milestone Project' (2014) p. 18 <https://www.abim.org/Media/qeuhualp/internal-medicine-milestones-project.pdf> accessed 5 March 2024.
77 ibid.
78 Neil Hamilton and Jeff Maleska (n 28) 198.
79 ibid 200–202.
80 ibid 201.
81 ibid.
82 ibid.
83 ibid 215.

supporting students to graduate through relevant phases, which are presented in the subsequent text.

Student-led Strategies

Some strategies require students to engage explicitly with intercultural competency. A foundational strategy is for students to self-assess in a broad sense. This involves students identifying the various cultures to which they belong so that they can, firstly, understand which cultures are different from their own,[84] and, secondly, assess their own cultural background to consider what 'impact that [background] could have.'[85] Students can also explore their biases, as the 'reality is that all people have biases.'[86] This type of self-assessment is 'an ongoing life-long journey'[87] for lawyers, but, as Falati says, only when they take this 'first step'[88] to become aware of their own cultural background can they progress towards providing effective legal representation. There are various assessment tools available.[89]

American Legal Practice does not engage students in an explicit intercultural self-assessment task, but there are learning activities to prompt students to think along those lines. One example is our use of STAR discussions, which are held at the start of most workshops. We incorporate STAR discussions to provide formative spaces for interviews, where such questions are commonplace, and develop deeper insight into *who* our students are so we might better advise them. These discussions involve students (and academics) sharing answers to a behavioural question, for example 'Tell me about a time when you had to resolve conflict or collaborate with someone you find challenging.' Everyone is encouraged to shape their responses according to the STAR framework, and it is my experience that answers often intersect with culture, with stories about having an accent, being from a marginalised group, dealing with inappropriate workplace behaviour, and resolving family disputes springing to mind as examples.

Scholars recommend more targeted assessments too. For instance, Hamilton and Maleska propose that students (and lawyers) 'choose a cross-cultural area'[90] – for example, physical ability, gender, or race – and complete a developmental self-assessment centred on that area, using one or more of the developmental models available. Students should be encouraged to select an

84 ibid 188.
85 Falati (n 29) 644.
86 ibid 646.
87 ibid 644.
88 ibid.
89 University of Michigan, 'Assessing Intercultural Competence' (*umich.edu*) <https://crlt.umich.edu/interculturalcompetence> accessed 5 March 2024.
90 Neil Hamilton and Jeff Maleska (n 28) 195.

area that would benefit them.[91] Applying this idea to *American Legal Practice*, students could target cultures that would make them a stronger applicant for a desired internship. For example, a student wanting to intern in a southern border town might want to learn more about Hispanic cultures, whereas a student wanting to intern with a non-profit organisation might wish to find out more about organisational cultures common to that sector. After completing their self-assessment, Hamilton and Maleska advise students to request peer assessment from people who have experience of them operating in a cross-cultural setting.[92] Considering *American Legal Practice* students, this could be someone at their part-time job, house-share, or place of worship or volunteering. This combination of self- and peer-assessment should give students an insight into how others perceive their intercultural competency, help calibrate their own perceptions, and guide self-reflection.[93] It can also inform a development plan, which is recommended to avoid the pitfalls of having a 'mere general intention to improve.'[94] Beyond fostering other professional skills, written development plans allow students to:

> [I]dentify specific experiences, set dates to achieve the desired competency, seek feedback from others on the plan and its implementation, reflect on the student's experiences and the feedback, and periodically revise the plan going forward.[95]

Development plans bring another strategy into focus, namely stretch experiences. These are experiences that challenge a student's 'present level of knowledge and skill with novel, complex, and ambiguous experiences, which in turn generate awareness of cross-cultural competency deficiencies and thus drive the student to improve their competency.'[96] Stretch experiences sit outside of a student's comfort zone and help develop a feeling of comfort with discomfort whilst in a supportive environment.[97] Again, these experiences can target specific areas of culture, and feature in development plans.

The internship element of *American Legal Practice* would widely be considered a stretch experience.[98] Yet, the stretch concept is embedded within the preparatory stage too. Student feedback, for example, often characterises the traffic light monitoring system in stretch-like terms, particularly in terms of it being novel and motivating. Further, the online learning portal houses a

91 ibid 203–204.
92 ibid 204.
93 ibid 195.
94 ibid 206.
95 ibid.
96 ibid 207.
97 ibid.
98 ibid ('[M]ost research focuses on the benefit of stretch experiences in the context of foreign study or work').

CV Building Opportunities tile, where we signpost, albeit without the label, stretch experiences, for example student editor roles with *BJALS*. Another example is the interview assessment, which requires students to describe a time (using STAR) when they have had to learn about another culture to resolve a problem. This task, in effect, requires students to consider a previous stretch experience.

Module Design Strategies

Module convenors can promote intercultural competence through module design. To start, we can dedicate a learning outcome to intercultural competency, a practice implemented in several US law schools and manifested through various activities, from simulations to coaching.[99] Scholars caution these approaches can encounter student resistance, but through making sure relevant learning objectives drive a learning programme that speaks to 'students' self-interest in meaningful employment'[100] educators can neutralise concerns.

The learning programme must also scaffold safe spaces for students to learn about culture, and to confront bias and stereotypes. With 'careful course design'[101] educators can 'infuse cultural competency'[102] through, for example, embedding cultural issues and biases within problem questions and reading lists.[103] *American Legal Practice* incorporates both techniques. With regards to the former, several themes within Quarter 2 revolve around a simulation exercise, including a client conference. In this exercise, students 'meet' a client (played by a staff member) to determine the nature of their legal issues so they can carry out legal research and produce a legal memo of advice. The scenario centres on a client who is complaining about their prison cell conditions. To fully advise, however, students must go beyond facts about temperature and hygiene; they must recognise cues relating to culture, like the client's medical history and social ties. We have taken several steps to make this a safe learning experience for students. The first is to hold a dedicated preparatory workshop where students can prepare together with academic support. The second is to schedule simulations to take place 1-to-1 online so that students feel less exposed as they tread new ground and can have the exercise recorded for future review. The third is to schedule simulations to build in time for feedback.

In terms of an example of targeted reading, each year we aim to co-host an online session – *Legal Education and Imposter Syndrome* – with Georgetown

99 Neil Hamilton and Jeff Maleska (n 28) 209–214.
100 ibid 215.
101 Falati (n 29) at 659.
102 ibid.
103 ibid 656–8.

University Law School's Federal Habeas Practicum Class. The session connects *American Legal Practice* students with US law students who are also enrolled in a class focused on preparing students for legal practice. The session emerged from discussions about ways to support law students to overcome Imposter Syndrome – 'a feeling of phoniness in people who believe that they are not intelligent, capable or creative despite evidence of high achievement'[104] – noting intersectional disparities are linked with how students might experience such feelings.[105] In preparation, students are required to read *The Phantom Menace to Professional Identity Formation and Law Success: Imposter Syndrome*[106] and prepare to answers to the following questions, which we use to structure class discussion:

1. Do you recognise some of the feelings/experiences associated with Imposter Syndrome? If so, in what context and how did they impact you?
2. Have you used any of the strategies recommended in the article? If so, which ones, in what context, and what was the result?

In our experience, the class stirs a rich conversation, especially about how our perception of failure can be shaped by other factors, like gender, class, and social groups.

A final strategy is to regularly update the learning programme. This is an important 'mindset for educators and institutions'[107] wanting to become culturally proficient. Of course, as educators we update our materials as a matter of routine and good practice, but it's fair to say the demands of higher education might conspire to limit the time we have to do this. To that end, I have devised ways to streamline certain updating exercises for *American Legal Practice*. For example, it's critical that students are presented with contemporary information about internships, including what hosts expect and students experience. To do this, at the end of Quarter 4, I bring all interning students together online to record a discussion about their experiences, including budgets, accommodation, daily routines, challenges and highlights, and what advice they would give to future interns. I then embed the recording as lecture

104 David A. Grenardo, 'The Phantom Menace to Professional Identity Formation and Law Success: Imposter Syndrome' (2022) 47 U. Dayton L. Rev. 369, 371. (American Bar Association, 'Imposter Syndrome? 8 tactics to combat the anxiety,' (*americanbar.org*) <https://www.americanbar.org/news/abanews/publications/youraba/2018/october-2018/tell-yourself-_yet--and-other-tips-for-overcoming-impostor-syndr/> accessed 5th March 2024.

105 Helen Hewertson & Faith Tissa, 'Intersectional Imposter Syndrome: How Imposterism Affects Marginalised Groups' (2022). 10.1007/978-3-030-86570-2. <https://www.researchgate.net/publication/361969300_Intersectional_Imposter_Syndrome_How_Imposterism_Affects_Marginalised_Groups> accessed 5th March 2024.

106 Grenardo (n 104).

107 Falati (n 29) 641.

content and schedule a TEAMsTALK to give new students the opportunity to meet previous interns.

Institutional Strategies

Institutions, or perhaps more practically organisational units (like schools or colleges), must also commit to supporting intercultural competency.[108] Falati suggests there are five elements to an institution being 'culturally competent.'[109] These are that the institution values diversity, can periodically self-assess, remains 'curious and conscious'[110] to intercultural dynamics, has institutionalised cultural knowledge and know-how, and adapts to diversity.[111] Ideas for 'facilitating and promoting'[112] an institutional environment that fosters culturally competent students include providing opportunities for students to learn additional languages, experience international foods, attend cultural cabarets, engage in multi-faith talks, and travel internationally.[113] Obviously, the final idea speaks directly to *American Legal Practice*, with internships providing an 'immersion experience.'[114]

Moran notes that students express considerable satisfaction with immersion experiences,[115] which aligns with my experience of feedback tending to be overwhelmingly positive, and, rightly, celebrated by all stakeholders. There is, however, in my view, an important space to explore here, in amongst the feel-good vibes, and that is what institutions can do to, one, maximise the number of students who can take up immersion experiences, and two, offer meaningful consolation experiences for those who, despite everything, cannot.

I propose interrogating these spaces because if I was asked to name – in a single word – the most common challenge students encounter, it would be the *resource* they need to make an internship a reality. For some this does, indeed, relate to funding. For others it's about another type of resource they need – family support, information and communication technology (ICT) equipment, cover at a part-time job, well-being, and disability support. Moreover, identifying these needs works both ways – sometimes students flag them to us, and sometimes we flag them to students. As such, it is critical that an institution's commitment to intercultural competency in the context of maximising international travel opportunities runs the full gamut of students' resource needs, be that offering travel bursaries, ensuring access to institutional

108 ibid 667.
109 ibid.
110 ibid.
111 ibid.
112 ibid.
113 ibid 667–676.
114 Aldana (n 34) 3 ('My focus here is principally on summer abroad programs and on service-learning opportunities that include student immersion in rich cross-cultural exchanges').
115 Moran (n 35) 113.

well-being services abroad, and/or offering flexible part-time working opportunities and ICT equipment loans. These are just some initial ideas, inspired by existing institutional practices, like study abroad schemes,[116] and support for well-being,[117] ICT,[118] and employment.[119]

Following on from this, though, institutions must also find ways to bring the international experience *to* those students that cannot – for whatever reason – amass the resources they need to travel abroad. One way we have sought to bridge our BCU classrooms with the US is through harnessing the institutional Academic Visitor Scheme,[120] which has allowed us to welcome several US students, scholars, and practitioners to join our community.[121] This has given students the chance to build US contacts, and experience what US law students do in terms of teaching styles. On *American Legal Practice*, we have also harnessed their presence to creatively introduce aspects of daily American culture. This can be as light touch as engaging our guests in light banter about sports and music, or to frame an entire learning activity. For instance, we have organised pop quizzes as games of hit US TV show *Jeopardy!* and framed the public speaking simulation in Quarter 2 as *Show and Tell*, a popular school activity in the US where class members bring in an object (e.g., a photograph or a trophy) and talk to their peers about it. Described as 'central to assertive American culture,'[122] we have scheduled *Show and Tell* to co-inside with the arrival of our Visiting Academics, thereby merging the benefits of the simulation exercise with a culturally familiar way for our guests to build rapport with students.

116 Birmingham City University, 'Go Abroad' (*bcu.ac.uk*) <https://www.bcu.ac.uk/student-info/why-study-at-bcu/go-abroad> accessed 5 March 2024.

117 Birmingham City University, 'Mental Health and Wellbeing' (*bcu.ac.uk*) <https://www.bcu.ac.uk/student-info/student-support/mental-health-and-wellbeing> accessed 5 March 2024.

118 Birmingham City University, 'IT, Computer Networks and Printing' (*bcu.ac.uk*) <https://www.bcu.ac.uk/student-info/learning-support/it-computer-networks-and-printing> accessed 5 March 2024.

119 Birmingham City University, 'Employability' (*bcu.ac.uk*) <https://www.bcu.ac.uk/student-info/why-study-at-bcu/employability> accessed 5 March 2024.

120 Birmingham City University, 'Academic Visitors' (*bcu.ac.uk*) <https://www.bcu.ac.uk/international/academic-visitors> accessed 5 March 2024.

121 British Association for American Studies, 'Masterclass: American Democracy in the Spotlight – British Association for American Studies' (*baas.ac.uk*) <https://baas.ac.uk/news-and-events/2023/03/masterclass-american-democracy-in-the-spotlight/> accessed 5 March 2024.

122 Judit Szitó, 'Show and Tell "The Significance of a Children's Genre in Culture and Education"' (2017) Freeside Journal <https://www.freesideeurope.com/articles/-show-and-tell-the-significance-of-a-children-s-genre-in-culture-and-education-72> accessed 5 March 2024.

Conclusion

This chapter reveals educators have a rich foundation from which to build better environments for supporting students to develop intercultural competency. Modules like *American Legal Practice* offer a dynamic space to trial innovations, refine good practices, and emphasise the need to cultivate inclusive institutions. As educators, we can maximize our students' potential to thrive as 'multicultural beings,'[123] ensuring they are well-prepared for the complexities of rights and justice in action on a global stage. For me, researching and writing this chapter has offered the opportunity to critically reflect on how I can enhance my own practice in service to all *American Legal Practice* stakeholders, especially students and hosts. For now, though, I have set myself three goals. The first is to explicitly label intercultural competency aspects within the module, and the second is to embed a self-assessment exercise so students can evaluate and chart progress. Thirdly, I want to explore the views of students and hosts. What does intercultural competency mean to them? What strategies, if any, speak to them? In short, I have been inspired to contribute further to this space through creating a new research inquiry. What this might look like is beyond the scope of this chapter. For now, though, I'm more excited than ever for class.

Bibliography

Aldana, R., 'Intercultural Legal Sensibility As Transformation' (2016) 25 *S. Cal. Interdisc. L.J.* 1–59.

Ali, F., 'Globalizing the U.S. Law School Curriculum: How Should Legal Educators Respond?' (2013) 41 *Int'l J. Legal Info.* 249–282.

American Bar Association, 'Bar Admissions' (americanbar.org) <https://www.americanbar.org/groups/legal_education/resources/bar_admissions/> accessed 5 March 2004.

American Bar Association, *Imposter Syndrome? 8 Tactics to Combat the Anxiety* (American Bar Association 2018) <https://www.americanbar.org/news/abanews/publications/youraba/2018/october-2018/tell-yourself-_yet--and-other-tips-for-overcoming-impostor-syndr/> accessed 5 March 2004.

American Bar Association, 'Schedule of Law fees' (americanbar.org) <https://www.americanbar.org/groups/legal_education/accreditation/schedule-of-law-school-fees/> accessed 5 March 2004.

American Board of Internal Medicine's, 'The Internal Medicine Milestone Project' (2014) 18 <https://www.abim.org/Media/qeuhualp/internal-medicine-milestones-project.pdf> accessed 5 March 2004.

Berman, W.L., 'Why Not an International Clinical Legal Exchange Program? It Is Worth the Schlep' (2014) 21 *Clinical L. Rev.* 171–199.

Bhasin, R., 'Cultural Competence: An Essential Skill for Success in an Increasingly Diverse World' (2014) 13(2) *LAWPRO MAG.* 9–14.

123 Aldana (n 34) 6.

Birmingham City University, 'Academic Visitors' (bcu.ac.uk) <https://www.bcu.ac.uk/international/academic-visitors> accessed 5 March 2004.

Birmingham City University, 'British Journal of American Legal Studies - School of Law' (bcu.ac.uk) <https://www.bcu.ac.uk/law/research/centre-for-american-studies/british-journal-american-legal-studies> accessed 5 March 2004.

Birmingham City University, 'Employability' (bcu.ac.uk) <https://www.bcu.ac.uk/student-info/why-study-at-bcu/employability> accessed 5 March 2004.

Birmingham City University, 'Go abroad' (bcu.ac.uk) <https://www.bcu.ac.uk/student-info/why-study-at-bcu/go-abroad> accessed 5 March 2004.

Birmingham City University, 'IT, Computer Networks and Printing' (bcu.ac.uk) <https://www.bcu.ac.uk/student-info/learning-support/it-computer-networks-and-printing accessed 5 March 2004.

Birmingham City University, 'Law with American Legal Studies – LLB (Hons) – 2024/25 Entry' (bcu.ac.uk) <https://www.bcu.ac.uk/courses/law-with-american-legal-studies-llb-2024-25> accessed 5 March 2004.

Birmingham City University, 'Mental Health and Wellbeing' (bcu.ac.uk) <https://www.bcu.ac.uk/student-info/student-support/mental-health-and-wellbeing> accessed 5 March 2004.

Birmingham City University, 'Research Streams – School of Law' (bcu.ac.uk) <https://www.bcu.ac.uk/law/research/centre-for-american-studies/research-clusters> accessed 5 March 2004.

Blumberg, J., 'Sitting by the Well: The Case for Intercultural Competency Training in International Experiential Learning' (2014) 43 *U. Balt. L. Rev.* 395–396.

British Association for American Studies, 'Masterclass: American Democracy in the Spotlight - British Association for American Studies' (baas.ac.uk) <https://baas.ac.uk/news-and-events/2023/03/masterclass-american-democracy-in-the-spotlight/> accessed 5 March 2004.

Bryant, S., 'The Five Habits: Building Cross-Cultural Competence in Lawyers' (2001) 8 *Clinical L. Rev.* 33–38.

Claire, Kramsch, *Context and Culture in Language Teaching* (1st ed, Oxford University Press 1993).

Connor, T., et. al., 'Becoming Global Citizens and Global Lawyers: Incorporating International Work and Study Experiences into the Australian Law School Curriculum' (2018) 25 *Clinical L. Rev.* 63–94.

Edward, D. Cavanagh, 'Countering the Big Lie: The Role of the Courts in the Post-Truth World' (2022) 107 *Cornell L. Rev. Online* 64 <https://live-cornell-law-review.pantheonsite.io/wp-content/uploads/2022/06/Cavanagh-online-essay-final-version-1.pdf> accessed 5 March 2004.

Falati, S., 'The Makings of A Culturally Savvy Lawyer: Novel Approaches for Teaching and Assessing Cross-Cultural Skills in Law School' (2020) 49 *J.L. & Educ.* 627–684.

Greenaway, J.A., and Joseph, A., 'Greenaway Jr Lecture Series on Law and Justice: Speak at Your Own Peril' (2020) 9 *Brit. J. Am. Legal Stud.* 1–15.

Grenardo, D.A., 'The Phantom Menace to Professional Identity Formation and Law Success: Imposter Syndrome' (2022) 47 *U. Dayton L. Rev.* 369, 371.

Hainsworth, A., 'Dobbs and the Post-Roe Landscape' (2022) 66(4) *Boston B.J.* 9.

Hamilton, N., and Maleska, J, 'Helping Students Develop Affirmative Evidence of Cross-Cultural Competency' (2017) 19 *Scholar: St. Mary's L. Rev. & Soc. Just.* 187–215.

Harvard Law School, 'Joseph Greenaway' (his.harvard.edu) <https://hls.harvard.edu/faculty/joseph-greenaway/> accessed 5 March 2004.

Hewertson, H., and Tissa, F., 'Intersectional Imposter Syndrome: How Imposterism Affects Marginalised Groups' (2022) https://doi.org/10.1007/978-3-030-86570-2. <https://www.researchgate.net/publication/361969300_Intersectional_Imposter_Syndrome_How_Imposterism_Affects_Marginalised_Groups> accessed 5 March 2004.

Hodge, S.D. Jr., 'Revolutionizing Justice: Unleashing the Power of Artificial Intelligence' (2023) 26 *SMU Sci. & Tech. L. Rev.* 217–223.

House of Commons Library, 'Cost of living and inflation' (commonslibrary.parliament.uk) <https://commonslibrary.parliament.uk/cost-of-living-and-inflation/#:~:text=Further%20reading-,Overview,was%204.0%25%20in%20December%202023> accessed 5 March 2004.

IDR Institute, 'The Developmental Model of Intercultural Sensitivity' (idrinstitute.org) <https://www.idrinstitute.org/dmis/> accessed 5 March 2004.

Inside Higher Education, 'Benefits, Challenges, and Sample Use Cases of Artificial Intelligence in Higher Education' (2023) <https://www.insidehighered.com/sites/default/files/2023-10/Benefits%2C%20Challenges%2C%20and%20Sample%20Use%20Cases%20of%20AI%20in%20Higher%20Education.pdf> accessed 5 March 2004.

King Institute, 'Freedom Summer' (kinginstitute.stanford.edu) <https://kinginstitute.stanford.edu/freedom-summer> accessed 6 February 2024.

Law Careers. Net, 'Law Course Fees: A Guide for Students' (lawcareers.net) 5 December 2023 <https://www.lawcareers.net/Explore/Features/05122023-Law-course-fees-a-guide-for-students#:~:text=You%27re%20likely%20to%20be,14%2C300%2C%20depending%20on%20the%20provider> accessed 5 March 2004.

Maranville, D., et al., 'Building on Best Practices: Transforming Legal Education in a Changing World' (eds., 2015). (Carolina Academic Press).

Merriam-Webster Dictionary, 'Culture' (merriamwebster.com) <https://www.merriam-webster.com/dictionary/culture> accessed 5 March 2004.

Moran, R., 'When Intercultural Competency Comes to Class: Navigating Difference in the Modern American Law School' (2013) 26 *Pac. McGeorge Global Bus. & Dev. L.J.* 109–115.

Office for National Statistics, 'Student Voices: Experiences of the Rising Cost of Living' (ons.gov.uk) <https://www.ons.gov.uk/peoplepopulationandcommunity/educationandchildcare/articles/studentvoicesexperiencesoftherisingcostofliving/2023-09-06> accessed 5 March 2004.

Routledge & CRC Press, 'Controversies in American Constitutional Law: Controversies in American Constitutional Law - Book Series' (routledge.com) <https://www.routledge.com/Controversies-in-American-Constitutional-Law/book-series/CONTROVERSIES> accessed 5 March 2004.

Solicitors Regulation Authority, 'Risk Outlook report: The Use of Artificial Intelligence in the Legal Market' (sra.org.uk) <https://www.sra.org.uk/sra/how-we-work/reports/risk-outlook/report-use-artificial-intelligence-legal-market.page> accessed 5 March 2004.

Szitó, J., '"Show and Tell" The Significance of a Children's Genre in Culture and Education' (2017) Freeside Journal <https://www.freesideeurope.com/articles/-show-and-tell-the-significance-of-a-children-s-genre-in-culture-and-education-72> accessed 5 March 2004.

Turing Scheme, 'Turing Scheme' (turing-scheme.org.uk) <https://www.turing-scheme.org.uk> accessed 5 March 2004.

U.K. Parliament, 'The Governance of Artificial Intelligence: Interim Report' (publications.parliament.uk) <https://committees.parliament.uk/publications/16471/governance-of-ai-interim-report> accessed 5 March 2004.

U.S. Government Publishing Office, 'Select January 6th Committee Final Report and Supporting Materials Collection' (govinfo.gov) <https://www.govinfo.gov/collection/january-6th-committee-final-report?path=/GPO/January%206th%20Committee%20Final%20Report%20and%20Supporting%20Materials%20Collection> accessed 5 March 2004.

United Nations, 'Treaty Series – View Details' (treaties.un.org) <https://treaties.un.org/Pages/ViewDetails.aspx?src=TREATY&mtdsg_no=IV-11&chapter=4&clang=_en> accessed 5 March 2004.

United Nations, 'United Nations: Peace, Dignity and Equality on a healthy planet' (un.org) <https://www.un.org/en/> accessed 5 March 2004.

United States Government, 'COVID-19 International Travel Advisories' (usa.gov) <https://www.usa.gov/covid-international-travel#;>~:text=COVID%2D19%20testing%20and%20vaccine,fully%20vaccinated%20against%20COVID%2D19> accessed 5 March 2004.

University of Michigan, 'Assessing Intercultural Competence' (umich.edu) <https://crlt.umich.edu/interculturalcompetence> accessed 5 March 2004.

Ward, C. M., and Miller, N. P., 'The Role of Law Schools in Shaping Culturally Competent Lawyers' (2010) *Mich. B.J.*

Cases

Dobbs v. Jackson Women's Health Org. (2022) 597 U.S. 215

Roe v. Wade (1973) 410 U.S. 113

9 UK Politics and Human Rights

From New Labour's Human Rights Act 1998 to the Conservative's Bill of Rights Bill

Chris Monaghan and Josie Welsh

Introduction

It hard to understate the importance of human rights as a notion however, the particular ways in which such rights are defined, protected and enforced remains a site of much debate both in the United Kingdom and abroad. While these debates make this a topic rich in opinion, information and challenging discussions – the question is how should these complexities be appropriately reflected in how we teach the subject of 'human rights.'

A student recently said to one of the authors that human rights are 'at best aspirational.' This insight firstly impressed the author then made the author reflect upon why they had reached this conclusion. In later discussions, it transpired that having studied the long history of 'rights' within English law it had left the student unsure of what had been achieved but most importantly, how much there was still do be done.

Teaching human rights prompts often highly-personal thoughts about the nature of justice, the nature of right and wrong and can also draw on difficult and unpleasant histories and lived experiences. For this reason, teaching human rights is, on the one hand, hugely interesting and varied and on the other, incredibly difficult to know how best to present information.

This chapter seeks to initially reflect upon part of the history of rights in the United Kingdom, particularly emphasising the political nature of the rights and the context in which debates often arise. The chapter will address the inherent tensions often presented by human rights cases and discuss the importance of reconciling the need for both intellectual honesty and impartiality. Ultimately, however, this chapter explores the different ways in which we can foster an interest and engagement in human rights law for the students we teach.

Looking at the History of Rights – What Lessons Might We Learn?

History is often a dangerous thing if it is not approached properly. The historic achievements of the Common Law in protecting rights and liberties can be used to distract from any shortcomings, or the Human Rights Act 1998

DOI: 10.4324/9781003457985-9

(HRA) critiqued as a product of the left, whilst not acknowledging the traditional reluctance of the left (as opposed to the political right) to incorporate the European Convention on Human Rights (ECHR) into domestic law.

The Long Road to Incorporation

The case for giving domestic effect to the United Kingdom's obligations under the European Convention on Human Rights, a rights framework that was largely drafted by Conservative politicians who were lawyers, took a long time to be taken seriously by a government.[1] This is perhaps surprising, as the former High Court judge, Sir Michael Tugendhat, argued that the Convention was a Conservative achievement and not one warmly embraced by Labour politicians (with Tugendhat describing them as either 'indifferent, or event hostile').[2] Tugendhat was clear that 'the European Convention on Human Rights in 1950, marked the achievement of the British war aim. The ECHR was largely a project of Churchill, Maxwell-Fyfe, and other conservatives, both in the UK and amongst the victorious powers in Europe.'[3] The United Kingdom's dualist legal system meant that Convention rights could only be enforced against the United Kingdom where an applicant brought a case to the European Court of Human Rights based in Strasbourg. This right to access the Court (which heard its first case in 1961) was only granted by Harold Wilson's Labour government in 1966. This did not mean that incorporation was championed or proposed by those on the political left. However, it was (and if often the case remains) complicated. As Francesca Klug observed:

> Margaret Thatcher, whose 1979 Manifesto promised all party talks on 'a possible Bill of Rights.' Once in power, this commitment evaporated. When lobbyists like myself, from pressure groups such as Liberty and Charter 88, attempted to engage the Thatcher or Major Governments on this commitment, the customary response was similar to this 1989 letter from Thatcher to Baroness Ewart-Biggs: 'the government considers that our present constitutional arrangements continue to serve us well and that the citizen in this country enjoys the greatest degree of

1 In her foreword to 'The Conservative Case for the Human Rights Act,' Shami Chakrabarti, the then Director of Liberty, stated that the ECHR 'was largely drafted by British conservative lawyers.' See J. Norman and P. Oborne, 'Churchill's Legacy: The Conservative Case for the Human Rights Act' Liberty, October 2009, available at: https://www.libertyhumanrights.org.uk/wp-content/uploads/2023/10/Churchills_Legacy.pdf. See also M. Duranti, *The Conservative Human Rights Revolution: European Identity, Transnational Politics, and the Origins of the European Convention* (Oxford University Press 2016).

2 M. Tugendhat, 'The Conservative Case for Human Rights' (2019) 90(3) *The Political Quarterly* 368, 372.

3 ibid 372.

liberty that is compatible with the rights of others and the vital interests of the state.'[4]

Whatever the reluctance of either Margaret Thatcher or John Major to enact a Human Rights Act, this does not equate to reluctance on the part of leading Conservative politicians. As Tugendhat observed it was Lord Hailsham who:

> In 1968… proposed that there be a bill of rights, by which Parliament would voluntarily limit its right to pass legislation which was to the detriment of the rights of individuals. He proposed that the judges in the UK should have the powers to adjudicate upon claims that the UK had violated the rights of individuals under the ECHR. Individuals would no longer have to take such claims to the European Court in Strasbourg. He was thus the first to propose what was to be later enacted in the Human Rights Act.[5]

The case for incorporation via a Human Rights Act was championed by the then Labour leader, John Smith, in 1993, as 'the quickest and simplest way of achieving democratic and legal recognition of a substantial package of human rights.'[6] Smith who was tipped as the next Prime Minister, died before the next General Election, and his party and his successor Tony Blair continued to campaign for a Human Rights Act.

It is vital to appreciate that to many the British constitution was considered as a success, as it protected the rights of the subject. Therefore what was to be gained from human rights legislation? According to Dicey:

> the securities for personal freedom are in England as complete as the laws can make them… every man's legal rights or liabilities are almost invariably determined by the ordinary Courts of the realm, and each man's individual rights are far less the result of our constitution than the basis on which that constitution is founded.[7]

These freedoms may have been developed and protected the Common Law, yet these were at the mercy of Parliament and times when those in power might see rights as a barrier to the interests of the state. The cornerstone of the United Kingdom's constitution is Parliamentary Sovereignty. Parliament can legislate as

4 S. Chakrabarti, H. Kennedy, F. Klug, M. McWilliams and A. Miller, 'Common Sense: Reflections on the Human Rights Act' *Liberty*, June 2010, available at: https://www.lse.ac.uk/sociology/assets/documents/human-rights/publications/commonSense.pdf, 9.

5 M. Tugendhat, 'The Conservative Case for Human Rights' (2019) 90(3) *The Political Quarterly* 368, 373.

6 ibid 10.

7 Cited by C. O'Cinneide, 'How Well Does the UK's Democracy Protect Human Rights and Civil Liberties' Democratic Audit, 28 November 2018, available at: https://www.democraticaudit.com/2018/11/28/how-well-does-the-uks-democracy-protect-human-rights-and-civil-liberties/.

it wishes, even if this means legislating contrary to fundamental rights. This was a view endorsed by Lord Hoffmann in *Exp Simms*[8] and taken to the extreme by Leslie Stephen's in his *The Science of Ethics* that was originally published in 1882. The only restraints are political and not legal. Whilst Sir Edward Coke in *Dr Bonham's Case*[9] may have seen the Common Law as the ultimate controller of law, is does not reflect constitutionality reality. Lord Camden's judgment in *Entick v Carrington*[10] may be championed as a cause celebre in the development of the rule of law, however less than four decades later Habeas Corpus was suspended by Parliament at the request of William Pitt the Younger's government.[11] In the early 1940s Lord Atkin in his (in)famous dissent in *Liversidge v Anderson*[12] was scathing of the use of detention without trial:

> In this country, amid the clash of arms, the laws are not silent. They may be changed, but they speak the same language in war as in peace. It has always been one of the pillars of freedom, one of the principles of liberty for which on recent authority we are now fighting, that the judges are no respecters of persons and stand between the subject and any attempted encroachments on his liberty by the executive, alert to see that any coercive action is justified in law. In this case I have listened to arguments which might have been addressed acceptably to the Court of King's Bench in the time of Charles I.[13]

Lord Bingham, the former Senior Law Lord, observed that Lord Atkin's dissent was a 'eloquent and courageous' assertion of:

> older, nobler, more enduring values: the right of the individual against the state; the duty to govern in accordance with law; the role of the courts as guarantor of legality and individual right; the priceless gift, subject only to constraints by law established, of individual freedom.[14]

8 *R v Secretary of State for the Home Department, ex parte Simms [1999] UKHL 33.*
9 *(1610) 8 Co. Rep. 107.*
10 (1765) 19 Howell's State Trials 1029.
11 William Pitt's government suspended the Habeas Corpus Act 1679 on 23 May 1794. As Clive Emsley stated, '[t]he Act itself did not guarantee freedom from arrest without due charge and without subsequent trial; rather, it was a piece of legal machinery which enabled a dubious arrest to be tested in the courts. But eighteenth-century Englishmen could use the Act to boast that unlike their unfortunate continental neighbours, they were not subject to arbitrary arrest and the threat of a lettre de cachet.' (C Emsley, 'Repression, "Terror" and the Rule of Law in England during the Decade of the French Revolution' (1985) 100(397) *The English Historical Review* 801, 807). Indeed, as Emsley observed, '[s]uspending the Habeas Corpus Act was a drastic step, but it was not an unheard of occurrence in eighteenth-century England' (ibid 808).
12 [1942] AC 206. For commentary see G.W. Keeton, 'Liversidge v. Anderson' (1942) 5(3/4) *The Modern Law Review* 162,
13 ibid 244.
14 Lord Bingham, 'The Case of Liversidge v. Anderson: The Rule of Law Amid the Clash of Arms' (2009) 43(1) *The International Lawyer* 33, 38.

This can be contrasted with the expediency of the government, as Bingham noted, 'it was no doubt easy to feel that exceptional circumstances called for exceptional remedies, that it was no time for legal niceties.'[15]

The problem of Parliamentary Sovereignty was articulated by Anupam Chander in 1991, when he questioned whether, 'If a bill of rights were passed in the United Kingdom in 1992, could Parliament pass a Bill of Rights Repeal Act the following year.'[16] The answer being yes, even if this meant 'contravening the provisions of a bill of rights.' Chander observed that there is a 'dilemma of a bill of rights that strives to restrict the power of the state in a land where Parliament is by tradition sovereign, and thereby omnipotent.'[17]

As Colm O'Cinneide observed, this older view about suitability of the constitution protecting rights was eroded, as 'this Diceyan consensus gradually began to be called into question. The parliamentary restraint needed was not always forthcoming.' O'Cinneide gives examples including '[t]he wide-ranging discretionary powers enjoyed by public authorities were also prone to abuse, especially when it came to colonial governance in the British empire.'[18] It is telling that the most recent abuse of colonial power occurred in the 1960s and 1970s with the forced depopulation of the Chagos Islands, even if the legal attempts to challenge a renewed exclusion of the population in 2004 was not adequately protected by either the Common Law or the Human Rights Act 1998.[19]

In the late 1970s Anthony Lester QC considered the operation of rights within the United Kingdom. Lester acknowledged the positives of the British constitutional and political system, arguing that:

> one should not dismiss the virtue of the British system too readily. Human rights may not be 'fundamental' in a constitutional sense, but it is arguable that they are as well protected and that the spirit of liberty is as strong in the United Kingdom as in those democratic societies that have written constitutions, Bills of Rights, and comprehensive systems of administrative law.[20]

15 ibid 38.

16 A. Chander, 'Sovereignty, Referenda, and the Entrenchment of a United Kingdom Bill of Rights' (1991) 101(2) *The Yale Law Journal* 457.

17 ibid 458.

18 C. O'Cinneide, 'How Well Does the UK's Democracy Protect Human Rights and Civil Liberties' Democratic Audit, 28 November 2018, available at: https://www.democraticaudit.com/2018/11/28/how-well-does-the-uks-democracy-protect-human-rights-and-civil-liberties/.

19 For discussion see S. Allen and C. Monaghan (eds), *Fifty Years of the British Indian Ocean Territory: Legal Perspectives* (Springer 2018) and TT Arvind, '"Though it Shocks One Very Much": Formalism and Pragmatism in the "Zong" and "Bancoult"' (2012) 32(1) *Oxford Journal of Legal Studies* 113.

20 A. Lester, 'Fundamental Rights in the United Kingdom: The Law and the British Constitution' (1976) 125(2) *University of Pennsylvania Law Review* 337, 341.

However, Lester was clear that a system driven by the absolute observance of Parliamentary Sovereignty had its shortcomings in terms of the protection of human rights. Drawing upon the previous century of Irish political history which had seen Ireland gain independence, whilst creating Northern Ireland and the consequential human rights issues that arose because of sectarianism and British control, Lester observed that '[o]ne is bound to ask whether human rights might not have been better protected during the half century of devolved government in Northern Ireland with the support of a Bill of Rights liberally interpreted and actively enforced by the judiciary.'[21]

To Lester the then British system, because of:

> [t]he absence of constitutional standards... means that laws are made that may affect fundamentals, such as those defined and protected in your Bill of Rights, yet their fundamental implications tend to become apparent in Britain only if vigilant and well-informed individual Parliamentarians or journalists make them so.[22]

New Labour's Achievements

The enactment of the Human Rights Act 1998 was a considerable achievement. The rationale for incorporation was clear and rooted in unfairness and a rights-based lacuna. As the Labour Government observed in its Rights Brought Home: The Human Rights Bill:

> The effect of non-incorporation on the British people is a very practical one. The rights, originally developed with major help from the United Kingdom Government, are no longer actually seen as British rights. And enforcing them takes too long and costs too much. It takes on average five years to get an action into the European Court of Human Rights once all domestic remedies have been exhausted; and it costs an average of £30,000. Bringing these rights home will mean that the British people will be able to argue for their rights in the British courts – without this inordinate delay and cost. It will also mean that the rights will be brought much more fully into the jurisprudence of the courts throughout the United Kingdom, and their interpretation will thus be far more subtly and powerfully woven into our law. And there will be another distinct benefit. British judges will be enabled to make a distinctively British contribution to the development of the jurisprudence of human rights in Europe.[23]

21 ibid 344.
22 Ibid 349–350.
23 The original text of the Bill is available here: https://assets.publishing.service.gov.uk/government/uploads/system/uploads/attachment_data/file/263526/rights.pdf

This was hardly a case of overselling the need for incorporation, as cases such as *R v Ministry of Defence, ex parte Smith*[24] and *Kaye v Robertson*[25] had demonstrated the shortcomings of domestic rights protection.

When the Act came into force in October 2000 few perhaps could have imagined the significance of the legislation on the United Kingdom, nor the hostility that would be generated by those opposed to the natural consequences of bringing rights home – namely, that if rights are brought home and the judiciary empowered and obligated by law to protect rights, then this might cause tensions between those who favoured a traditional political constitution and the judiciary.

A Mixed Reception

Arguably the main problems with the HRA 1998 are twofold. Firstly, it is seen as an imposition on the traditional British constitution – but not just an imposition, rather a foreign one, transplanting alien and undemocratic European rights into English law and empowering judges to rule against elected politicians. Secondly, it can easily be dismissed as a product of New Labour, too political, too radical and not appropriately respectful to constitutional norms. These two problems go to the heart of why it is difficult to teach human rights. Our Human Rights framework (albeit giving effect to the ECHR) has not been celebrated, but is rather viewed in some quarters with suspicion and disdain.

As has been discussed so far, such views do not reflect the reality. This is a point emphasised by Klug, as she observed that:

> Despite [its] heritage, the HRA is sometimes painted as a party political measure. Henry Porter implied last week that the HRA was a creature

24 [1996] 1 All ER 256. In this case a blanket ban of homosexuals serving in the armed forces was underpinned by stigma and historic homophobia. See for example Sir Thomas Bingham MR's judgment, where Bingham MR outlined the criticisms of the blanket ban made by counsel, 'Mr Pannick also criticised the second factor relied on by Sir John. He pointed out that any service member behaving inappropriately towards an under-age member of the service could be disciplined and punished in the same way as in society at large. He rejected the suggestion that homosexuals were less able to control their sexual impulses than heterosexuals. Again he suggested that the policy of the ministry was pandering to ignorant prejudice.'

25 [1991] FSR 62. In his judgment Bingham LJ noted the lack of legal protected accorded to Gordon Kaye (a famous British actor in the 1980s and 1990s) due to the violation of his privacy. Bingham LJ stated, 'The defendants' conduct towards the plaintiff here was "a monstrous invasion of his privacy"... If ever a person has a right to be let alone by strangers with no public interest to pursue, it must surely be when he lies in hospital recovering from brain surgery and in no more than partial command of his faculties. It is this invasion of his privacy which underlies the plaintiff's complaint. Yet it alone, however gross, does not entitle him to relief in English law... We cannot give the plaintiff the breadth of protection which I would, for my part, wish.'

> of the left, used by Labour as a 'figleaf' behind which to attack our freedoms. Conservative MPs also sometimes refer to 'Labour's Human Rights Act'. Anyone acquainted with the sequencing that led to the Act will be struck by the awkwardness of this phrase. It was the Society of Conservative Lawyers which recommended in its 1976 report, Another Bill of Rights?, that 'the ECHR should be given statutory force as overriding domestic law.'[26]

The key supporters in the 1970s and 1980s for a Bill of Rights were leading Conservative politicians, precisely because it would protect liberty from state intervention. A similar point was made by Tugendhat:

> The tabloid press frequently portrays human rights as being 'soft' on criminals and immigrants, thus endangering the rest of the population's security. So, people might be forgiven for thinking that human rights are the concern of left-wing politicians. Yet this perception of human rights is misplaced. Conservative values lie at the heart of the centuries-long development of human rights in the UK.[27]

The criticism of the Human Rights Act 1998 is considerable and sustained in political discourse and in the right-wing tabloid press. Colm O'Cinneide's assertion that '[p]oliticians regularly subject the HRA to criticism, and bemoan the influence exerted by the jurisprudence of the European Court of Human Rights (ECHR) over UK law,' is both sound and indicative of how a critique of rights (both through domestic and European enforcement) are (in our view, very often) played for political capital.[28]

The 'Wrong' People

There is the other question of 'universalism.' This engages public debate sometimes more than the specific rights' question itself. For example, in the debate about whether the United Kingdom's blanket ban on prisoners' voting rights was incompatible with the ECHR, more focus was placed upon the (potential) rights-holders – prisoners – rather than the matter of enfranchisement and public feeling about 'the right to vote' itself.[29] It was equally the case that the decision in *Hirst v United Kingdom (No2)*[30] and the debate it prompted

26 https://www.lse.ac.uk/sociology/assets/documents/human-rights/publications/commonSense.pdf 14–15

27 https://onlinelibrary.wiley.com/doi/epdf/10.1111/1467-923X.12713, 368

28 Supra n 16.

29 This debate was prompted by the first challenges under the HRA in 2001 by three convicted prisoners. John Hirst, one of the claimants, appealed to the European Court of Human Rights.

30 *(2006) 42 EHRR 41.*

'largely focused on the constitutional issues raised by the judgment.'[31] The problem here is that the matter remains politically-charged which makes it more difficult to extricate – and sometimes understand – the nuances of the legal issues involved. When the then Prime Minister David Cameron infamously stated that he was 'sickened'[32] by the prospect of prisoners having the right to vote and would not be giving prisoners' the vote, one can see why it may be challenging to return the focus to the legal question of the Representation of the People Act 1983, the ECHR and the HRA.[33]

In 2006, the narrative of one of the architects of 'bringing rights home' was starting to change on this question of universalism: Tony Blair. His position was clarified, and plans developed for a 'radical overhaul' of the HRA rights regime, following a High Court judgment which he publicly called, 'an abuse of common sense.[34] The decision confirmed that nine Afghan refugees – who had, in 2000, 'hijacked an aircraft on an internal flight in Afghanistan in order to flee from the Taliban regime' – were to be given discretionary leave to enter and remain in the United Kingdom, reviewable every six months.[35] The then Director of Liberty, Baroness Shami Chakrabarti, termed Blair's change in stance regarding the reach and use of the HRA a 'sinister twist.'[36]

But these changing political narratives around rights, rights-holders and the protection to be offered by the state is an ongoing feature of social debate about human rights. Over 20 years after the enactment of the HRA, there has been clear focus on protecting the rights of some groups by limiting the rights of others within political debate, demonstrating perhaps the invitation to antagonism by human rights questions. Suella Braverman, then Home Secretary, told the Conservative party conference in October 2023, that the HRA should be renamed the 'Criminal Rights Act' and warned her audience of the 'hurricane' of mass migration.[37] The demonising of some social groups within debates about rights appears to undermine any initial hopes that it may be possible to recognise 'the equal and inalienable rights of all members of the human family.'[38]

31 House of Commons Library, Research Briefing 'Prisoners' voting rights' 9 August 2023 https://commonslibrary.parliament.uk/research-briefings/cbp-7461/

32 https://www.thetimes.co.uk/article/cameron-sickened-by-prisoner-vote-j3zf67bbm2t

33 https://www.theguardian.com/society/2012/oct/24/prisoners-vote-david-cameron

34 Joint Committee on Human Rights, Thirty-Second Report, Session 2005–06 https://publications.parliament.uk/pa/jt200506/jtselect/jtrights/278/27802.htm [Para. 10]

35 *S. and others v Secretary of State for the Home Department* [2006] EWCA Civ 1157

36 https://www.theguardian.com/uk/2006/aug/04/immigration.immigrationpolicy

37 https://www.theguardian.com/politics/2023/oct/03/suella-braverman-claims-hurricane-of-mass-migration-coming-to-uk

38 United Nations, Preamble to the Universal Declaration of Human Rights https://www.un.org/en/about-us/universal-declaration-of-human-rights

Reflecting on Teaching Experience/Practice in Developing Our Pedagogical Approaches

Often, understanding the 'best' way to do something comes through practice and reflection. In teaching, it is usually reflecting upon what has *not* worked which helps us to develop a practice that is more effective. This is arguably the case when teaching human rights. There are several variables in this task and as such, what may be best practice in one moment may change in another. Firstly, the landscape of rights and what Mary-Ann Glendon termed 'rights-talk' changes. In a disciplinary sense, the attitudes of constitutional lawyers, of public law practitioners and even of the judiciary may evolve depending upon the changing context. Glendon speaks of how the intellectual environment surrounding rights in 1980s America had been 'infused with the romance of rights.'[39] As discussed above, in the United Kingdom since the enactment of the HRA, we can see plenty of contributions to the debates about what rights are, should be and whose responsibility it is to protect them. This presents a first difficulty which is to know how best to present this changing landscape to students. Is the 'best approach' one which dispassionately reports on events and maps out the detail but leaves students the room to form their own opinions?

The second challenge here is acknowledging how the student body changes. Not only will the composition and dynamics of a single cohort change between academic years, there is the possibility that human rights are taught across a degree programme, at different levels and for different reasons. Take, for example, a first year undergraduate student group learning about the HRA and ECHR for the first time, compared to an advanced final year module offering a smaller group of students the chance to study human rights in more detail. Compare these to the integration of human rights questions in areas such as employment law, media law or property law. This must again affect how we 'teach' human rights and the decisions we take as teachers in deciding upon content.

Finally, as teachers and as academics we change. In our academic careers, through research and teaching experiences, we are unlikely to deliver the same session five years apart – and nor should we. However, when teaching human rights this could possibly verge on negligence given the way in which understandings develop, the evolution of legislation and case law and the vast – and often unpredictable – ways in which society and its attitudes evolve. Consider the important cases relating to questions of gender reassignment and rights' protection as an example. The case of *Bellinger v Bellinger* illustrates the importance of precision, accuracy but social awareness when teaching.[40] In the UK House of Lords judgment, Lord Nicholls takes five paragraphs at the outset of

39 Mary-Ann Glendon, *Rights Talk: The Impoverishment of Political Discourse* (The Free Press, 1991) 5.

40 [2003] UKHL 21.

the judgment to carefully explain terminologies including trans-sexual people, inter-sexual people, gender dysphoria and the differences between transsexual, transvestite and homosexual.[41] To teach students about this case and the issues it raises in 2003 would have been vital in raising awareness, improving understanding of society at that time but most importantly in respecting and reflecting the rights of all. To teach students about this case 20 years later in 2023, would require careful and similarly important consideration of the state of society today. As teachers, is this an opportunity for us to reflect on our understandings but to encourage students to talk about their reflections too. Again, human rights are about everyone and to neglect these conversations or the issues faced by individuals in the cases we read would be a disservice.

Intellectual Honesty

It seems, therefore, that the teaching of human rights must seek a balance between intellectual honesty. If we recognise the fact that rights talk is inherently antagonistic then we begin our work from a realistic perspective. We know that when we present information, such on whether prisoners should have the right to vote or whether asylum seekers must be protected from deportation, there could be people in the room who disagree with the view. One key approach is not to make any assumptions on the views of others.

Perhaps one way to reconcile this is to understand that impartiality in this context is not adopting a 'vanilla' approach to teaching human rights. By their nature, the rights questions we pose via cases, social issues or campaigns, will prompt critical thought. In contrast to some areas of legal education, there is, in some ways, less to do to engage, enthuse or evoke responses from students to help them develop that critical mind. Therefore, our role is more about offering a range of views and opinions and consider the arguments they present in a fair-minded manner. We should not, as academics, shy away from expressing (hopefully) informed opinion and encourage our students to be open-minded and to reach their own assessment. However, there is a real danger – that we are seen as siding with one view (anti-government).

The Dilemma

The teacher is torn as how to teach human rights over what could be one or indeed several weeks of teaching. Do we pitch human rights as a roller coaster from pre-Second World War, to the formation of the Council of Europe, the drafting of the ECHR, the establishment of the European Coirt of Human Rights, the position in the United Kingdom before October 2000, the enactment of the HRA, criticism of the HRA, and the lead up from 2010 to the ill-fated Bill of Rights (Bill)? Is the HRA to be viewed as an achievement, even

41 *Bellinger v Bellinger* [2003] UKHL 21, [5–10].

if we acknowledge any shortcomings on how the Act was drafted or has been relied upon by the Courts (think *R v A (No.2)*[42] or *R (on the application of Ullah) v Special Adjudicator*),[43] something that must be treated as a central to our discussion of human rights? Do we perhaps take a broader view and treat the HRA as just one way to protect rights and give effect to the ECHR? How then are we to teach the criticism of the HRA, Policy Exchange and the ill-fated Bill of Rights Bill? Surely, a large part of this will be dependent on our own views, subconscious (or not) biases and political and constitutional outlook. Should we pretend or actively strive to be neutral when we teach human rights, should we acknowledge our own biases and call these out whilst bringing in the counter argument, and if so, how much weight should we give to contrary views, even if such views are in the minority and may appear to be unsatisfactory and driven by (political) ideology? It feels as though the best approach may come via communication and openness. In resolving these questions for ourselves, we can involve students as a means of illustrating these difficulties surrounding human rights. That in itself is a lesson, Answering the question of why there is a dilemma at all begins to unpack the nature and nuances of rights.

Hypotheticals

The biggest challenge when teaching human rights in a Public Law or Constitutional Law context is engaging students and responding to a myriad

42 [2001] UKHL 25. The use of section 3 of the Human Rights Act 1998 has been criticised, see for example R. Ekins and G. Gee, 'Submission to the Joint Committee on Human Rights: 20 years of the Human Rights Act' 18 September 2018, available at: https://policyexchange.org.uk/wp-content/uploads/2018/10/JPP-submission-to-the-JCHR-inquiry-18-September-2018.pdf. Ekins and Gee take the view that, '[t]he HRA is a standing risk to legal certainty, with section 3 very often being a ground on which courts may twist and subvert the meaning of statutes or invalidate regulations altogether' ([23]). For a contrary view see See F. Powell and S. Needleman, 'How Radical an Instrument Is Section 3 of the Human Rights Act 1998?' U.K. Const. L. Blog (24 March 2021) (available at https://ukconstitutionallaw.org/). Powell and Needleman's view is that 's.3 is a well-crafted interpretative tool that is rarely relied on by the courts, but when it is used, the courts have done so to protect Convention rights in way which maintains the constitutional separation of power.' See also A. Wagner and G. Barth, 'Judicial Interpretation or Judicial Vandalism? Section 3 of the Human Rights Act 1998' (2016) *Judicial Review* 99.

43 [2004] UKHL 26. For commentary on the mirror principle that was advanced by Lord Bingham see R. Masterman, 'The Mirror Crack'd' UK Const. L. Blog (13 February 2013) (available at http://ukconstitutionallaw.org). Masterman is clear that 'the Bill of Rights debate has emphasised that while the legal influence of the *Ullah* principle is considerable, it has arguably had a damaging effect on political perceptions of the HRA and the link the Act creates between domestic law and the Convention jurisprudence. The relationship between domestic courts and the European Court of Human Rights that *Ullah* embodies is out of touch with the widely-held view that the content of our domestic human rights law should not be 'dictated' to us by the European Court.' See also Lord Irvine, 'A British Interpretation of Convention Rights' [2012] *Public Law* 237, and J Straw, *Aspects of Law Reform: An Insider's Perspective* (Cambridge University Press 2013).

of differing views, ideas, assertions and assumptions. In this section we have constructed a hypothetical group of students to attend our imaginary seminar. These students are hypothetical but represent some of the opinions/questions that those teaching might be faced with. We would emphasise that this is a hypothetical exercise and is designed to be provocative, rather than necessarily reflecting the day-to-day reality of our teaching experience. Imagine the following questions arising in a discussion:

- Student One: 'Human Rights are too European.'
- Student Two 'Human Rights Lawyers are left wing activists.'
- Student Three: 'Any critique of "Bill of Rights"/reform is anti-Tory.'
- Student Four: 'I'm here to learn the law and not to hear about your political views.'
- Student Five: 'Human Rights protect the wrong people at the expense of the majority.'
- Student Six: 'The judiciary is pale, state and male – why do we empower them?'
- Student Seven: 'Surely elected politicians are better at protecting rights than judges? (ECtHR as well?)'
- Student Eight: 'Are the criticisms of the Human Rights Act unsound and why do we even discuss them.'
- Student Nine: 'I wish I had learnt about human rights at school.'
- Student Ten: 'The Human Rights Act is a terrorist charter.'
- Student Eleven: 'Didn't the government try and repeal it? Why are we learning about human rights.'
- Student Twelve: 'Didn't we Brexit?'

We ask you here to consider how you might respond. Is there a 'right' answer? Is there a 'best' answer? Or are there circumstances where we, as academics, ought not to respond at all? For us, these questions – and the wider ideologies, misconceptions or reflections – illustrate just how challenging it can be to *teach* human rights. As we have suggested previously, part of the role here is to prompt thought and to engage students to the extent that they wish to even ask these questions. Perhaps, given the challenges of the position we might hold in such a hypothetical situation, we are best to allow space for others to answer or for some questions to remain unanswered. One reason for this, it can be argued, is that there are times where it may seem like teachers are there to give the single, 'right' answer. Where human rights are concerned, there rarely is a single answer to the question.

Conclusions

Speaking from some experience, however, it appears that a student body is often as conflicted by these questions as we are in answering them. Students are astute and realise the challenges and the perpetual tensions when seeking to provide legal solutions to what may appear inherently 'moral' questions. Human rights cause us to make judgement. As lawyers – or law students – we must confront this task but what is vital is that we refine our skills in determining how best to reach and rationalise those judgements. We must learn from the lessons of those judges, politicians and groups of litigants to work out how best to teach, respect and protect human rights.

What is clear is that we have access to an ever-growing body of literature, case law and political debate *about* human rights. We can – and should – be confident to make selections from that body of information in crafting teaching sessions and encouraging students to focus on particular issues or questions. We can do this with confidence because we know our subject, we get to know our students and we know that it remains a vital part of their legal education to learn the skills of talking about and debating human rights questions.

This subject allows us to show a wide range of perspectives and experiences. It allows us to explore the experiences of many different people and groups. It allows us to confront the histories of those rights and of those peoples too. The task is one of skill: *How* do we do all of these things? We do so with care, with information and with an open mind. Teaching human rights is not, we would argue, about being 'right,' it is about being human.

Bibliography

Bingham, L. 'The Case of Liversidge v. Anderson: The Rule of Law Amid the Clash of Arms' (2009) 43(1) *The International Lawyer* 33

Chander, A. 'Sovereignty, Referenda, and the Entrenchment of a United Kingdom Bill of Rights' (1991) 101(2) *The Yale Law Journal* 457

Ekins, R. and Gee, G. 'Submission to the Joint Committee on Human Rights: 20 years of the Human Rights Act', 18 September 2018

Emsley, C. 'Repression, "Terror" and the Rule of Law in England during the Decade of the French Revolution' (1985) 100(397) *The English Historical Review* 801

Glendon, M.-A. *Rights Talk: The Impoverishment of Political Discourse* (The Free Press, 1991)

Irvine, L. 'A British Interpretation of Convention Rights' (2012) (2) *Public Law* 237

Lester, A. 'Fundamental Rights in the United Kingdom: The Law and the British Constitution' (1976) 125(2) *University of Pennsylvania Law Review* 337

Masterman, R. 'The Mirror Crack'd', *UK Const. L. Blog*, 13th February 2013

Norman, J. and Oborne, P. 'Churchill's Legacy: The Conservative Case for the Human Rights Act', *Liberty* October 2009

O'Cinneide, C. 'How Well Does the UK's Democracy Protect Human Rights and Civil Liberties', Democratic Audit, 28 November 2018

Straw, J. *Aspects of Law Reform: An Insider's Perspective* (Cambridge University Press, 2013)

10 Upholding the Racial Hierarchy

The So-Called Perspectivelessness of Legal Study Skills

Sonya Onwu

Introduction

In 1988 after moving to Sydney, Australia, eight-year-old me was profoundly disturbed that the indigenous people whose land I had been told it was, were nowhere to be seen. When I asked where they were, my aunt told me that 'they weren't welcomed in the city so they didn't live there'[1]. Eight-year-old me did not understand how they could not be welcome when the land belonged to them, and wondered who it was that had the power to decide that they were not welcome on their own land. Two years later, we returned to England, where, as one of the first non-white families to move into the area, racist abuse and violence was an almost everyday occurrence. Every year on Halloween local racists would pelt the front of our house with dozens of eggs. One year, a traffic cone smashed through our front window, shattering glass all over the sofa from which my little brother had only just gotten up. When we called the police, the very people whose job it was to help and protect us from harm, they sighed, irritated, and said 'don't you know what day it is?' before hanging up the phone, as if having 24 eggs thrown at your house was normal because it was Halloween, and not because we were the only Brown family on our road and we were not welcome there. Shaped by the unapologetically virulent racism of 90s England, I learned three things early on. First, there was no justice to be found for people like me and the 'not present' indigenous people to whom the land belonged. Second, that we did not have rights or access to justice unless someone (a white someone) allowed us to, and third , that our welcome and hence our belonging was contingent upon the approval and acceptance of white people, be it white Australians 'allowing' the indigenous people to live in the cities, or the local racists 'allowing' us to live peacefully as part of the neighbourhood.

I listened to what the world *told* me law was – fair and impartial rules that keep order in society, freedom, human rights, democracy, justice, protection – and found there to be a huge disconnect with what I *knew* it to be. A lifetime

1 In over two years of schooling at three different schools, I only ever met one Aboriginal student.

DOI: 10.4324/9781003457985-10

of racism has shown me the myriad ways that law, and all that it embodies, can, and has, failed me: as a woman, and more specifically, as a woman of colour; as a descendent of the formerly colonised; as a Brown woman born and raised in the United Kingdom denied the security of belonging; as a survivor of sexual violence; and as a Muslim. It is through the lens of this knowledge and experience that I think about Euro-modern law.[2] As a racialised woman I bring the weight of my whole history, and the history of my ancestors to the question of how to empower global majority students to own their knowledge and experience so as to 'interrogate the very premises of law'.[3] For me, questions of rights and justice are about the rights of, and justice for the global majority,[4] rights which Euro-modern law has consistently failed to recognise, respect and protect, and a justice thus far denied to us.

Law schools, particularly elite law schools, deliberately choose not to make the (denial of) rights of the global majority a focus of legal knowledge.[5] . To do so, they would need to recognise how the construction of what constitutes legal thinking and legal reason continues to perpetuate the denial of rights and justice to the global majority. Nowhere are the racially imbued norms of objectivity and neutrality that permeate legal thinking more pertinent and intrinsic to law students than in the teaching of foundational legal study skills. Emphasis on and protection of a rules-based approach to legal analysis, thinking and problem solving relies upon a conception of reason and reasoning that is rooted in colonial norms. The effect is to teach global majority students to deny their lived experience in pursuit of the perspectivelessness that comes with thinking like a lawyer.[6]

This chapter will set out the three main challenges to teaching legal study skills in a way that empowers and gives voice to global majority students. First, it will show how the colonial history and subsequent Enlightenment ideas around reason not only allowed for but were central to the planned

2 'Euro-modern law is law which began in Europe, but also arose out of colonial activities in the Americas, Africa, Asia and Oceania'. Foluke Adebisi, *Decolonisation and Legal Knowledge: Reflections on Power and Possibility* (Bristol University Press 2023) 46.

3 Issa G. Shivji, 'Law's Empire and Empire's Lawlessness: Beyond the Anglo-American Law' (2003) (1) *Law, Social Justice & Global Development Journal (LGD)* <http://www2.warwick.ac.uk/fac/soc/law/elj/lgd/2003_1/shivji2/> accessed 26 August 2023.

4 Global Majority is a collective term that first and foremost speaks to and encourages those so-called to think of themselves as belonging to the global majority. It refers to people who are Black, Asian, Brown, dual-heritage, indigenous to the global south, and or have been racialised as 'ethnic minorities'. Rosemary Campbell-Stephens, 'Global Majority; Decolonising the Language and Reframing the Conversation About Race' <https://www.leedsbeckett.ac.uk/-/media/files/schools/school-of-education/final-leeds-beckett-1102-global-majority.pdf> accessed 12 August 2023.

5 Doing otherwise would require a complete overhaul of their curriculum, content and ideology, thorough discussion of which is beyond the scope of this analysis.

6 Kimberlé W. Crenshaw, 'Toward a Race-Conscious Pedagogy in Legal Education' (1988) 11(1) *National Black Law Journal* 1, 2.

project of the dehumanisation of the colonised to facilitate the denial of their rights. Second, it will highlight how the erasure of subjectivity and lived experience from legal reasoning preserves the image of Euro-modern law and consequently, the practice of legal study skills as objective and perspectiveless, rendering concerns about race and racial injustice are emotional ,irrational and contrary to thinking like a lawyer. It will set out the ways that law schools, as white spaces, serve to preserve and reinforce racial hierarchies, before finally outlining my thus far unsuccessful efforts in my Legal Study Skills (LSS) module, to try and get students, particularly those from the global majority, to acknowledge and centre their own perspectives. .

The contention of this piece is that the racist norms and values of Euro-modern law and hence legal thinking and legal reason, forces global majority students to deny their lived experiences in pursuit of the perspectivelessness of thinking like a lawyer. The problem is that this perspectivelessness is a myth designed to render consideration of the racism inherent within Euro-modern law contrary to the exercise of legal reason.

The Problem with Reason

To understand the deep rootedness of the bias within legal method, we need to chart the racist origins of Euro-modern law which continues to shape how we think about and study modern liberal legality[7] to expose how it appears to be 'without history, genesis or any possible derivation'.[8] The problem of course, is that the history and genesis of Euro-modern law and modern liberal legality is a colonial one. The effect of this genesis is twofold – first, in its dehumanising effect and denial of rights and personhood to the colonised, and second, in its elevation of objectivity and reason to an almost transcendent, immutable status. The consequence of this is the denial, negation and violation of the rights of the global majority; and the devaluing and erasure of subjectivity and perspective in legal reasoning.

The continued denial of rights to the colonised required a more permanent fabrication of incapacity. Progress and civilisation, or rather the lack of it, was measured using 'reason as the appropriate yardstick',[9] a standard that was forever unattainable by the colonised. To justify itself, the colonial project thus required the positing of the colonised as forever lacking in the capacity to reason, and therefore to be politically excluded as a matter of necessity. This perceived capacity to reason accordingly required a move away from 'irrational' beliefs towards choices made through the exercise of logic and

7 This phrase is utilised to connote law, 'legal instrumentalities, discourse, and legal consciousness'. David Theo Goldberg, *The Racial State* (Blackwell Publishers 2002) 139.

8 Jacques Derrida (trans. A. Ronell), 'Before the Law' in *Acts of Literature* (Routledge 1992) 191.

9 Uday Mehta, *Liberalism and Empire: A Study in Nineteenth Century British Liberal Thought* (University of Chicago Press 1999) 82.

rational thought, for to 'think and act without consistent reason [is to act] irrationally'.[10] The problem with rationality so construed of course, is that it ignores the fact that rationality is exercised in conjunction with experience, perception, and situation,[11] and so is *always* value-laden. The centrality of the liberal individual to the colonial project of dehumanisation cannot be underestimated.[12] The liberal human – rational, autonomous, possessing of reason and full rights and freedoms within the economic (contractual) and political realm, served to obscure the 'inclusionary pretensions of liberal theory and the exclusionary effects of liberal practices'.[13] In contrast, the construction of the colonised as lacking in objectivity and rationality facilitated the denial of their personhood, their very *humanness* and justified not only the denial of their rights, but their very *human* right to those human rights.

The emphasis upon reason and rationality during the rise of science and the ensuing period of Enlightenment[14] transformed not only conceptions of the liberal individual (read human) but also thought about the nature of law to one in which objectivity and reason became inextricably intertwined with law.[15] Within this schematic, positivistic law becomes viewed as the expression of society's rational mind.[16] Reason is framed as operating from behind a 'veil of ignorance'[17] that posits a reasoned position as independent from the context in which it is exercised. This imputed unboundedness to reason enables its characterisation as objective and untainted by bias or prejudice. Reason dictates the resolution of problems and the making of decisions through an (allegedly) neutral, uninvolved process which conceives of a framework where lived experience must necessarily be set to one side in pursuit of the perspectivelessness of so-called objectivity.

The conception of reason as devoid of perspective is, in fact, the embodiment of a racist history which facilitates a construction of reason as a process of knowing that deliberately fails to take account of various experiential

10 John M Finnis, 'On Positivism and Legal Rational Authority' (1985) 5(1) Oxford J Legal Stud 74, 83.

11 Nancy Levit, 'Critical of Race Theory: Race, Reason, Merit, and Civility' (1999) 87 *Georgetown Law Journal* 795, 801–802.

12 Ratna Kapur, *Erotic Justice: Law and the New Politics of Postcolonialism* (Glasshouse Press 2005) 139.

13 Mehta (n 9) 46.

14 Bertrand Russell, *History of Western Philosophy* (Routledge 2000) 512–525. The establishment of science as the primary mechanism for knowledge ostracised traditional patterns of thought and belief and paved the way for the technological, scientific and medical advances seen in today's society, however, its parallel effect was to 'make science rather than God, central to society and ...[to] relegate religious beliefs to the inner realm of private life'. Alain Touraine, *Critique of Modernity* (Blackwell Publishers Ltd 1995) 9.

15 Finnis (n10).

16 Catherine A. MacKinnon, 'Feminism, Marxism, Method, and the State: Toward Feminist Jurisprudence' (1983) 3 *Signs* 635, 658.

17 John Rawls, *A Theory of Justice* (Oxford University Press 1999) 17.

standpoints. In so doing, experiences of oppression and dominance which impact upon the reasoning process can be 'written' or rather, 'reasoned' out of the equation. The *nomos*, that is, the 'normative universe'[18] within which we live, is designated as a liberal one and this liberal *nomos* is legitimated by Euro-modern law. 'The creation of legal meaning – 'jurisgenesis' – takes place always through an essentially cultural medium',[19] and it is suggested that this cultural medium is a racialised framework dependent upon distorted biases and illegitimate constructions rooted in colonialism which are insulated by reason itself from critical challenge. Jurisgenesis has been hijacked by dominant western thought in a manner which forcibly excludes other understandings, and which remains distorted by an imperialistic bias dependent upon the binary construction of the *other*. This appropriation of reason as non-situated episteme thus excludes the possibility of reason as situated and personal.

The racialisation of the space of the *nomos* and the culturally imbued nature of jurisgenesis makes implicit the privileging of certain values over others. Thus, legal reason and reasoning informed by these same culture specific norms and values necessarily denies inclusion of *other* norms and values. If values then are preferences, and the preference within Euro-modern law is for seemingly objective rationalisation, then it can be logically concluded that Euro-modern law is predicated upon the normative embodiment of a particular conception of reason and rationality that paradoxically posits the rejection of truths about the world informed by ones experiences of racism, unjustifiable by reference to reason and logic. Yet, if one explores this 'reasoning' what can be seen is an inherent failure within Euro-modern law to reconcile itself. Reason becomes privileged over values.To profess a *preference* for western conceptions of law, democracy, human rights or freedom, however defined, is to elevate some *values* over others to the point where their status as values is denied. As Charles Wright Mills notes:

> No individual can be logical unless there be agreement among the members of his universe of discourse as to the validity of some general conception of good reasoning... the principles of logic... are shaped and selected by the instrumental character of discourse, by the goals of inquiry and discourse.[20]

Thus, reason so defined is dependent upon and constitutive of hierarchies; indeed, it forms the basis for the construction of hierarchical orderings of meaning and value. It is reason so construed which is central to how we understand legal reasoning.

18 Robert M. Cover, 'Nomos and Narrative' (1983) 97 Harv. L. Rev. 4.

19 ibid 11.

20 Charles Wright Mills, 'Language, Logic, and Culture' (1939) 4(5) *American Sociological Review* 670, 673.

The Problem with Thinking Like a Lawyer

The standardisation of the law school curriculum and the emphasis on the analysis of case law 'to facilitate the internalisation of the doctrinal logic used in the judicial process'[21] embedded a particular idea of legal education centred around the idea of training law students to 'think like a lawyer', by engaging in legal reasoning as somehow distinct from other types of reasoning.[22]

At the core of the legal curriculum is an emphasis on rule-based reason, nowhere more evident than in problem questions. These are designed specifically to test students' ability to identify the issues and relevant rules, apply these to the facts of the problem scenario and draw a conclusion, using the IRAC (Issue-Rule-Application-Conclusion) structure to simulate syllogistic processes of judicial reason. There is no scope within a problem question answer to consider the normative value of the decision. Problem questions are concerned only with the application of the legal rules.[23] Indeed, students are explicitly told to limit their answers to the application of the law as it is, and to keep questions of its merits or demerits[24] for their essays:[25]

> It is ironic the method involved in problem solving causes so many headaches for students, but in reality and stripped of its legal content, the process of demystifying a question to be answered, the applicable rule, and combining the two to reach a conclusion is one that we all do, all of the time, as part of everyday life: eligibility for a discount, complying with a shop's refund policy, nightclub opening hours, and even reading a train timetable all involve a similar process of identification and application of a general rule to a particular factual situation.[26]

The legal rules, as the product of judicial decisions, are held up as an exercise in objective reason. Legal reasoning is typically taught as a deductive process, enacted through the application of the syllogism.[27] Insistence upon the syllogism as the method of judicial reasoning gives a veneer of objectivity to the

21 Wendy Leo Moore, *Reproducing Racism: White Space, Elite Law Schools, and Racial Inequality* (Rowman & Littlefield 2008) 16.
22 Frederick F Schauer, *Thinking Like a Lawyer: A New Introduction to Legal Reasoning* (Harvard University Press 2009) 2.
23 Susan McMahon, 'What We Teach When We Teach Legal Analysis' (2023) 107 Minn L Rev 2511, 2533.
24 Samuel E. Stumpf, 'Austin's Theory of the Separation of Law and Morals' (196) 14 *Vanderbilt Law Review* 117.
25 Emily Finch and Stefan Fafinski, *Legal Skills* (7th edn, Oxford University Press 2019) 331.
26 ibid 332.
27 ibid.

judge's decision,[28] and in doing so, suffuses it with an air of legitimacy that mystifies its similarities to everyday reasoning.

Criticisms of the syllogism are well established.[29] As Davis notes, 'We no longer imagine law… to be a matter of simple deduction. Instead, we understand that law is created by people – people who reason within a culture, from a perspective, and with a set of sensibilities'.[30] However, it seems that this understanding is the preserve of legal scholars[31] and not law students. Criticism of formal legal reasoning and the syllogism are typically taught within jurisprudence/legal theory modules, separate to the core foundational law modules, such as Contract, Tort or Property.[32] Thus, whilst students might engage with criticisms of legal reasoning and its claims to objectivity within a module on legal theory, these criticisms are rarely, if ever, applied to analysis of judgments outside of these modules. If legal reasoning is understood as no different to the reasoning of a doctor, a carpenter or even a first-year law student, and 'there is [therefore] nothing special about law',[33] why the curricular façade?

To answer this, we must return to the colonial construction of reason that Euro-modern law is premised upon. The 'constructed dichotomy between the rational – read non-racial and non-personal – and the emotional – read racial and experiential'[34] is instrumental in ensuring three things. First, that the exercise of legal reason whether by a judge or a law student, is never emotional (read racial). The effect is to perpetuate the illusion that the predominantly elite White male judges exercise their reason from a position of non-race. Second, this insistence on the supposed perspectivelessness of legal reason trains law students – the future lawmakers – to '*not* problematise the connection between law and domination'.[35] Third, that concern for, and indeed righteous anger about the denial of the rights of, and justice for the global majority is read as emotional ***and*** racial, and therefore indicative of the absence of reason, a failure in the ability to think like a lawyer and an obstacle to success.

28 Jerzy Wroblewski, 'Legal Syllogism and Rationality of Judicial Decision' (1974) 5 *Rechtstheorie* 33, 34.
29 ibid.
30 Peggy C. Davis, 'Contextual Legal Criticism: A Demonstration Exploring Hierarchy and "Feminine" Style' (1991) 66 NYU L Rev 1635.
31 ibid.
32 See for example the course descriptors for jurisprudence/legal theory modules at Queen Mary University of London; University of Surrey; Durham University; London School of Economics; University of Birmingham. Indeed, even the textbook *Legal Skills* by Finch and Fafinski includes discussion of legal reasoning and the syllogism in its chapter on legal theory. Finch and Fafinski (n25) 253–256.
33 Nancy B Rapoport, 'Is Thinking Like a Lawyer What We Really Want to Teach?' (2002) 1 J Ass'n Legal Writing Directors 91, 95.
34 Crenshaw (n6) 6.
35 Wendy Leo Moore, 'The Mechanisms of White Space(s)' (2020) 64(14) *American Behavioural Scientist* 1946, 1952.

As Moore notes, 'while the process of teaching students to think like lawyers is generally presented as a neutral, impartial endeavour, the law school space is clearly marked by class, gender, and racial hierarchies'.[36] The law school's *nomos* is dependent upon an insistence on objectivity and its construction in opposition to experience. The racialised global order which protects and promotes white privilege and supremacy is inherently dependent on these dichotomies and hierarchies.[37] It is suggested then, that the process and purpose of teaching students to think like a lawyer is not so much about legal reasoning as a special and distinct skill. Rather, what we are actually doing is training students to uphold the hierarchy by 'reify[ing] and reproduce[ing] White privilege and power within the institutional setting of legal education'.[38] The effect of this reification is the reaffirming of colonial matrixes of humanness as a marker of those who are worthy of protection, and those who are not. As Upendra Baxi asserts, 'outside the foundational natural right inherent in colonialism (the *natural right to an Empire for European nations*), colonial legal tradition repudiates firmly any *jusnaturalist* construction of rights.'[39] What we, as educators are up against then, is the dismantling of a curriculum centred around a conception of law and legal reason that embodies and perpetuates colonial hierarchies.

The Problem with Law Schools

The problem is a socialisation into the narrative of Euro-modern law that occurs before students even get to law school. At the start of each teaching year, I begin by asking my students: What is law? In over 20 years of teaching at various law schools, irrespective of the law school, or the students own background or identity, most answer with something to the effect of 'the rules that keep order in society without which we would have disorder, anarchy and chaos', 'human rights', 'justice', 'fairness', 'truth', 'morality', with the occasional 'supposedly' tacked on. When I question them on this, they say "well... if you look at how they treat group X"[40] at which point, there is much nodding in agreement amongst the cohort. Yet in spite of this they still insist that ultimately, law is the (objective and impartial) rules. And so, when I come to the question of how to equip students with the skills to be able to engage with the treatment of the global majority, and the *denial* of their very right to these rights, it is with students for whom there is very often, a disconnect between

36 Moore (n21) 20.

37 Zeus Leonardo, 'The Color of Supremacy: Beyond the Discourse of "White Privilege"' (2004) 36(2) *Educational Philosophy and Theory* 137.

38 Moore (n35) 1955.

39 Upendra Baxi, 'The Colonialist Heritage' in Pierre Legrand and Roderick Munday, *Comparative Legal Studies: Traditions and Transitions* (Cambridge University Press 2009) 46–76, 72.

40 Group X inevitably being the global majority.

the realities of the world around them, and the narrative of law that they have been socialised into. As Subedi notes:

> the mainstream school curriculum socializes students into systems of knowledge that foster complacency... Such an outlook may emphasize a curriculum that does not explore the material realities and everyday subaltern experiences in the world... Because of the disjunction between the material realities of the world and those to which students are exposed, the nature of knowledge students learn rarely becomes relevant in critically analyzing global events and experiences. Thus, students often fail to learn to critique their place in the world as well as the intersection of power and privilege that creates inequities and oppression in local and global contexts. For this reason, students who are socialized into the dominant curriculum become unaware, reluctant, or opposed to learning about global issues that raise questions about racism, oppression, and inequities.[41]

Law modules are designed around teaching students the 'core' of each subject – the legal rules that they need to know, and how these have been interpreted and applied in cases. Each teaching week is devoted to setting out a different legal element, principle, issue or crime, with little interest in and/or time for questioning the racialised norms, values or history embodied in these rules, or the underlying racist and racialised assumptions implicit in the case-law.[42] This Eurocentric approach to curriculum and module design further cements the law student's socialisation into epistemic complacency.

The political location of law schools is one built upon a system of white supremacy that remains dependent on a legal structure that facilitated the 'construction of political and social racial domination... [and] simultaneously justifies, normalizes, and enforces the racial oppression of the state'.[43] Law schools then 'rationalize and normalize the legal structure; socialize those who will have the most control over the legal structure to uncritically internalize the ideological frames of the law'.[44] The function of law schools, particularly elite law schools, is to create leaders who will continue to uphold the global political order. The law school as an institution is thus fundamentally and necessarily opposed to creating legal thinkers wired to engage in or dismantle these power relations. As Adebisi, Jivraj, and Tzouvala notes:

41 Binaya Subedi, 'Decolonizing the Curriculum for Global Perspectives' (2013) 63(6) *Educational Theory* 621, 626.

42 See Suhraiya Jivraj, 'Towards Anti-racist Legal Pedagogy: A Resource' (SLSA 2020).

43 Moore (n21) 18.

44 ibid.

> law schools, especially in elite universities, remain disproportionately rich and white in the Global North... This means that many of our students and colleagues will be indifferent to or even hostile towards efforts to remake our curricula and classroom practices insofar as the legal system protects their material interests and reproduces their worldview.[45]

The deliberate and continued exclusion of the voices of the global majority from the law curriculum and the demand for perspectivelessness serves to keep law students complicit in and non-critical *about* the treatment of the global majority.

Neo-liberal universities and their law schools are sites of reproductions of colonialist power relations,[46] with the exercise of legal reason predicated on a myth of objectivity when in reality it is anything but. This leads us to question: Is it possible to tackle this structurally embedded cognitive dissonance? Can we equip students with the skills to be able to think about and engage with questions of justice for the global majority if the tools that we give them, and the site from within which we ourselves operate, are tainted?

Dismantling the Hierarchy

If the purpose of legal education is to maintain the status quo and uphold racial hierarchies then we can simply continue to use the master's tools.[47] However, is it possible to think beyond this, to consider whether it is in fact possible to equip students with the skills to dismantle the master's house? What might this dismantling look like, and where would it start from? In thinking through this, I continually come back to the weight of my history, and that of my ancestors. The violence and racism experienced during my younger years and beyond was so formative to my understanding of the world that it made it impossible for me to engage in the cognitive dissonance required to internalise the mythology of Euro-modern law. For students to be able to engage with the ways in which Euro-modern law oppresses the global majority, perspective must be at the forefront of everything that they do.

> Critical analysis begins from the objective experiences of the oppressed in order to understand the dynamics of structural power relations. It also makes sense to say that it is not in the interest of racially dominated groups to mystify the process of their own dehumanization.'[48]

45 Foluke I Adebisi, Suhraiya Jivraj and Ntina Tzouvala, *Decolonisation, Anti-Racism, and Legal Pedagogy: Strategies, Successes, and Challenges* (Routledge 2024) 2.

46 See Gurminder Bhambra, Dalia Gebrial, and Kerem Nişancıoğlu (eds), *Decolonising the University* (Pluto Press 2018); Rahul Rao, 'Neoliberal anti-racism and the British university' 2(8) *Radical Philosophy* 47.

47 Audre Lorde, *The Master's Tools Will Never Dismantle the Master's House* (Penguin 2018).

48 Leonardo (n37) 141.

If we take as our starting point the objective experiences of the oppressed, we need to ask ourselves the following questions: What is it that we want and need to teach students? How can we centre perspective? How can we let the subaltern speak and allow them the authority of their knowledge?[49] What might legal academic skills look like?

> If we are to challenge white space, while teaching a legal framework that is within the white frame, we must begin to be vigilant about exposing that power relations that the law facilitates... Thinking like a lawyer should mean being able to assess whose interests particular doctrines serve... we [would] have to reject traditional notions of objectivity in favour of more nuanced conception of the term.[50]

These questions have been central to my thinking on how to teach my course 'Legal Study Skills' (LSS). LSS is a compulsory, non-assessed course for all first year undergraduate Law, and Law and Anthropology students at the London School of Economics (LSE) Law School. The aim of LSS is twofold: to assist students in transitioning to study at university, and to teach them the skills needed to study law. These skills include how to read statutes, case law and articles, how to write essays and answer problem questions and how to take effective notes. Material for LSS is drawn from the reading lists of their core first year modules. The module is taught via hour-long classes. At the start of each session, we spend time working through the skill of that week as a class, before they are put into small groups to work on a designated task centred around the application of that skill. Two years ago, I added a lecture to the start of the course – LSS' only lecture. In this lecture, I ask students to tell me their answer to the question, 'What is law?' before asking them to think about the question 'Who are you?' In this part of the lecture, I take them through a snapshot of my life and identity as a Brown, Muslim woman, a mother, a survivor of sexual violence, a socialist, growing up in Newham (one of the poorest boroughs in London) and the racism I experienced living in an area where the British National Party (BNP) and National Front roamed freely. I also talk about the texts that were instrumental in shaping my thinking around law, amongst these, Franz Fanon's *Wretched of the Earth*, Aime Cesaire's *Discourse on Colonialism*, Makau Mutua's 'Savages, Victims, and Saviours: The Metaphor of Human Rights', Issa Shivji's 'Law's Empire and Empire's Lawlessness: Beyond Anglo-American Law' and Ratna Kapur's *Erotic Justice: Law and the New Politics of Postcolonialism*. At this point, I again pose the question, 'What is law?' and ask them to think about examples or events that *for them*, best illustrate what law is, before moving to highlight

49 Gayatri Spivak, 'Can the Subaltern Speak?' in Cary Nelson and Lawrence Grossberg (eds) *Marxism and the Interpretation of Culture* (Macmillan 1988).
50 Moore (n21) 175.

my own examples – the French ban on the hijab; police violence towards the global majority, particularly Black people; ownership of cultural property; and the decolonising the curriculum movement. Throughout the lecture I encourage them to think about their own experiences and/or the experiences of those around them, and what these tell them about law and the narratives around it. Student feedback post lecture has been overwhelming positive, with many saying how 'inspirational' they found it, how it gave them 'lots to think about', and how excited they were by the questions I had raised. After each lecture, I was inundated with students wanting to hear more about my thoughts on law, politics and decolonising. (It is worth noting that the students who approached me were all, without exception, global majority and/or self-described feminists, to whom my lecture spoke most loudly to.)

I begin classes, always with a request and reminder to the students to think about their 'lens', their perspective. I encourage them to start with their worldview, whatever that might be – feminist, anti-racist, conservative, capitalist, positivist – and to approach each skill, each module, each issue from the starting point of their positional, experiential lens, and in each class I gave them examples of how I would approach these from my own perspective. However, whilst students were enthusiastic about my lecture, and its 'inspiring' content, they struggled to apply it to their own studies in their core modules. Whilst they could engage to some extent with each of the questions that I had posed, they did so in a disconnected way, treating these as disparate, unrelated albeit interesting questions, separate to their study and analysis of law. Their life experiences were relegated to the margins of their legal study,[51] and this marginalisation was further compounded by the perspectivelessness of analysis in their other core first year modules.

The question then is whether it is in fact possible to empower students from the global majority to stand firm in their perspectives when law schools and legal thinking are premised upon 'the myth of perspectivelessness [that] is often analytically and emotionally disempowering'.[52] The disavowal and disconnection of their lived experience acts as a self defence mechanism that enables them to 'play the game right [by assuming] a stance that denies their own identity and requires them to adopt an apparently objective stance as the given starting point of analysis'.[53] It is this apparently objective starting point that I attempt to disrupt in my lecture, and through my continued insistence on, and encouraging of the centring of their worldview. Yet this in itself is not enough to counter the epistemic harm[54] that has been done to them. Many elite law schools resist calls to decolonise their curriculum because doing so

51 L. Danielle Tully, 'Race and Lawyering in the Legal Writing Classroom' (2022) 26 J Legal Writing Inst 195, 198.

52 Crenshaw (n6) 12.

53 ibid 5.

54 Terrell Carter and Rachel Lopez, 'If the Subaltern Could Speak' (Feb 2024) *Minnesota Law Review* (forthcoming) 1.

necessitates recognising their own complicity in upholding the racial hierarchy. In the absence of a complete overhaul of the curriculum, we need to teach the students seemingly innocuous yet disruptive ways to approach legal study skills. The first step is to recognise that asking students to own their perspective goes against a lifetime of educational complacency and conformity. From an LSS perspective, this means building upon the initial lecture to draw out illustrative key 'follow up' questions to encourage the centring of their worldview in a more seemingly objective way. For instance, what themes or issues (for example, racism, oppression, hierarchy, power, injustice), emerge from your examples that illustrate law? How might you apply these themes to your other modules? How do definitions of harm in tort or the harm principle in criminal law impact upon different individuals or groups? What does parliamentary supremacy tell us about power? How has race and racism fed into understandings of the reasonable person? Whose interests do these rules and decisions serve? Who is (disproportionately) impacted by these rules? Do these rules reflect a particular bias or worldview? What narratives or ideologies do these rules produce and perpetuate? Presenting these questions within the lecture itself will hopefully enable me to lead the global majority students towards the application of their own standpoint, whilst taking the onus for being too 'emotional' off them. Choosing articles or cases which represent 'controversial' or unfair views or decisions (not necessarily race related) will allow students to disagree with the content, whilst giving them the space to 'learn how to analyze an opinion that carries the air of authority but which nevertheless deny a reality that its readers feel they know'.[55] Another approach is to ask them to reflect upon the introductory lectures for their core modules, Contract, Tort, Criminal and Public Law, and to consider how these aims align with their own perspectives, and then locate the focus of the essay question within this understanding.

In Lieu of a Conclusion

There are a number of challenges to attempts to teach legal skills in a way that counteracts the problematic subject that is Euro-modern law. First, Euro-modern laws colonial heritage and its shaping of reason as objective and value-free to both exclude and deny rights to the colonised. Second, the conceptualisation of legal reason as perspectiveless and unemotional (read: non-racial) to further silence global majority students under the guise of thinking like a lawyer. Finally, the fact that law schools exist as key sites of 'hierarchy, deference to authority, [and]rationalisation of power and violence'.[56] Ultimately, a decolonial approach to legal study skills which places perspective at the forefront of critical analysis can only go so far. Without a dismantling

55 Crenshaw (n6) 13.
56 Adebisi, Jivraj and Tzouvala (n45) 1.

of the master's curriculum that confronts the racism of Euro-modern law and embeds perspective across the entire curriculum, it makes it difficult to empower global majority students to unsilence themselves. What is clear is that how we teach legal thinking is central to maintaining the racial hierarchy that Euro-modern law is premised upon. It is difficult to see how it is possible to dismantle the masters curriculum when it is this very curriculum that upholds the racialised global order and keeps the masters house belonging to the master.

Bibliography

Adebisi, F.I., Jivraj, S., and Tzouvala, N., *Decolonisation, Anti-Racism, and Legal Pedagogy: Strategies, Successes, and Challenges* (Routledge 2024)

Adebisi, F.I., Jivraj, S., and Tzouvala, N., 'Decolonising the Law School: Presences, Absences, Silences. . . and Hope' (2020) 54(4) *The Law Teacher* 471

Bhambra, G., Gebrial, D., and Nişancıoğlu, K., (eds), *Decolonising the University* (Pluto Press 2018)

Campbell-Stephens, R., 'Global Majority: Decolonising the Language and Reframing the Conversation about Race' <https://www.leedsbeckett.ac.uk/-/media/files/schools/school-of-education/final-leeds-beckett-1102-global-majority.pdf> accessed 12 August 2023

Carter, T. and Lopez, R., 'If the Subaltern Could Speak' (Feburary 2024) *Minnesota Law Review*

Conaghan, J., 'Schlag in Wonderland' (2003) 57 *University of Miami Law Review* 543

Cover, R.M., 'Nomos and Narrative' (1983) 97 *Harvard Law Review* 4

Crenshaw, K.W., 'Toward a Race-Conscious Pedagogy in Legal Education' (1988) 11(1) *National Black Law Journal* 1

Danielle Tully, L., 'Race and Lawyering in the Legal Writing Classroom' (2022) 26 *Legal Writing: The Journal of the Legal Writing Institute* 195

Derrida, J., *Acts of Literature* (Routledge 1992)

Finch, E., and Fafinski, S., *Legal Skills* (7th edn, Oxford University Press 2019)

Fitzpatrick, P., *The Mythology of Modern Law* (Routledge 1992)

Goldberg, D.T., *The Racial State* (Blackwell Publishers 2002)

Jivraj, S., *Towards Anti-Racist Legal Pedagogy: A Resource* (SLSA 2020) <https://research.kent.ac.uk/decolonising-law-schools/wp-content/uploads/sites/866/2020/09/Towards-Anti-racist-Legal-Pedagogy-A-Resource.pdf> accessed 25 September 2023

Kapur, R., *Erotic Justice: Law and the New Politics of Postcolonialism* (Glasshouse Press 2005)

Kennedy, D., 'The Politics of Law' (1982) 32(4) *Journal of Legal Education* 591

Kerr, J., 'Western Epistemic Dominance and Colonial Structures: Considerations for Thought and Practice in Programs of Teacher Education' (2014) 3(2) *Decolonization: Indigeneity, Education & Society* 83

Lacey, N., *Unspeakable Subjects: Feminist Essays in Legal and Social Theory* (Hart 1998)

Leonardo, Z., 'The Color of Supremacy: Beyond the Discourse of 'White Privilege'' (2004) 36(2) *Educational Philosophy and Theory* 137

Levit, N., 'Critical of Race Theory: Race, Reason, Merit, and Civility' (1999) 87 *Georgetown Law Journal* 795

Lorde, A., *The Master's Tools Will Never Dismantle the Master's House* (Penguin 2018)

MacKinnon, C.A., 'Feminism, Marxism, Method, and the State: Toward Feminist Jurisprudence' (1983) 3 *Signs* 635

Matiluko, O., 'Decolonising the Master's House: How Black Feminist Epistemologies Can be and are Used in Decolonial Strategy' 54(4) *The Law Teacher* 547

McMahon, S.A., 'What We Teach When We Teach Legal Analysis' (2023) 107 *Minnesota Law Review* 2511

Mehta, U., *Liberalism and Empire: A Study in Nineteenth Century British Liberal Thought* (University of Chicago Press 1999)

Mill, J.S., *On Liberty and Other Essays* (Oxford University Press 1991)

Moore, W.L., 'The Mechanisms of White Space(s)' (2020) 64(14) *American Behavioral Scientist* 1946

Moore, W.L., *Reproducing Racism: White Space, Elite Law Schools, and Racial Inequality* (Rowman and Littlefield Publishers 2008)

Nandy, A., *The Intimate Enemy: Loss and Recovery of Self Under Colonialism* (Oxford University Press 1983)

Rao, R., 'Neoliberal Anti-Racism and the British University' 2(8) *Radical Philosophy* 47

Rapoport, N.B., 'Is Thinking Like a Lawyer Really What We Want to Teach' (2002) 1 *Journal of the Association of Legal Writing Directors* 91

Rawls, J., *A Theory of Justice* (Oxford University Press 1999)

Russell, B., *History of Western Philosophy* (Routledge 2000)

Schauer, F.F., *Thinking Like a Lawyer: A New Introduction to Legal Reasoning* (Harvard University Press 2009)

Stumpf, S.E., 'Austin's Theory of the Separation of Law and Morals' (196) 14 Vanderbilt Law Review 117

Subedi, B., 'Decolonizing the Curriculum for Global Perspectives' (2013) 63(6) *Educational Theory* 621

Touraine, A., *Critique of Modernity* (Blackwell Publishers Ltd 1995)

Wroblewski, J., 'Legal Syllogism and Rationality of Judicial Decision' (1974) 5 *Rechtstheorie* 33

11 Human Rights Education in Times of Adversity

UK Government Agenda on Refugee Issues

Radu Cinpoes

Introduction

One of the key areas of focus on the agenda of the UK government concerns the issue of refugees. Public and political debates about refugees and about migration more broadly have gained prominence at least since the 2010 elections when the Conservative Party gained power. Since then, migration has been a salient issue in British politics, polarising public opinion and informing the way political parties position themselves in terms of electoral promises. In the last few years, however, the articulation of the 'legal/illegal' dichotomy in relation to refugees has become particularly problematic, especially in terms of how it relates to national and international human rights law.

As recently as January 2023, the 'stop the boats' slogan adopted by the Conservative Party in Government was incorporated by Prime Minister (PM) Rishi Sunak into his five key pledges shaping his cabinet's agenda.[1] Subsequently, and part of the plan to stem the number of asylum seekers crossing the Channel on small boats, the government managed to pass through the Parliament the Illegal Migration Act 2023 – a controversial piece of legislation, which entrenches the concept of 'illegal migration' and facilitates quick removal of those who are not deemed to meet conditions of 'entry clearance'.[2]

This phenomenon linked to refugee issues is part of a wider backlash against human rights in general. As far back as 2006, the then leader of the Conservative Party (in opposition) David Cameron pledged in a speech made at the Centre for Policy Studies that once in Government, his party would repeal the Human Rights Act 1998, and replace it with a British Bill of Rights.[3] This commitment was later nuanced in successive Conservative Party electoral manifestos (in 2015, 2017 and 2019). Furthermore, Rishi Sunak (when he

1 Prime Minister's Office, 10 Downing Street and The Rt Hon Rishi Sunak MP, 'PM Speech on Building a Better Future: 4 January 2023' (Gov.UK, 4 January 2023), <PM speech on building a better future: 4 January 2023 - GOV.UK (www.gov.uk)> accessed 1 May 2024.

2 Illegal Immigration Act 2023.

3 Peter Munce, 'The Conservative Party and Constitutional Reform: Revisiting the Conservative Dilemma through Cameron's Bill of Rights' (2014) 67(1) *Parliamentary Affairs* 80.

DOI: 10.4324/9781003457985-11

was Prime Minister) had hinted that he would support leaving the European Convention on Human Rights if it interfered with the government's refugee policy, a move that has been previously advocated by important right-wing figures in the Conservative Party, including former Home Secretary Suella Braverman.[4]

Against the background of this public, political and legal context in the United Kingdom, this chapter is concerned with normative questions about higher education teaching. More specifically, it aims to engage with questions about the language of the international human rights legal documents compared with that in current government policy, and about how the (over-) use of the word 'illegal' shapes the public understanding of refugee issues, with a view to ultimately tackle the problem of how academics approach these dynamics in teaching human rights in higher education.

To do so, the chapter acknowledges the added challenge that all these debates are situated within an epistemic paradigm shaped by 'post-truth' and anti-intellectualism. Thus, the chapter is divided into three parts. The first part conceptualises the notion of 'post-truth' and 'post-factual' politics and discourse, as well as that of anti-intellectualism, with a view to highlight the parameters of the current context. The second part deals specifically with the language of 'illegal migration' that characterises the current government's discourse and policy on refugee issues and contrasts it with current international legal norms regulating refugee issues. Finally, drawing on these dynamics, the chapter aims to sketch some key principles in addressing emerging challenges in higher education teaching. In particular, the chapter will address the challenges associated with distinguishing between 'neutral' and 'objective' approaches to such controversial issues and will discuss the role research-informed teaching practices have in engaging with students in the critical examination of current legal and political issues.

Conceptual Issues: Post-truth, Post-factual Politics and Anti-intellectualism

In 2016, Oxford Dictionaries declared 'post-truth' to be the word of the year. While first used in the early 1990s, the events surrounding the Brexit referendum and the election of Donald Trump in the United States led 'post-truth' to being labelled 'one of the defining words of our time'.[5] Since then, a growing body of scholarly work has emerged, focusing on the one hand on establishing

4 Christopher McKeon, 'Sunak Hints that the UK Could Leave ECHR if Rwanda Plan Blocked' *The Independent* (4 April 2024) <Sunak hints that UK could leave ECHR if Rwanda plan blocked | The Independent> accessed 1 May 2024.

5 BBC News, '"Post-truth" Declared Word of the Year by Oxford Dictionaries' *The BBC* (16 November 2016) <'Post-truth' declared word of the year by Oxford Dictionaries - BBC News> accessed 1 May 2024.

a working definition that depicts the reality behind the word appropriately, and on the other clarifying which label captures that reality better.

The *Oxford English Dictionary* defines post-truth as 'relating to or denoting circumstances in which objective facts are less influential in shaping public opinion than appeals to emotion and personal belief'. By virtue of having entered common parlance (at the expense of other equivalents), post-truth remains the dominant marker in the literature. Scholars such as Bufacchi, Conrad (et al.), Lockie or Lo Schiavo have provided thorough attempts to examine the multi-faceted nature of the phenomenon.[6] Despite the growing and diverse literature on post-truth, there is an emergent common ground that highlights two defining features: the relationship post-truth has with emotion and with truth. As the *Oxford English Dictionary* definition suggests, the appeal to emotion at the expense of facts constitutes one of the key strengths post-truth has in terms of shaping public opinion. What matters about claims is not factual evidence; instead, what is important is 'whether those listening to those claims would like them to be true'.[7] The persuasive power of such claims lies in their ability to resonate at an emotional level with the listener. Thus, counter-acting such claims with evidence that proves their falsehood is ineffective. The Brexit campaign slogans about the need to 'take back control' or 'get our country back', for instance, are meaningless and vacuous in terms of any concrete, factual basis, but they were effective in rallying support for the 'leave' camp. Similarly, the claim about 350 million pounds going to the European Union every day, that could be shifted towards the National Health Service seemed to be very effective, despite numerous attempts by the 'remain' supporters to offer concrete evidence undermining it.

While the emotive power that is generated by such claims coupled with the disregard for proof are important in understanding their salience, the most relevant aspect is the fact that post-truth needs to be differentiated from mere lying, because of the different relationship is has with the truth. The dissemination of disinformation and misinformation is supported by new technological developments that have created pervasive digital media infrastructures.[8] More importantly, what we see is a visible shift from general political lying to this new category of post-truth. As Newman puts it, there is 'an important

6 See Vittorio Bufacchi, 'Truth, Lies and Tweets: A Consensus Theory of Post-truth' (2021) 47(3) *Philosophy & Social Criticism* 347, Maximilian Conrad et al. (eds), *Europe in the Age of Post-truth Politics: Populism, Disinformation and the Public Sphere* (Palgrave 2023); Stewart Lockie, 'Post-truth Politics and the Social Sciences' (2017) 3(1) *Environmental Sociology* 1; Lidia Lo Schiavo, 'From Post-democracy to Post-truth Politics: the Crisis of Contemporary Democracy in Three Analytical Moves' (2019) 6(2) *Soft Power* 207.

7 Stewart Lockie, 'Post-truth Politics and the Social Sciences' (2017) 3(1) *Environmental Sociology* 1.

8 Maximilian Conrad and Guðmundur Hálfdanarson, 'Introduction: Europe in the Age of Post-Truth Politics' in Maximilian Conrad et al. (eds), *Europe in the Age of Post-truth Politics: Populism, Disinformation and the Public Sphere* (Palgrave 2023) 4.

qualitative difference between the post-truth politician and the spin doctors of yore'.[9] Similarly, Newman acknowledges that while lying is nothing new in politics, post-truth points to 'a new condition'. He explains that the 'political lie, in its transgression of the truth, at the same time confirmed truth's moral authority'.[10] In the past, truth remained a reference point that lying aligned itself against. Equally, as a politician, being caught lying – that is having been proven to have steered away from the truth – would normally have moral consequences (erosion of trust) and political ones (loss of support). Post-truth generates its own reality that is not concerned with the truth and is instead characterised by 'the complete shamelessness of these lies and manipulations' and by an utter 'indifference to any ethical norms of political discourse'.[11] The 'Partygate' scandal in the United Kingdom is reflective of statements that construct their own reality that is unscrupulously in complete denial of the truth. During his prime-ministership, Boris Johnson was criticised (alongside members of his cabinet) for repeatedly breaching the Covid-19 restrictions to public gathering that they, themselves, imposed. In response to such accusations, Boris Johnson and various other Conservative politicians questioned by journalists on this issue maintained – despite photographic evidence leaked to the press – that no parties had taken place and no breaches to Covid-19 restrictions occurred. Eventually, investigations were carried out by the police, and fines were issues in some cases. Moreover, the cross-party House of Commons Privileges Committee found in their report following a year-long investigation, that Boris Johnson had misled the House of Commons by continuously claiming that rules were observed and also found Boris Johnson in contempt of Parliament.[12]

The attempt to capture accurately the nature of the phenomenon has generated debates in the literature about the appropriate label that ought to be attached to it. While the term post-truth has gained significant currency, other concepts are employed in order to explain this new reality. Wardle and Derakhshan articulate the concept of ***information disorder***, which looks at three dimensions of information: the types, the phases and the elements of information.[13] The focus on types of information (dis-information, mis-information

9 Lockie (n 7) 1.

10 Saul Newman, 'Post-Truth, Postmodernism and the Public Sphere' in Maximilian Conrad et al. (eds), *Europe in the Age of Post-truth Politics: Populism, Disinformation and the Public Sphere* (Palgrave 2023) 14.

11 ibid 14.

12 For details, see: BBC News, 'Partygate: a Timeline of Lockdown Parties' *The BBC* (21 March 2023) < Partygate: A timeline of the lockdown parties - BBC News> accessed 1 May 2024; BBC News, 'Boris Johnson Report: Key Findings from the Partygate Inquiry' *The BBC* (15 June 2023) <Boris Johnson report: Key findings from the Partygate inquiry - BBC News> accessed 1 May 2024.

13 Claire Wardle and Hossein Derakhshan, 'Information Disorder: Towards an Interdisciplinary Framework for Research and Policy Making' *Council of Europe* (2017) <168076277c (coe.int)> accessed 1 May 2024.

and mal-information), on the phases (creation, production and distribution) and on elements of information (agent, message and interpreter) provides a nuanced understanding of the mechanics of the process of information disorder. However, the concept does not capture fully the broader epistemic impact of this new form of communication. MacMullen's notion of *post-factual politics* is concerned precisely with the wider implications of the epistemic dimension of post-factualism (which he adds to the unconscious, the metaphysical and the motivational ones), which in combination with the other three constitutes the current 'post-factual political culture'.[14] I employ the concept of post-factualism over the post-truth one because of how such claims are received by those who are persuaded by them. Rather than being disconnected from truth, post-factual statements make claims about 'truth' – what calls an *alt-epistemic stance*.[15] It is, however, a different kind of truth: one that does rely on empirical evidence. Moreover, empirically grounded truth is relativised, and opinions are formulated based on emotional and ideological values. As MacMullen puts it: 'epistemic post-factualism leads to a complete suspension of belief on the empirical matter in question [...] epistemic post-factualism leads to ideological, tribal, and/or partisan approaches to politics, but it does so in a distinctive manner'.[16] Picking up on the notion of an epistemic shift, Dahlgren goes further and suggests that we are witnessing an *epistemic crisis of democracy*: 'a sort of epistemic cacophony, where even the descriptions of basic social realities are often contested', which leads to 'an emerging political culture of distrust that undermines shared assumptions about social reality and the pathways to legitimate knowledge', all of these undermining trust and the character of democracy.[17]

Coupled with the post-factual condition and enhancing the epistemic crisis is the increased prevalence of anti-intellectual attitudes. Broadly defined, anti-intellectualism is characterised by 'a generalized suspicion and mistrust of intellectuals and experts of whatever kind'.[18] In terms of its key features, Rigney identifies three important aspects that define anti-intellectualism: anti-rationalism (as rejection of critical thinking), unreflexive instrumentalism (as prioritisation of short-term material gains over long-term goals) and anti-elitism (as

14 Ian MacMullen, 'Survey Article: What Is "Post-factual" Politics?' (2020) 28(1) *The Journal of Political Philosophy* 97.

15 Kjetil Rommetveit, 'Introduction: Post-truth – another Fork in Modernity's Path' in Kjetil Rommetveit (ed), *Post-truth Imaginations: New Starting Points for Critique of Politics and Technoscience* (Routledge 2022).

16 ibid 109.

17 Peter Dahlgren, 'Media, Knowledge and Trust: the Deepening Epistemic Crisis of Democracy' (2018) 25(1–2) *Javnost: the Public*, 20, 25–26.

18 Eric Merkley, 'Anti-intellectualism, Populism, and Motivated Resistance to Expert Consensus' (2020) 84(1) *Public Opinion Quarterly* 24, 26.

lack of trust in experts).[19] As is the case with political lying, anti-intellectualism is not a new phenomenon: Richard Hofstadter – on whose work Rigney picks up – engaged with the concept in relation to the American society in the early 1960s, claiming that it was older than the country's national identity itself.[20] However, as in the case of post-truth and post-factual politics and grafted onto the cumulative effect results in the epistemic crisis highlighted earlierthe result is not only a lack of trust in political institutions, but rather, broader transformations 'in the processes of production of knowledge' that go beyond basic anti-intellectualism and constitute 'aggressive attacks on basic Enlightenment premises'.[21]

The stark anti-intellectualism operating in the context of post-factual narratives is epitomised by the much-quoted statement made by Michael Gove (from his then position of Justice Secretary and prominent figure in the 'Leave' campaign in the Brexit referendum) that 'people had enough of experts'.[22] Later on, Gove suggested that he was mainly referring to economics and social scientist who often get it wrong in their predictions. Much more concerning than this statement, was the letter – again, in the context of the Brexit referendum – by Conservative MP Chris Heaton-Harris to universities in the United Kingdom requesting the names of academics teaching European affairs, as well as copies of the curricula on these topics and links to online materials. The request was labelled as 'chilling' and reminding of McCarthyism by university leaders.[23]

Government Agenda and the Language of 'Illegal Migration'

Having provided a conceptual framework that considers the combined effect of post-factualism and anti-intellectualism, this section aims to explore how these practices feature in the UK government's discourse and inform the agenda in relation to refugee issues. It focuses specifically on the 'illegal migration' narrative that has shaped both public opinion and – more importantly – government policy, by comparing it with current international legal frameworks relating to refugees.

19 Daniel Rigney. 'Three Kinds of Anti-Intellectualism: Rethinking Hofstadter' (1991) 61(4) *Sociological Inquiry* 434.

20 Richard Hofstadter, *Anti-Intellectualism in American Life* (Random House 1962).

21 Dahlgren (n 17) 26.

22 Michael Gove later nuanced his statement. See BBC News, 'Michael Gove Clarifies Stance on Experts' *The BBC* (27 February 2017) <Michael Gove clarifies stance on experts - BBC News> accessed 1 May 2024.

23 Jack Sommers, 'Tory MP Condemned for "Chilling" Letter Asking Universities to Reveal Information on Brexit Teaching' *The Huffington Post* (24 October 2017) <Tory MP Condemned For 'Chilling' Letter Asking Universities To Reveal Information On Brexit Teachings | HuffPost UK News (huffingtonpost.co.uk)> accessed 1 May 2024.

Immigration has been a highly charged political issue in the United Kingdom for some decades. It seems that the 2010 elections represented a shift: a consensus emerged across the main political parties in terms of the need to limit migration drastically. For the Labour Party (and arguably for the Liberal Democrats, as well) this change in position was one of necessity. It was a calculated response to the Conservative criticism (supported and reinforced by the right-wing press) that the Labour Party had had an 'open door policy' on migration which gained significant purchase with the voters. Illustratively, in the first televised party leaders' debate ahead of the 2010 elections, none of them made a positive case for migration.[24] From then on, this cross-party convergence shifted the immigration paradigm further towards more restrictive approaches to immigration.[25] In 2019, the Conservative Party electoral manifesto still focused on reducing the number of migrants into the United Kingdom. While it aimed to reduce the number of people coming from outside the European Union (EU) (given that free movement for people from the EU ended following the United Kingdom's withdrawal from the EU), it nonetheless did not yet make the explicit connection between illegal migration and refugees. (Incidentally, the manifesto borrowed the 2010 Labour pledge to introduce an Australia-style point-based system.)[26]

With the appointment by then PM Boris Johnson of Priti Patel as Home Secretary and in the context of an increase in the number of people attempting to cross the English Channel and come to the United Kingdom in search of asylum (with Britain not part of the EU Dublin regime concerning asylum and migration management) the shift towards conflating debates about illegal migration on the one hand and about asylum on the other happened in earnest. In May 2021, Priti Patel outlined her immigration plans in a speech where she explicitly labelled attempts at crossing the Channel in small boats as illegal and articulated the prevention mechanisms in terms of preventing 'more lives being lost' in the crossing and protecting people from placing 'their lives in the hands of people smugglers'. At the same time, she articulated the drive

24 Mehdi Hasan, 'Election 2010: Silent on Immigration? Hardly' *The Guardian* (18 April 2010) <Election 2010: Silent on immigration? Hardly | Mehdi Hasan | The Guardian> accessed 1 May 2024.

25 Interestingly, the shift is very visible in the case of the Labour Party. Their 2005 electoral manifesto committedly states that 'immigration has been good for Britain'. By contrast, their 2010 electoral manifesto places immigration alongside crime and talks about the need to 'control immigration through our Australian-style points-based system'. See: The Labour Party, 'The Labour Party Manifesto 2005: Britain Forward not Back' (2005) <Layout 1 (deryn.co.uk)> accessed 1 May 2024; The Labour Party, 'The Labour Party Manifesto 2010: A Future Fair for All' (2010) <TheLabourPartyManifesto-2010.pdf (deryn.co.uk)> accessed 1 May 2024.

26 The Conservative Party, 'Get Brexit Done, Unleash Britain's Potential: the Conservative and Unionist Party Manifesto 2019' (2019) <Conservative Party Manifesto 2019 (conservatives.com)> accessed 1 May 2024.

towards 'speeding up the removal of those with no legal right to be in the UK'.[27]

This became the official party stance on asylum with various prominent figures reinforcing the message. In his April 2022 speech, then PM Boris Johnson distinguishes between 'safe and legal routes' for seeking protection and 'a parallel illegal system'. In true post-factual fashion, he talks, on the one hand, about those attempting to cross the Channel as both 'men under 40, paying people smugglers to queue jump' calling the attempts as crossing 'perverse'. On the other hand, he also refers to these asylum seekers as victims, claiming that 'vile people smugglers are abusing the vulnerable and turning the Channel into a watery graveyard, with men, women and children, drowning in unseaworthy boats' – a reference to the number of people drowning while attempting to cross the Channel into the United Kingdom. Finally, he explicitly distinguishes between a 'legal' and an 'illegal' route into the UK asylum system, based on the form of entry which the then proposal for a Nationality and Borders Bill (which was passed into law later that month) was meant to address, as it allowed the authorities 'for the first time to distinguish between people coming here legally and illegally, and for this distinction to affect how your asylum claim progresses and your status in the United Kingdom if that claim is successful'.[28]

Suella Braverman (Priti Patel's successor as Home Secretary) continued this trend and by proposing what became in July 2023 the Illegal Immigration Act. Thus, the 'illegal' label attached to undocumented entries by people aiming to claim asylum became the norm in the Government's discourse shaping the legislative agenda. The legislative proposal was part of a wider strategy that involved an agreement with the Republic of Rwanda (brokered by Priti Patel) that would effectively 'outsource' the asylum process for those entering the United Kingdom in an undocumented way. In relation to the legislative proposal, Suella Braverman declared in December 2022 that: 'if you come here irregularly or illegally – on a small boat, putting yourself and others at risk – you will be detained and swiftly removed to a safe country or to Rwanda for your asylum claim to be processed'.[29] The 'illegal migration' label and the 'stop the boats' slogan became the hallmark of the government approach to refugee issues. Prime Minister Rishi Sunak repeatedly pushed this narrative,

27 Home Office and The Rt Hon Priti Patel MP, 'Home Secretary Priti Patel Speech on Immigration' *Gov.UK* (25 May 2021) <Home Secretary Priti Patel speech on immigration - GOV.UK (www.gov.uk)> accessed 1 May 2024.

28 Prime Minister's Office, 10 Downing Street and The Rt Hon Boris Johnson, 'PM Speech on Action to Tackle Illegal Migration' *Gov.UK* (14 April 2022) <PM speech on action to tackle illegal migration: 14 April 2022 - GOV.UK (www.gov.uk)> accessed 1 May 2024.

29 Lizzie Dearden and Bel Trew, 'Suella Braverman Insists Rwanda Deportation Policy Is "Humane" but Is Unable to Give Start Date' *The Independent* (19 December 2022) <Suella Braverman insists Rwanda deportation policy is 'humane' but is unable to give start date | The Independent> accessed 1 May 2024.

even using the 'stop the boats' slogan to emblazon his lectern during press conferences.[30]

With the Illegal Immigration Act 2023 receiving royal assent in July 2023, Rishi Sunak's cabinet faced further challenges in carrying out the plan to deport asylum seekers that entered the country via informal routes, when the Supreme Court unanimously ruled that the government plan to send asylum seekers to Rwanda was unlawful, due to refoulment risks.[31] To circumvent the court's decision, and it true postfactual vein – legislating that a country is safe – the government pushed through Parliament the Safety of Rwanda (Asylum and Immigration) Act 2024, which came into force in April. This piece of legislation has been strongly criticised both in parliamentary debates and by organisations concerned with refugee rights, including the United Nations (UN) High Commissioners for Human Rights and for Refugees. As for the idea 'that a country will remain "safe" regardless of what happens there', this is – as McKee directly puts is – 'simply ludicrous'.[32]

In understanding challenges raised by the 'illegal migrant' narrative and by legal developments informed by it (namely the Illegal Immigration Act 2023 and the Safety of Rwanda (Asylum and Immigration Act 2024)), it is important to contrast them with existing international norms relating to refugee protection and broader human rights frameworks. The key starting point in this is the United Nations 1951 Convention Relating to the Status of Refugees (The Refugee Convention in short) and its 1967 Protocol of which the United Kingdom is a signatory state. One defining feature of the 'illegal migrant' narrative is to distinguish between those who enter the territory of the United Kingdom via formal routes (e.g., visas, specific country routes, family routes, resettlement routes, etc.) and those coming via informal routes (e.g., via small boats, in and undocumented way), to label the latter 'illegal' and to punish them by removing various rights to asylum. In this regard, the Refugee Convention states in Article 31.1 that

> The Contracting States shall not impose penalties, on account of their illegal entry or presence, on refuges who, coming directly from a territory where their life and freedom was threatened in the sense of article 1, enter or are present in their territory without authorization, provided

30 See a discussion about the backlash caused by this in Graeme Demianik, '"Dystopian": Rishi Sunak's New "Stop the Boats" Lectern Prompts Backlash' *The Huffington Post* (7 March 2023) <Rishi Sunak's 'Stop The Boats' Lectern Prompts Backlash | HuffPost UK Politics (huffingtonpost.co.uk)> accessed 1 May 2024.

31 Jonathan Este, 'Supreme Court Rules Rwanda Plan Unlawful: A Legal Expert Explains the Judgement, and What Happens Next' *The Conversation* (15 November 2023) <Supreme court rules Rwanda plan unlawful: a legal expert explains the judgment, and what happens next (theconversation.com)> accessed 1 May 2023.

32 Martin McKee, 'The Safety of Rwanda Act: A Pointless Exercise in Performative Cruelty' (25 April 2024) 38 *The BMJ*, doi: https://doi.org/10.1136/bmj.q947.

> they present themselves without delay to the authorities and show good cause for their illegal entry or presence.[33]

Thus, the principle of no penalty on unlawful entry lies in stark contrast with the default labelling and treating of people entering via informal routes as 'illegal'. Moreover, semantically classing such individuals as 'illegal *migrants*' places them in a broader category on human mobility that takes away the specific character of potential forced displacement and 'well-founded fear' that describes the conditions in which these people are in. Other principles in the Refugee Convention that are jeopardised in the government's approach to 'illegal migration' pertain to the access to courts (Art. 16), non-refoulment (Art. 33). Ahead of being passed into law, a detailed analysis of the constitutional implications of the Illegal Migration Bill found a significant number of 'very likely' breaches of international human rights law, including of the Refugee Convention, of the European Convention on Human Rights, of the Council of Europe Convention on Action against Trafficking in Human Beings, the United Nations Convention on the Rights of the Child, the United Nations Convention Relating to the Status of Stateless Persons, as well as undermining parliamentary sovereignty, the rule of law, devolution and the separation of powers.[34]

Importantly, the report highlights the fact that the Illegal Migration Bill and the government's insistence that refugees ought to claim asylum in 'the first safe country they reach' constitutes a desertion from the Refugee Conventions principle that refugee protection 'should be a shared responsibility among states', a point raised by the UN High Commissioner for Refugees, as well.[35]

Despite the distance from international legal framework, the concept of 'illegal migration' has become – through repetition – the common label when referring to asylum seekers coming via informal routes to the point where most of the media outlets are using it, with few exceptions of instances when journalists attempt to correct politicians when they are making false claims in relation to the issue. An example of such an exception is the instance when journalist Krishnan Guru-Murthy corrected and took to task the then Immigration Minister Robert Jenrick on his claims. In that interview, Jenrick falsely stated several times that the UN Refugee Convention required that people seek refuge in the first safe country.[36] One of the most astonishing

33 1951 Convention Relating to the Status of Refugees and 1967 Protocol, Art.3.1.

34 Public Law Project et al., 'The Illegal Migration Bill: Constitutional Implications' <The-Illegal-Migration-Bill-Constitutional-Implications.pdf (publiclawproject.org.uk)> accessed 1 May 2024.

35 ibid 22–24.

36 See a section of the recorded interview and transcript in Graeme Demianyk, 'Robert Jenrick Called Out for False "Asylum Shoppers" Claim' *The Huffington Post* (10 May 2023) <Robert Jenrick Called Out For 'Asylum Shoppers' Claim | HuffPost UK Politics (huffingtonpost.co.uk)> accessed 1 May 2024.

post-factual statements on the issue, however, was made by then Home Secretary, Suella Braverman, who – in an article written for the *Daily Mail* newspaper – claimed: 'There are 100 million people displaced around the world, and likely billions more eager to come here if possible'.[37] She made a similar claim in Parliament, on the same day: 'There are 100 million people around the world who could qualify for protection under our current laws. Let's be clear. They are coming here'.[38] This was a claim she maintained even when questioned subsequently in an interview, when journalists pointed out that the 100 million figure was of people displaced worldwide, of which over a quarter had left their own country.[39]

While creating this alternative reality, which is enhanced by the use of incendiary language such as 'invasion' or 'hurricane' in relation to migration,[40] anti-intellectualism is employed to stem any criticism against such claims, completing a narrative fuelling an adverse environment for the protection of human rights and more broadly for empirical truth. The labels placed on people opposing the government policies on refugees – such as 'lefty lawyers', 'activist lawyers', 'lefty human rights lawyers', 'do-gooders' have become commonly used insults, causing members of the legal profession to voice their concerns.[41] In a different context, an epitome of this phenomenon was Suella Braverman's blaming 'the Guardian-reading, tofu-eating wokerati' for disruptive environment protest.[42]

37 Suella Braverman, 'The British People Have Had enough of Migrants Pouring over the Channel… That's Why Stopping the Boats Is My Top Priority' *Mail Online* (7 March 2023) <SUELLA BRAVERMAN: The British people have had enough of migrants pouring over the Channel… | Daily Mail Online> accessed 1 May 2023.

38 Channel 4 News, 'Migrants Arriving on Small Boats Will Be Swiftly Removed' *YouTube* (7 March 2023) <Migrants arriving on small boats will be 'swiftly removed' (youtube.com)> accessed 1 May 2024.

39 Adam Forrest, 'Suella Braverman again Rebuked by Stats Watchdog for Saying "Millions of Migrants" could Come to UK' *The Independent* (10 May 2023) <Suella Braverman rebuked by watchdog for saying 'millions' could come to UK | The Independent> accessed 1 May 2024.

40 See Becky Morton, 'Minister Warns on Language after Suella Braverman "Invasion" Comment' *The BBC* (1 November 2022) <Minister warns on language after Suella Braverman 'invasion' comment - BBC News> accessed 1 May 2024; David Hughes, 'Suella Braverman Faces Backlash for "Incendiary" Language in Tory Conference Speech' *The Standard* (4 October 2023) <Suella Braverman faces backlash for 'incendiary' language in Tory conference speech | Evening Standard> accessed 1 May 2024.

41 See Davin Renton, 'In Defence of Lefty Lawyers' *The Spectator* (10 April 2021) <In defence of lefty lawyers | The Spectator> accessed 1 May 2024; Owen Bowcott, 'Government QCs Call for an End to Ministers' Attacks on "Lefty" Lawyers' *The Guardian* (6 November 2020) <Government QCs call for end to ministers' attacks on 'lefty' lawyers | Law | The Guardian> accessed 1 May 2024; Rowena Mason, '"An Activist Blob": Tory Party Attacks on Lawyers – a Timeline' *The Guardian* (16 August 2023) <'An activist blob': Tory party attacks on lawyers – a timeline | Conservatives | The Guardian> accessed 1 May 2024.

42 Guardian News, 'Suella Braverman Blames "Guardian-reading, Tofu-eating Wokerati" for Disruptive Protests' *YouTube* (18 October 2022) <Suella Braverman blames 'Guardian-reading, tofu-eating wokerati' for disruptive protests (youtube.com)> accessed 1 May 2024.

Human Rights Education in the Context of Post-factualism and Anti-intellectualism

Having contextualised the emergence of a post-factual era, coupled with anti-intellectualism, it is important to recognise the challenges this new paradigm poses to teaching in higher education, in particular on issues related to human rights. These challenges are raised by both the fact that higher education institutions are increasingly being attacked for being out of touch bastions of 'wokeness',[43] and by the fact that people coming to university are increasingly operating in a post-factual world with competing claims to 'truth' and 'knowledge'. In this context, the purpose of this section is to try to sketch some directions in response to these challenges, with a view to supporting students with tools to navigate these difficulties. These suggestions are focused on two broad areas: on the one hand on addressing the epistemic symmetry principle, and on the other on assuming a fallibilist epistemological relativism.

The first area for discussion concerns the epistemic symmetry principle that treats all knowledge claims symmetrically. In attempting to address the relationship between authoritative knowledge and power and redress the balance by enabling marginalised knowledge claims to be considered on an equal playing field, the symmetry principle postulated a 'value-neutral relativism', which 'combines neutrality in methods' which applies consistent and equal criteria to conflicting claims, 'with partiality in outcomes' which assigned 'true' and 'false' labels to competing.[44] The post-factual context opened the gate for a distortion of the principle that points to a neutrality that affects outcomes, where knowledge claims are assigned 'true' values indiscriminately. This has been facilitated – as Söderberg further observes – by the fact that neutrality leads inadvertently to partiality, because it privileges the 'epistemically disadvantaged actors'. At the same time, the principle 'does not guarantee that the opinions of marginalised actors are sound and just, but their marginality suffices to warrant an "epistemological preferential treatment"'.[45] The debate about climate change is illustrative in this respect: climate change-denying claims are often given equal voice and credibility with the dominant scientific arguments, because they are seen as marginal and disadvantaged in comparison to the dominant, authoritative truth.

43 See for instance, Andrew Lilico, 'Britain Needs New "Non-woke" Universities' *The Telegraph* (28 November 2021) <Britain needs new 'non-woke' universities (telegraph.co.uk)> accessed 1 May 2024, and a defence of universities from accusations of 'wokeness' in Gavin Esler, 'Too "Woke"? Universities in Europe Are Unfairly Attacked' *The National News* (12 October 2021) <Too 'woke'? Universities in Europe are being unfairly attacked (thenationalnews.com)> accessed 1 May 2024.

44 Johan Söderberg, 'The Moment of Post-truth for Science and Technology Studies' in Kjetil Rommetveit (ed), *Post-truth Imaginations: New Starting Points for Critique of Politics and Technoscience* (Routledge 2022) 97.

45 ibid 97–98.

Post-factualism also facilitates the blurring of the relationship between what can be regarded as the dominant authoritative voice (with the power mechanisms associated to it) and the disadvantaged voices, though a process of self-victimisation by actors that represent themselves as marginalised. One of the curiosities of the 'illegal migration' narrative is that actors articulating it portray it as a marginalised voice, despite being very strongly represented in the media and public discourse and having the government's political clout and communication machine behind it.

As educators, to counteract these tendencies, it is important to address the balance between neutrality and objectivity. This requires undermining epistemic processes that result in neutrality of outcomes. The first step is to encourage students to recognise disparities between the different voices and to investigate these critically. This can be done by stimulating scientific literacy, supporting students in familiarising themselves with different ways in which science is communicated and ultimately 'inoculating students against misleading scientific communication techniques'.[46] In the context of refugee issues, this would make it easier to discern the 'truth' value of statements suggesting – for instance – that there is a danger that millions (if not billions!) of people may seek refuge in the United Kingdom, in comparison with consistent evidence that the vast majority of displaced people remain within the borders or their own countries, or within the same geographical regions. Similarly, debates about human rights can at least offer a legal-positivist reference point that could help in counteracting some of post-factual narratives. The 'illegal migration' label attached to refugees, for instance, can easily be refuted by referring to what international legal instruments say (about no penalties for irregular entry). Whether the legal instruments available are appropriate or not is a different matter and should certainly be subjected to informed critical debate and deliberation; what they state in their current form is less so.

How we respond to counter-factual narratives is the second important area that – as educators – we need to bear in mind, and this applies equally to wider public debates. Rommetveit remarks that scholarly responses to post-factualism tended to either amount to 'epistemic pearl-clutching rushing to the defence of fact, truth, and rationality' or 'defensive positions [...] on the social (and political) roles and uses of knowledge, and of critique of knowledge'.[47] Both of these stances ultimately reinforce a certain 'intolerant parochialism' and 'expert hubris'[48] that refuses to take the other side seriously and to acknowledge their voices and (often) legitimate concerns. In the Brexit referendum

46 See Sarit Barzilai and Clark A. Chinn, 'A Review of Educational Responses to the "Post-truth" Condition: Four Lenses on Post-truth Problems' (2020) 55(3) *Educational Psychology* 107, 111–112.

47 Kjetil Rommetveit (n 15) 2.

48 Brian Wynne, 'Truth as What Kind of Functional Myth for Modern Politics? A Historical Case Study' in Kjetil Rommetveit (ed), *Post-truth Imaginations: New Starting Points for Critique of Politics and Technoscience* (Routledge 2022) 40, 58.

debate, lay people supporting the 'leave' camp complained (often justifiably) that they were treated condescendingly by those in the 'remain' camp (labels like 'ignorant', 'brain-washed', etc. being hurled against them). The display of epistemic certitude, especially by experts and members of the scientific community, and disdain for alternative positions (even post-factual ones) builds resentment, fuels anti-intellectualism, and – most importantly – removes the possibility for critical, reasoned exchanges. Fostering 'epistemic humility, curiosity and courage'[49] in students creates a framework for constructive exchange of ideas and critical learning.

At the other end of the spectrum, post-factualism as an unintended consequence of (potentially misinterpreted) sceptical postmodernism[50] has arguably led to a situation where 'postmodernist ideas that "truth" was "unstable, contingent, contested" could easily guide students to question received wisdom without giving them the tools or inclination to defend important ideals'.[51] Linked to the earlier point about epistemic symmetry, post-factualism's extreme relativism that postulates that alternative truths are as legitimate as any other established knowledge and can replace it (see for instance flat earth arguments gaining ground) requires epistemic humility. A grounded fallibilist epistemological relativism can provide solutions to education. The acknowledgment that our knowledge is potentially flawed can counteract the hubris of epistemic certainty, prompting a constant subjecting of knowledge to critical testing and re-evaluation. Using immanent critique – by subjecting a claim to criticism from its own standpoint – allows students to 'discuss and evaluate disagreement on how to know' leading to a 'better understanding of scientific practice'.[52] Thus, what is needed is a more focused approach to achieving a critical, objective (not neutral) and solution-driven understanding of the current challenges in the field of human rights. As Philip Alston puts it, 'critical scholarship [that] is formulaic, and unfocused' can lead to losing sight of 'unintended consequences'[53] that can manifest in legitimising post-factual and anti-intellectual stances. On the refugee issue in particular, it is important to consider all perspectives critically, but at the same time to

49 Norma A. Marrun et al., 'Indifferent, (Un)critical, and Anti-intellectual: Framing How Teachers Grapple with Bans on Teaching Truth about Race and Racism, and Critical Race Theory' (2024) 27(1) *Race Ethnicity and Education* 75.

50 See the debate between Perrin and Delton regarding the links between post-truth and postmodernism in Andrew J. Perrin, 'Stop Blaming Postmodernism for Post-Truth Politics' (4 August 2017) *The Chronicle of Higher Education* <Stop Blaming Postmodernism for Post-Truth Politics (chronicle.com)> accessed 1 May 2024, and Jennifer Delton, 'Don't Absolve Postmodernism so Quickly' (15 August 2017) *The Chronicle of Higher Education* <Letters: Don't Absolve Postmodernism So Quickly (chronicle.com)> accessed 1 May 2024.

51 Rick Szostak, 'Interdisciplinarity versus Anti-Intellectual and Anti-Democratic Impulses' (2018) 36(2) *Issues in Interdisciplinary Studies* 267, n.3.

52 Sarit Barzilai et al. (n 46) 15.

53 Philip Alston, 'The Populist Challenge to Human Rights' (2 February 2018) 9(1) *Journal of Human Rights Practice* 1.

distinguish emotion-driven and ideologically grounded postulations of truth and evidence-based claims knowledge that can sustain continuous scrutiny.

Conclusion

This chapter identified as its starting point the current political debates concerning refugee issues in the United Kingdom. It acknowledged that there is a strong government agenda according to which these debates have been cast into a narrative about 'illegal migration' and that this narrative has shaped policy making. The recently-come-into-force Illegal Immigration Act 2023 and Safety of Rwanda (Asylum and Immigration) Act 2024 are the last controversial chapters in this saga.

Within this context, the aim here was to situate the current events within a broader phenomenon that is characterised on the one hand by the proliferation of post-truth and post-factual politics and on the other (and convergently) by increased anti-intellectualism. These trends are not only visible within the public life, but they are further accentuated by the current government, who uses these stances in order to advance its goals. The chapter engaged with scholarly work on post-truth and post-factualism and argued that this phenomenon represents a concerning shift from political lying, not only through its endemic spread, but also qualitatively by signalling the advent of a new form of discourse that is not simply distorting facts and diverting from the truth. Instead, it is not concerned with factual accuracy altogether and aims to articulate a different reality (an alt-truth) that is legitimised by the response it generates at an emotional level rather than by facts or common sense. The rejection of expert views and empirical facts contributes to the exacerbation of this phenomenon.

Having established some brief conceptual parameters, I have shown that the current government agenda on refugees both illustrates and embeds more deeply this post-factual stance. As a result, through constant repetition and reinforcement, the 'illegal migration' narrative has been accepted widely by the public and the media, with relatively weak challenges. Criticism to the narrative has been dismissed effectively through anti-intellectual arguments that reduce critical voices to out of touch, 'lefty' and 'woke' elites.

This environment raises significant challenges to teaching and learning in higher education. The final section of the chapter engaged with some of these challenges and outlined some directions for action. In particular, it suggested the need to address the distortion of the epistemic symmetry principle that leads to a situation where methodological neutrality is replaced by a neutrality of outcome. To counteract that, it is important to clarify the difference between neutrality and objectivity in debates and to support students in developing the skills to identify critically disparities between voices and asses the truth value of claims accordingly. Linked to that, it argued that the responses to post-factualism should steer away from either epistemic parochialism and hubris, and from extreme relativism. Instead, it suggested that a fallible epistemological relativism that is characterised by constant critique and a more sophisticated understanding of scientific practice can counteract the effects of post-factualism.

Bibliography

Alston, P., 'The Populist Challenge to Human Rights' (2 February 2018) 9(1) *Journal of Human Rights Practice* 1.

Barzilai, S., and Chinn, C.A., 'A Review of Educational Responses to the "Post-truth" Condition: Four Lenses on Post-truth Problems' (2020) 55(3) *Educational Psychology* 107.

BBC News, 'Boris Johnson Report: Key Findings from the Partygate Inquiry' *The BBC* (15 June 2023) <Boris Johnson report: Key findings from the Partygate inquiry - BBC News> accessed 1 May 2024.

BBC News, 'Michael Gove Clarifies Stance on Experts' *The BBC* (27 February 2017) <Michael Gove clarifies stance on experts - BBC News> accessed 1 May 2024.

BBC News, 'Partygate: A Timeline of Lockdown Parties' *The BBC* (21 March 2023) <Partygate: A timeline of the lockdown parties - BBC News> accessed 1 May 2024.

BBC News, '"Post-truth" Declared Word of the Year by Oxford Dictionaries' *The BBC* (16 November 2016) <'Post-truth' declared word of the year by Oxford Dictionaries - BBC News> accessed 1 May 2024.

Bowcott, O., 'Government QCs Call for an End to Ministers' Attacks on "Lefty" Lawyers' *The Guardian* (6 November 2020) <Government QCs call for end to ministers' attacks on 'lefty' lawyers | Law | The Guardian> accessed 1 May 2024.

Braverman, S., 'The British People Have Had Enough of Migrants Pouring over the Channel… That's Why Stopping the Boats Is My Top Priority' *Mail Online* (7 March 2023) <SUELLA BRAVERMAN: The British people have had enough of migrants pouring over the Channel… | Daily Mail Online> accessed 1 May 2023.

Bufacchi, V., 'Truth, Lies and Tweets: A Consensus Theory of Post-truth' (2021) 47(3) *Philosophy & Social Criticism* 347.

Channel 4 News, 'Migrants Arriving on Small Boats Will Be Swiftly Removed' *YouTube* (7 March 2023) <Migrants arriving on small boats will be 'swiftly removed' (youtube .com)> accessed 1 May 2024.

Conrad, M. and Hálfdanarson, G., 'Introduction: Europe in the Age of Post-Truth Politics' in Maximilian Conrad et al. (eds), *Europe in the Age of Post-truth Politics: Populism, Disinformation and the Public Sphere* (Palgrave 2023) 4.

Conrad, M. et al. (eds), *Europe in the Age of Post-truth Politics: Populism, Disinformation and the Public Sphere* (Palgrave 2023).

Dahlgren, P., 'Media, Knowledge and Trust: the Deepening Epistemic Crisis of Democracy' (2018) 25(1–2) *Javnost: The Public* 20–25.

Dearden, L. and Trew, B., 'Suella Braverman Insists Rwanda Deportation Policy Is "Humane" but Is Unable to Give Start Date' *The Independent* (19 December 2022) <Suella Braverman insists Rwanda deportation policy is 'humane' but is unable to give start date | The Independent> accessed 1 May 2024.

Delton, J., 'Don't Absolve Postmodernism so Quickly' (15 August 2017) *The Chronicle of Higher Education* <Letters: Don't Absolve Postmodernism So Quickly (chronicle .com)> accessed 1 May 2024.

Demianik, G., '"Dystopian": Rishi Sunak's New "Stop the Boats" Lectern Prompts Backlash' *The Huffington Post* (7 March 2023) <Rishi Sunak's 'Stop The Boats' Lectern Prompts Backlash | HuffPost UK Politics (huffingtonpost.co.uk)> accessed 1 May 2024.

Demianyk, G., 'Robert Jenrick Called Out for False "Asylum Shoppers" Claim' *The Huffington Post* (10 May 2023) <Robert Jenrick Called Out For 'Asylum Shoppers' Claim | HuffPost UK Politics (huffingtonpost.co.uk)> accessed 1 May 2024.

Esler, G., 'Too "Woke"? Universities in Europe Are Unfairly Attacked' *The National News* (12 October 2021) <Too 'woke'? Universities in Europe are being unfairly attacked (thenationalnews.com)> accessed 1 May 2024.

Este, J., 'Supreme Court Rules Rwanda Plan Unlawful: A Legal Expert Explains the Judgement, and What Happens Next' *The Conversation* (15 November 2023) <Supreme court rules Rwanda plan unlawful: a legal expert explains the judgment, and what happens next (theconversation.com)> accessed 1 May 2023.

Forrest, A., 'Suella Braverman Again Rebuked by Stats Watchdog for Saying "Millions of Migrants" Could Come to UK' *The Independent* (10 May 2023) <Suella Braverman rebuked by watchdog for saying 'millions' could come to UK | The Independent> accessed 1 May 2024.

Guardian News, 'Suella Braverman Blames "Guardian-reading, Tofu-eating Wokerati" for Disruptive Protests' *YouTube* (18 October 2022) <Suella Braverman blames 'Guardian-reading, tofu-eating wokerati' for disruptive protests (youtube.com)> accessed 1 May 2024.

Hasan, M., 'Election 2010: Silent on Immigration? Hardly' *The Guardian* (18 April 2010) <Election 2010: Silent on immigration? Hardly | Mehdi Hasan | The Guardian> accessed 1 May 2024.

Hofstadter, R., *Anti-Intellectualism in American Life* (Random House 1962).

Home Office and The Rt Hon Priti Patel MP, 'Home Secretary Priti Patel Speech on Immigration' *Gov.UK* (25 May 2021) <Home Secretary Priti Patel speech on immigration - GOV.UK (www.gov.uk)> accessed 1 May 2024.

Hughes, D., 'Suella Braverman Faces Backlash for "Incendiary" Language in Tory Conference Speech' *The Standard* (4 October 2023) <Suella Braverman faces backlash for 'incendiary' language in Tory conference speech | Evening Standard> accessed 1 May 2024.

Lilico, A., 'Britain Needs New "Non-woke" Universities' *The Telegraph* (28 November 2021) <Britain needs new 'non-woke' universities (telegraph.co.uk)> accessed 1 May 2024.

Lockie, S., 'Post-truth Politics and the Social Sciences' (2017) 3(1) *Environmental Sociology* 1.

MacMullen, I., 'Survey Article: What Is "Post-factual" Politics?' (2020) 28(1) *The Journal of Political Philosophy* 97.

Marrun, N.A. et al., 'Indifferent, (Un)critical, and Anti-intellectual: Framing How Teachers Grapple with Bans on Teaching Truth about Race and Racism, and Critical Race Theory' (2024) 27(1) *Race Ethnicity and Education* 75.

Mason, R., '"An Activist Blob": Tory Party Attacks on Lawyers – a Timeline' *The Guardian* (16 August 2023) <'An activist blob': Tory party attacks on lawyers – a timeline | Conservatives | The Guardian> accessed 1 May 2024.

McKee, M., 'The Safety of Rwanda Act: A Pointless Exercise in Performative Cruelty' (25 April 2024) 38 *The BMJ*, https://doi.org/10.1136/bmj.q947.

McKeon, C., 'Sunak Hints that the UK Could Leave ECHR if Rwanda Plan Blocked' *The Independent* (4 April 2024) <Sunak hints that UK could leave ECHR if Rwanda plan blocked | The Independent> accessed 1 May 2024.

Merkley, E., 'Anti-intellectualism, Populism, and Motivated Resistance to Expert Consensus' (2020) 84(1) *Public Opinion Quarterly* 24–26.

Morton, B., 'Minister Warns on Language after Suella Braverman "Invasion" Comment' *The BBC* (1 November 2022) <Minister warns on language after Suella Braverman 'invasion' comment - BBC News> accessed 1 May 2024.

Munce, P., 'The Conservative Party and Constitutional Reform: Revisiting the Conservative Dilemma through Cameron's Bill of Rights' (2014) 67(1) *Parliamentary Affairs* 80–101.

Newman, S., 'Post-Truth, Postmodernism and the Public Sphere' in Maximilian Conrad et al. (eds), *Europe in the Age of Post-truth Politics: Populism, Disinformation and the Public Sphere* (Palgrave 2023) 14.

Perrin, A.J., 'Stop Blaming Postmodernism for Post-Truth Politics' (4 August 2017) *The Chronicle of Higher Education* <Stop Blaming Postmodernism for Post-Truth Politics (chronicle.com)> accessed 1 May 2024.

Prime Minister's Office, 10 Downing Street and The Rt Hon Boris Johnson, 'PM Speech on Action to Tackle Illegal Migration' *Gov.UK* (14 April 2022) <PM speech on action to tackle illegal migration: 14 April 2022 - GOV.UK (www.gov.uk)> accessed 1 May 2024.

Prime Minister's Office, 10 Downing Street and The Rt Hon Rishi Sunak MP, 'PM Speech on Building a Better Future: 4 January 2023' *Gov.UK* (4 January 2023) <PM speech on building a better future: 4 January 2023 - GOV.UK (www.gov.uk)> accessed 1 May 2024.

Public Law Project et al., 'The Illegal Migration Bill: Constitutional Implications' <The-Illegal-Migration-Bill-Constitutional-Implications.pdf (publiclawproject.org.uk)> accessed 1 May 2024.

Renton, D., 'In Defence of Lefty Lawyers' *The Spectator* (10 April 2021) <In defence of lefty lawyers | The Spectator> accessed 1 May 2024.

Rigney, D., 'Three Kinds of Anti-Intellectualism: Rethinking Hofstadter' (1991) 61(4) *Sociological Inquiry* 434.

Rommetveit, K., 'Introduction: Post-truth – Another Fork in Modernity's Path' in Kjetil Rommetveit (ed), *Post-truth Imaginations: New Starting Points for Critique of Politics and Technoscience* (1–5) (Routledge 2022).

Schiavo, L.L., 'From Post-democracy to Post-truth Politics: The Crisis of Contemporary Democracy in Three Analytical Moves' (2019) 6(2) *Soft Power* 207.

Söderberg, J., 'The Moment of Post-truth for Science and Technology Studies' in Kjetil Rommetveit (ed), *Post-truth Imaginations: New Starting Points for Critique of Politics and Technoscience* (Routledge 2022) 86–110.

Sommers, J., 'Tory MP Condemned for "Chilling" Letter Asking Universities to Reveal Information on Brexit Teaching' *The Huffington Post* (24 October 2017) <Tory MP Condemned For 'Chilling' Letter Asking Universities To Reveal Information On Brexit Teachings | HuffPost UK News (huffingtonpost.co.uk)> accessed 1 May 2024.

Szostak, R., 'Interdisciplinarity versus Anti-Intellectual and Anti-Democratic Impulses' (2018) 36(2) *Issues in Interdisciplinary Studies* 267.

The Conservative Party, 'Get Brexit Done, Unleash Britain's Potential: The Conservative and Unionist Party Manifesto 2019' (2019) <Conservative Party Manifesto 2019 (conservatives.com)> accessed 1 May 2024.

The Labour Party, 'The Labour Party Manifesto 2005: Britain Forward not Back' (2005) <Layout 1 (deryn.co.uk)> accessed 1 May 2024.

The Labour Party, 'The Labour Party Manifesto 2010: A Future Fair for All' (2010) <TheLabourPartyManifesto-2010.pdf (deryn.co.uk)> accessed 1 May 2024.

Wardle, C. and Derakhshan, H., 'Information Disorder: Towards an Interdisciplinary Framework for Research and Policy Making' *Council of Europe* (2017) <168076277c (coe.int)> accessed 1 May 2024.

Wynne, B., 'Truth as What Kind of Functional Myth for Modern Politics? A Historical Case Study' in Kjetil Rommetveit (ed), *Post-truth Imaginations: New Starting Points for Critique of Politics and Technoscience* (Routledge 2022) 33–64.

Legislation:

Convention Relating to the Status of Refugees (adopted 28 July 1951, entered into force 22 April 1954) 189 UNTS 137 (Refugee Convention).

Human Rights Act 1998.

Illegal Immigration Act 2023.

Safety of Rwanda (Asylum and Immigration Act) 2024.

12 Teaching and Debating the Legal Protection of Philosophical Belief in the Workplace in a University Law School

Stephen Hurley

Introduction

Teaching and debating what no one feels very strongly about brings its own challenges – primarily that of making the subject matter relevant, interesting and understandable to students. However, when the subject matter being taught is not just controversial but contains material and issues which some students (and academic staff) feel passionately about – even perhaps touching the core of their very identity and/or existence – the challenge becomes infinitely greater, requiring empathetic and sensitive management.

In this chapter, the writer will consider the challenge of teaching and debating the legal protection of philosophical belief in the workplace, in a university law school. The prime focus will be on UK law schools but where appropriate lessons and issues from outside the jurisdiction, in particular the United States, will be included.

Note the chapter is not intended as an extended discussion of the technical law concerning philosophical belief in the workplace. Nor is it intended as a 'how-to' guide to teach law: many others are far better qualified to provide such guidance. The writer's aspiration is simply that the reader will learn something both interesting and useful for their own teaching practice and their understanding of the law in this area.

The Legal Definition of Philosophical Belief

The Equality Act 2010 sets out the main framework for the protection against unlawful discrimination in the United Kingdom. The Act's protection is centred primarily around the concept of 'protected characteristics'.[1] There are nine such characteristics listed in the Act. One of them is 'religion or belief'.[2] 'Belief' is defined in the Act as 'any religious or philosophical belief and a reference to belief includes reference to a lack of belief'.[3]

1 Listed in s4 Equality Act 2010.
2 S10.
3 S10(2).

DOI: 10.4324/9781003457985-12

While there is already much case law and academic commentary concerning the legal protection of religion, only in recent years has the case law begun to expand in the United Kingdom regarding the area of philosophical belief.

To amount to a philosophical belief protected by the Act, the case law that has developed has set out a number of criteria, all of which must be satisfied. These are referred to as the '*Grainger* criteria'.

They specify that:

(i) the belief must be genuinely held;
(ii) it must be a belief and not an opinion or viewpoint based on the present state of information available;
(iii) it must be a belief as to a weighty and substantial aspect of human life and behaviour;
(iv) it must attain a certain level of cogency, seriousness, cohesion and importance; and
(v) it must be worthy of respect in a democratic society, not be incompatible with human dignity and not conflict with the fundamental rights of others.[4]

UK courts and Tribunals are also required to read and give effect to statutory provisions in a way which is, so far as possible, compatible with the European Convention on Human Rights.[5] Often in philosophical belief cases, Articles 9(1)[6] (freedom of thought, conscience and religion) and 10(1)[7] (freedom of expression) are relevant.

Important consequences follow if a particular belief is recognised as having legal protection. In particular, the belief can then benefit from Equality Act protections against direct and indirect discrimination and harassment. Such claims can be brought by a wide category of workers, without any qualifying period of service and, if successful, may result in unlimited compensation including sums for injury to feelings.[8] In addition, holders of beliefs may also

4 *Grainger plc v Nicholson* [2010] ICR 360 at para 24. For a recent review of the case law on the criteria, see K Patten, 'Protected beliefs under the Equality Act: Grainger questioned' *ILJ* 2024, 53(2), 239–267.

5 Ss 3 and 6 Human Rights Act 1998.

6 '1. Everyone has the right to freedom of thought, conscience and religion; this right includes freedom to change his religion or belief and freedom, either alone or in community with others and in public or private, to manifest his religion or belief, in worship, teaching, practice and observance'.

7 '1. Everyone has the right to freedom of expression. This right shall include the freedom to hold opinions and to receive and impart information and ideas without interference by public authority and regardless of frontiers'.

8 This compares much more favourably to another key employment claim of unfair dismissal under the Employment Rights Act 1996 where, generally, only employees may claim, who have been dismissed, they require two years' service, compensation is capped by statute and no injury to feelings awards are payable. Note though the intention of the new UK Government

find comfort in concluding that society (through the law) has at least confirmed that their belief is 'worthy of respect in a democratic society'.

Controversial Aspects of the Topic

Unsurprisingly, given the nature of the test, and perhaps in particular the rather vague wording of the fifth element, which essentially amounts to a value judgement of whether the belief is worthy of respect in a democratic society, there have been significant differences of opinion as to whose beliefs should get legal protection and whose should not.

Findings by Employment Tribunals (ETs) and courts that certain beliefs are protected has provoked little controversy. For example, holding as protected a belief in humanism, democratic socialism[9] or Scottish independence[10] is unremarkable. The courts are at pains to point out that the mere fact that any particular belief is held to qualify for legal protection does not mean that the judiciary have in any way endorsed as true or validated the accuracy or correctness of the belief in question.[11]

However, whether other beliefs should get legal protection has generated much more controversy. For example, the topical issue of so called 'gender critical beliefs' has been the subject of much debate. The Employment Appeal Tribunal (EAT) held in the case of *Forstater*,[12] that such beliefs were legally protected. Ms Forstater worked for a think tank in the United Kingdom. She believed that biological sex is real, immutable and not to be conflated with gender identity. Her consultancy contract was not renewed by her employer following complaints by some work colleagues who felt that some of her social media posts were 'transphobic', 'exclusionary or offensive' or made them feel 'uncomfortable'.

After at first losing her argument that her beliefs qualified for protection in the Employment Tribunal, she succeeded in the Employment Appeal Tribunal. The ET at first instance had held that it was

> a core component of her belief is that she **will** refer to a person by the sex she considered appropriate even if it violates their dignity and/or creates an intimidating, hostile, degrading, humiliating or offensive environment. The approach is not worthy of respect in a democratic society.[13]

---

to extend unfair dismissal protection to the wider category of 'workers' and provide protection from day one of service: Prime Minister's Office, *The King's Speech 2024 Background Briefing Notes* (17 July 2024), 20. See too now the Employment Rights Bill 2024.

9 *Olivier v Dept for Work and Pensions* ET/1701407/2013.

10 *McEleny v Ministry of Defence* S/4105347/2017.

11 See for example *Maya Forstater v CGD Europe & ors* (UKEAT/0105/20/JOJ) at para 55 b.

12 *Maya Forstater v CGD Europe & ors* (UKEAT/0105/20/JOJ).

13 ET decision, unreported, (18 December 2019) para 90 (emphasis added).

However, in a landmark decision in this area, the EAT held that Ms Forstater's beliefs were worthy of legal protection. Noting first that the issue in the case 'has generated strong feelings',[14] the EAT ruled that:

> it is only those beliefs that would be an affront to Convention principles in a manner akin to pursuing totalitarianism, or advocating Nazism, or espousing violence or hatred in the gravest forms, that should be capable of being not worthy of respect in a democratic society. Beliefs that are offensive, shocking or even disturbing to others, and which fall within the less grave forms of hate speech would not be excluded from the protection.[15]

In a highly unusual move, the EAT in its decision were at pains to make clear also what their decision did **not** mean. In para 79 they noted that the manifestation of such beliefs may, depending on the circumstances, justifiably be restricted under Article 9(2)[16] or Article 10(2)[17] as the case may be.

At para 118 they stressed that their decision did **not** mean that

> those with gender critical beliefs can 'misgender' trans persons with impunity. [Ms Forstater], like everyone else, will continue to be subject to the prohibitions on discrimination and harassment under the EqA. Whether or not conduct in a given situation does amount to harassment or discrimination ... will be for a tribunal to determine in a given case.[18]

When teaching controversial law topics, making use in class of such detailed judicial pronouncements of what the decision does **not** mean is essential, to

14 *Maya Forstater v CGD Europe & ors* (UKEAT/0105/20/JOJ) para 2.

15 *Maya Forstater v CGD Europe & ors* (UKEAT/0105/20/JOJ) para 79.

16 '2. Freedom to manifest one's religion or beliefs shall be subject only to such limitations as are prescribed by law and are necessary in a democratic society in the interest of public safety, for the protection of public order, health or morals, or for the protection of the rights and freedoms of others'.

17 '2. The exercise of these freedoms, since it carries with it duties and responsibilities, may be subject to such formalities, conditions, restrictions or penalties as are prescribed by law and are necessary in a democratic society, in the interests of national security, territorial integrity or public safety, for the prevention of disorder or crime, for the protection of health or morals, for the protection of the reputation or rights of others, for preventing the disclosure of information received in confidence, or for maintaining the authority and impartiality of the judiciary'.

18 For other recent cases where the concept of so called 'misgendering' was at issue see *Dr David Mackereth v Dept for Work and Pensions & anor* [2022] EAT 99, *Lister v Swindon College* ET Case No. 1404223/2022 and, on the related issue of email signature pronouns, *Orwin v East Riding of Yorkshire Council* ET Case No. 6000146/2022. See too on the issue of so called 'compelled speech', Rowbottom J 'Cakes, Gay Marriage and the Right against Compelled Speech', U.K. Const.L.Blog (16th Oct. 2018) (available at: https://ukconstitutionallaw.org/)

reduce scope for misunderstanding or inferring a meaning that a Tribunal did not intend.

The EAT's decision has been subject to significant criticism by some,[19] and when teaching it, there is the possibility that some students may find it personally challenging. Whilst acknowledging this before discussion, it is therefore essential to root the legal substance of the decision in the subsequent application of the principle by later courts and tribunals.

So, for example, the *Forstater* finding regarding gender critical beliefs being, prima facie,[20] legally protected has been followed by the EAT in the case of *Dr Mackereth*,[21] and the ET in recent decisions such as *Joanna Phoenix v The Open University*.[22] In addition, it was not subject to any adverse criticism in the EAT's subsequent decision also dealing with trans issues in *Mrs Kristie Higgs v Farmor's School & anor*.[23]

By acknowledging that the discussion may be challenging at the outset, and rooting it in a close analysis of the legal decision, it is possible to have a challenging debate in which students may profoundly disagree with each other – and even with the legal finding – but in an atmosphere of scholarly endeavour and respect.

Prohibitions on Harassment and 'Safe Spaces'

Such an atmosphere is not always encouraged at some university campuses. To protect students from perceived harm, some student unions have developed 'safe space' policies. Such policies 'seek to restrict the expression of certain views or words that can make some groups feel unsafe'.[24]

The belief by some that university classrooms should be 'safe spaces', not simply from unlawful harassment but also from being exposed to any opinions,

19 See for example: S Cowan et al., 'Should "Gender Critical" Views about Trans People Be Protected as Philosophical Beliefs in the Workplace? Lessons for the Future from *Forstater, Mackereth* and *Higgs*' (2022) *ILJ* 55(1) pp.1–37. For a particular focus on issues of manifestation, see M Foran, 'Discrimination and Manifestation of Belief: *Higgs v Farmor's School*' (2024) *ILJ* 53(2) pp.285–304.

20 Prima facie in the sense that, strictly, it is still for each claimant in a case to give evidence as to how **their** belief satisfies the *Grainger* criteria (unless conceded by the respondent). It is though highly likely that, as certain protected beliefs become more well known, respondents are more likely to concede the issue as a preliminary point, provided they believe the claimant genuinely holds the belief. See for example the partial concession noted at para 281 in the Tribunal's decision in *Ms Allison Bailey v Stonewall Equality Ltd & ors* Case No. 2202172/2020.

21 *Dr David Mackereth v Dept for Work and Pensions & anor* [2022] EAT 99, see the discussion paras 78-94 and the EAT's conclusion on this point at para 120.

22 Case No 3322700/2021 & 3323841/2021 at para 484.

23 *Higgs v Farmor's School & anor [2023] EAT 89 at para 79.*

24 House of Commons/House of Lords Joint Committee on Human Rights, *Freedom of Speech in Universities* (March 2018)(HC 589/HL Paper 111) p.27 Box 8.

views or ideas which make a student uncomfortable, poses a significant challenge to academic freedom and freedom of expression, and to law teachers.

The proper role and purpose of a university is of course (quite rightly) a debated topic. For most academics though, providing safe spaces should not be to the detriment of free thinking. As Professor Hannah Holborn Gray of the University of Chicago noted: 'education should not be intended to make people comfortable, it is meant to make them think'.[25]

The Joint Committee on Human Rights concluded that the concept of safe spaces was not helpful. They suggested that it often marginalised the views of minority groups, in practice, serving to 'prevent the free speech of those whose views they disagree with'.[26]Lukianoff et al. agree, and suggest that academics '[d]iscourage the creep of the word "unsafe" to encompass "uncomfortable"'.[27] Hume notes that the concept of 'safe spaces' 'risk turning campuses into soporific cocoons where students and academics are protected from anything that might wake them up or ask them to think differently'.[28]

Simon Fanshawe, one of the co-founders of Stonewall, argues that the concept is being fundamentally misunderstood. In the context of a typical workplace, he suggests that '[s]paces only become safe when trust is built. And trust is only built through the understanding that comes from exploring and experiencing differences'.[29] He concludes that: 'safe spaces must be safe *for* disagreement *not from* them to achieve the best and most satisfying results'.[30]

University law schools should be a space which is 'safe' for respectful debate and discussion of alternative viewpoints within the law – even if controversial, unpopular and discomforting. If a university cannot be safe in this sense, where in society can be?

25 Cited in N.A.G. Zelinsky et al., *Campus Speech in Crisis: What the Yale Experience Can Teach America* (Encounter Books 2016) 69.

26 House of Commons/House of Lords Joint Committee on Human Rights, *Freedom of Speech in Universities* (HC 589/HL Paper 111) p45, para 6. See too the concern re the operation of safe spaces by the Equality and Human Rights Commission who caution that 'care should be taken when applying any policies in a 'blanket manner', for example across campus, to make sure they do not restrict freedom of expression'. Equality and Human Rights Commission, *Freedom of expression: a guide for higher education providers and students' unions in England & Wales* (2019) 39.

27 G. Lukianoff et al., *The Coddling of the American Mind: How Good Intentions and Bad Ideas Are Setting Up a Generation for Failure* (Penguin 2018) 259.

28 M. Hume, *Trigger Warning: is the fear of being offensive killing free speech?* (William Collins 2015 concise edition) 104.

29 S. Fanshawe, *The Power of Difference: Where the complexities of diversity and inclusion meet practical solutions* (Kogan Page 2022) 207.

30 ibid 208.

Threats to Free Speech and Academic Freedom

Academic freedom is clearly pertinent to the educational discussion of philosophical beliefs in the workplace. Why does such a freedom matter?

In a number of cases, the US Supreme Court has articulated the reasoning behind the importance of academic freedom, while accepting that such freedom can never be absolute and unfettered. This encompasses the 1952 case of *Wieman v Updegraff*, in which Justice Frankfurter urged teachers to be 'exemplars of open-mindedness and free inquiry',[31] Chief Justice Warren's later assertion that '[t]o impose any straitjacket upon the intellectual leaders in our colleges and universities would imperil the future of our Nation'[32] and Justice Brennan's caution against any laws seeking 'to cast *a pall of orthodoxy* over the classroom ... The classroom is peculiarly the "*marketplace of ideas*".[33]

Some case law in the United States has held that a public university may regulate what lecturers say in class provided it is reasonably related to legitimate pedagogical objectives, for example, by banning offensive language.[34] However, there is a danger that banning offensive words from the classroom might progress into the separate and much more concerning process of banning certain topics. Bernstein speculates in the US context, 'under this line of cases, arguably a [public] university may even declare that certain controversial subjects, such as whether racial differences in IQ exist, are off-limits in the classroom because they are too distracting to students'.[35]

Indeed, there is some evidence of a trend by some seeking to ban certain topics from being researched and/or taught at university level in the United Kingdom.[36] Such a movement is at least consistent with slogans used by

31 *Wieman v Updegraff*, 344 U.S.183 (1952) at 196-197 (cited in L. Niehoff et al., *Free Speech: From Core Values to Current Debates* (CUP 2022) 196).

32 *Sweezy v State of New Hampshire*, 354 U.S. 234 (1957) at 250 (cited in L. Niehoff et al., *Free Speech: From Core Values to Current Debates* (CUP 2022) 197–198).

33 *Keyishian v Board of Regents of the University of the State of New York*, 385 U.S. 589 (1967) at 603 ((cited in L. Niehoff et al., *Free Speech: From Core Values to Current Debates* (CUP 2022) 199, new emphasis added).

34 D.E. Berstein, *'You can't say that! The growing threat to civil liberties from antidiscrimination laws'* (Cato Institute 2003) 66.

35 ibid 67.

36 See for example: https://www.theguardian.com/education/2021/nov/03/kathleen-stock-says-she-quit-university-post-over-medieval-ostracism; https://www.oxfordmail.co.uk/news/15787566.oxford-prof-defended-british-empire-branded-racist/; https://www.timeshighereducation.com/news/laura-favaro-gender-studies-groupthink-forcing-scholars-out; https://www.theguardian.com/education/2019/mar/20/cambridge-university-rescinds-jordan-peterson-invitation; https://www.judiciary.uk/wp-content/uploads/2024/01/Joanna-Phoenix-v-The-Open-University-Employment-Tribunal-Reserved-Judgment.pdf; https://www.cloisters.com/insights/reindorf-review-on-no-platforming. See too https://www.theguardian.com/education/2024/feb/05/uk-professor-suffered-discrimination-due-to-anti-zionist-beliefs-tribunal-rules . See too, making use in particular of the cases of *Phoenix* and *Miller*, N Waltham-Smith and J Murray, 'Academic Freedom and Protected Philosophi-

some pressure groups which have expressly stated 'no debate' in their policy positions.

Dame Sara Khan DBE, the Independent Adviser to the UK Government for Social Cohesion and Resilience, concluded in her March 2024 report ('the Khan Review') that there is a growing culture of what she termed 'freedom-restricting harassment' in the United Kingdom.[37] She defined this as 'when people experience or witness threatening, intimidatory or abusive harassment online and/or offline which is intended to make people or institutions censor or self-censor out of fear'.[38] Such harassment can affect the operation of whole institutions – for example, in cancelling a proposed research centre because of such alleged harassment.[39] Reflecting on the 'chilling effect' of such behaviour demonstrated in evidence given in her Review, she noted that:

> We heard shocking cases of the extent to which 'cancelling' was occurring – including cancelling the publication of academic books on legitimate areas of study. This was not because of any concerns about the content of the book but due to false reputational smears about the author.[40]

As will be explored in some detail in the following section, the enactment of the Higher Education (Freedom of Speech) Act 2023 is partly in response to the challenges identified here.

'Microaggressions', Cancel Culture and Academic Freedom

Another potential means of controlling which topics and ideas are permitted to be discussed is through an unhelpful side effect of the use of the concept of 'microaggressions'. This term is not used or defined in UK legislation, but as the Equality and Human Rights Commission Scotland makes clear, committing a microaggression is not necessarily an unlawful act, although repetition

---

cal Belief: Strenghtening the Legal Analysis' *Industrial Law Journal* (2024) (advance access publication 4 October 2024).

37 Dame Sara Khan DBE, *Threats to Social Cohesion and Democratic Resilience: A New Strategic Approach*, ('the Khan Review') March 2024.

38 Dame Sara Khan DBE, *Threats to Social Cohesion and Democratic Resilience: A New Strategic Approach*, ('the Khan Review') March 2024 p9. See generally Adekoya, R. et al, *Academic freedom in the UK: Protecting viewpoint diversity* (Policy Exchange 2020), M. Goodwin, *Is Academic Freedom Under Threat?* (Legatum Institute 2022), N. Hillman, '*You Can't Say That!' What Students Really Think of Free Speech on Campus"* (HEPI Policy Note 35, June 2022).

39 Dame Sara Khan DBE, *Threats to Social Cohesion and Democratic Resilience: A New Strategic Approach*, ('the Khan Review') March 2024 9. For the case study on the ill-fated proposed Centre for the Study of Political Islam at Bradford University's Peace Studies Department, see 47–48.

40 Dame Sara Khan DBE, *Threats to Social Cohesion and Democratic Resilience: A New Strategic Approach*, ('the Khan Review') March 2024, 57.

or escalation of them may be.[41] Other academic commentators concur with this view.[42]

Advance HE (a member led charity aiming to improve UK higher education) have defined 'microaggressions' as 'a term used for brief and commonplace daily verbal, behavioural or environmental indignities, whether intentional or unintentional, that communicate hostile, derogatory, or negative prejudicial slights and insults toward any group'.[43] In their examples, it is clear that most appear clearly to amount to inappropriate behaviour/stereotyping by the speaker and, depending on the circumstances, might even be unlawful acts of harassment under s26 Equality Act 2010 (e.g., 'You're Asian so you must be an IT expert, right?'). However, it is concerning that a small number of examples which it is accepted may give rise to offence in some listeners, may pose an unintended risk to academic freedom.

An example of a microaggression is given as follows:

> **Microaggression**: Questioning the purpose of Black History Month.
>
> **Why This Is Offensive**: Indicates that colonialism and slavery are history but not impacting our daily lives. Does not recognise that Black people are already underrepresented and historically not credited for achievements.

It could be argued that most fair-minded people (including the present writer) would not see any need to question the purpose or ongoing existence of Black History Month. However, by framing the mere posing of a question about the purpose of an annual event celebrated across higher education as an example of an aggressive act, this may well have a chilling effect on academic freedom. Surely if an academic or student wished to pose such a question in an educational context they should be able to, and not improperly deterred from doing so, provided that any discussion was undertaken in a responsible way, with all viewpoints carefully considered and respected?

Naturally, it's not necessary to classify a question or viewpoint as unlawful or officially banned in order to squash it. As George Orwell explained:

> Unpopular ideas can be silenced, and inconvenient facts kept dark, without the need for any official ban … At any given moment there is an orthodoxy, a body of ideas which it is assumed all right-thinking people will accept without question … Anyone who challenges the prevailing

41 Equality and Human Rights Commission Scotland, *Tackling Racial Harassment in Universities*, (undated article)(emphasis added).

42 A. Johnson et al. 'Are You Supposed to Be in Here?' Racial Microaggressions and Knowledge Production in Higher Education' in J. Arday et al. (editors) *Dismantling Race in Higher Education: Racism, Whiteness and Decolonising the Academy* (Palgrave Macmillan 2018).

43 Advance HE, *Microaggressions. Call it Racism.* (citing Prof. C.M. Pierce) (downloadable from https://wZAQww.advance-he.ac.uk/tackling-racism-campus/resources as part of pack 1).

> orthodoxy finds himself silenced with surprising effectiveness. A genuinely unfashionable opinion is almost never given a fair hearing.[44]

Inclusion is always a positive act. This is particularly true, for example, in developing a curriculum which does not exclude a diversity of cultures and viewpoints. Bhambra et al. argue that: 'the content of university knowledge remains principally governed by the West for the West. Disciplinary divisions, theoretical models and Eurocentric histories continue to provide intellectual materials that reproduce and justify colonial hierarchies'.[45] The desirability to be inclusive in what is taught in educational curricula was also highlighted as a recommendation in the Sewell Report.[46]

However, there is a danger that laudable attempts to be inclusive may have created an unusual paradox by inadvertently leading to the exclusion of open debate. Cultural commentator Stephen Fry observes that:

> It's a strange paradox that the liberals are illiberal in their demand for liberality. They are exclusive in their demand for inclusivity. They are homogenous in their demand for heterogeneity. They are somehow un-diverse in their call for diversity – you can be diverse, but not diverse in your opinions and in your language and in your behaviour. And that's a terrible pity.[47]

In the context of higher education, Professor Van de Noort, Vice Chancellor of the University of Reading, has recently warned of the risk of the universities being turned into 'uniformities'.[48]

As well as curriculum diversity, there is also an issue of classroom diversity. All things being equal, the more diverse the background of students, the more diverse the viewpoints one would expect to see join the debate – and the quality of that debate would be all the better for it. Universities have made genuine and largely successful efforts to ensure that every group in society feel

44 G. Orwell, 'The Freedom of the Press' (1945) cited in Appendix I to George Orwell, *Animal Farm* (Secker & Warburg 1987), 100 (cited in M. Hume, *Trigger Warning: Is the Fear of Being Offensive Killing Free Speech?* (William Collins 2015 concise edition) 104.

45 G.K. Bhambra et al., 'Introduction: Decolonising the University?' in G.K. Bhambra et al. (eds) *Decolonising the University* (Pluto Press 2018) 5.

46 Commission on Race and Ethnic Disparities, *Commission on Race and Ethnic Disparities: The Report* ('Sewell Report') March 2021, Recommendation 20, 89–93.

47 R. Griffiths, (editor), *Political Correctness: Dyson and Goldberg v Fry and Peterson (The Munk Debates)* (Oneworld Publications 2018) 97.

48 https://www.theguardian.com/education/2024/feb/27/universities-must-overcome-echo-chamber-and-self-censorship-says-reading-vc. See too on controversy caused by recent revisions to non-binding Subject Benchmark Statements by the Quality Assurance Agency (QAA): https://afcomm.org.uk/2024/07/16/the-qaa-tells-academics-to-decolonise-classics-and-maths/.

able to participate in higher education – the diversity of students benefitting all of them.

However, Stokes notes that some groups, such as white working class pupils, have been consistently ignored:

> the one group that has consistently been under-represented across the UK university sector is that of white working class young adults. Not only is this underrepresentation consistent over many years, but most universities have also not even bothered to draw up inclusion plans to address these forms of systemic discrimination.[49]

The Sewell Report also confirmed that: 'Male White British pupils eligible for [Free School Meals] are the least likely of all the main ethnic or social groups to progress to higher education by age 19'.[50] Only recently has the Office for Students begun to address this issue.[51] While acknowledging the efforts of some institutions to tackle this, Byrne et al conclude that: 'Too many universities do not do enough'.[52]

The extent of the problem of limiting free speech on UK university campuses is itself a matter of debate. In 2018, the UK Parliament's Joint Committee on Human Rights concluded that 'it is not a pervasive problem'.[53] Scott-Baumann et al agree, noting only that '[t]here is evidence that a minority of students do not feel as free to speak as they would wish to in the classroom – including students with right wing or socially conservative views'.[54] Goodwin makes a stronger assertion that: '[r]ecent studies suggest one in four of Britain's university students ... are self-censoring their voices in seminars

49 D. Stokes, *Against Decolonisation: Campus Culture Wars and the Decline of the West* (Polity Press 2023) 79. See too the House of Commons Education Committee report *The Forgotten: How White Working Class Pupils Have Been Let Down, and How to Change It* (June 2021) HC 85 3: 'The proportion of White British pupils who were [Free School Meals] eligible starting higher education by the age of 19 in 2018/19 was 16.0%, the lowest of any ethnic group other than traveller of Irish heritage and Gypsy/Roma ... FSM-eligible pupils from a Black Caribbean background had a participation rate of 31.8%'. Further, the Committee noted (para 30) a general educational attainment gap related to gender: 'Evidence highlighted the gender attainment gap. This exists in all ethnic and socio-economic groups and is stark for disadvantaged White boys'.

50 Commission on Race and Ethnic Disparities, *Commission on Race and Ethnic Disparities: The Report* ('Sewell Report') March 2021, 93. See generally on entry rates 93–96.

51 See further https://www.officeforstudents.org.uk/news-blog-and-events/press-and-media/why-are-some-white-students-left-behind-in-relation-to-higher-education-participation/

52 E. Byrne et al., *The University Challenge: Changing Universities in a Changing World* (Pearson 2020) 123.

53 House of Commons/House of Lords Joint Committee on Human Rights, *Freedom of Speech in Universities* (March 2018) (HC 589/HL Paper 111) 4.

54 A. Scott-Baumann et al., *Freedom of Speech in Universities: Islam, Charities and Counter-terrorism* (Routledge 2021) 120.

and lectures, fearful of what might happen to their … friendships if they reveal their views'.[55] Informed partly by their own recent survey evidence, Malcolm et al. conclude that, while the extent of the problem may be exaggerated, nevertheless, 'there are still worrying signs of a shift in which students increasingly think that some lawful views cannot be expressed in their universities'.[56]

This self censorship is not limited to students. Professor Arif Ahmed is England's first Director for Freedom of Speech and Academic Freedom.[57] He explains that: 'when an institution fails to protect, or punishes, legal speech, the effect goes well beyond the speaker. It casts a **penumbra of silence**. This is the chilling effect'.[58] A 2017 poll of University and College Union academics found that more than 1 in 3 UK academics (35%) surveyed was self-censoring.[59] Goodwin argues that there is a

> clear risk that Britain's universities … are now morphing into 'ideological monocultures', where liberal cosmopolitan and progressive values are completely dominant, those who do not share them feel they cannot speak, and political minorities, such as conservatives[60] and gender critical scholars, are either marginalized or openly discriminated against.[61]

55 M. Goodwin, *Values, Voice and Virtue: The New British Politics* (Penguin 2023) 127 (original footnote omitted).

56 See also F. Malcolm et al., *Freedom of Speech in UK Higher Education: recommendations for policy and practice* (The Policy Institute, King's College London, September 2023)September 2023) 14 available at: https://www.kcl.ac.uk/policy-institute/assets/freedom-of-speech-in-uk-higher-education.pdf.

57 He sits on the Board of the Office for Students and his role was created by statute.

58 Such a potential for a harmful 'chilling effect' to arise from even a relatively small number of incidents is also noted by the Joint Committee on Human Rights: House of Commons/House of Lords Joint Committee on Human Rights, *Freedom of Speech in Universities* (HC 589/HL Paper 111) 4.

59 Office for Students, *Transcript of Arif Ahmed's speech at King's College London*, published 10 October 2023 (available at https://www.officeforstudents.org.uk/news-blog-and-events/press-and-media/transcript-of-arif-ahmeds-speech-at-kings-college-london/) (emphasis added).

60 However, there is also evidence of non-conservative voices being silenced too. See on this point G. Lukianoff et al., *The Canceling of the American Mind: How Cancel Culture Undermines Trust, Destroys Institutions, and Threatens Us All* (Allen Lane 2023) 141–162. In striking down parts of Florida's 2022 Individual Freedom Law (also known as the Stop WOKE Act), the federal judge stated that the legislation was 'positively dystopian' in that it 'officially bans professors from expressing disfavoured viewpoints in university classrooms while permitting unfettered expression of the opposite viewpoints'. (G. Lukianoff et al. 147).

61 M. Goodwin, *Values, Voice and Virtue: The New British Politics* (Penguin, 2023) 127.

One does not have to look far for examples, either alleged or proven.[62] (The increasing use of digital management techniques may also be having a negative effect on academic freedom.)[63]

While we have touched upon the issue of microaggressions in this chapter given its relevance to teaching and debating controversial topics in a Law School, it is worth noting that some writers are highly critical of the concept of microaggressions, particularly if a definition is adopted which includes the giving of unintentional as well as intentional offence.[64] (This issue of intention, or lack of, is also relevant to the definition of harassment under s26 Equality Act 2010 and also whether a particular manifestation of a philosophical belief is within the law – see later.)

Lukianoff et al. note that:

> Many people from historically marginalized groups continue to face frequent acts of bias and prejudice. Sometimes people make thinly veiled bigoted remarks, and in cases where the speaker is expressing hostility or contempt, it seems appropriate to call it aggression … But *aggression* is not unintentional or accidental. If you bump into someone by accident

62 See for example: https://www.theguardian.com/education/2021/nov/03/kathleen-stock-says-she-quit-university-post-over-medieval-ostracism;https://www.oxfordmail.co.uk/news/15787566.oxford-prof-defended-british-empire-branded-racist/; https://www.timeshighereducation.com/news/laura-favaro-gender-studies-groupthink-forcing-scholars-out; https://www.theguardian.com/education/2019/mar/20/cambridge-university-rescinds-jordan-peterson-invitation; https://www.judiciary.uk/wp-content/uploads/2024/01/Joanna-Phoenix-v-The-Open-University-Employment-Tribunal-Reserved-Judgment.pdf; https://www.cloisters.com/insights/reindorf-review-on-no-platforming;https://afcomm.org.uk/2024/04/17/cambridge-race-realist-fired-for-rejection-of-edi/; https://feministlegal.org/law-lecturer-sacked-after-complaining-of-gender-identity-indoctrination/; https://www.theguardian.com/education/2024/feb/05/uk-professor-suffered-discrimination-due-to-anti-zionist-beliefs-tribunal-rules and *Miller v University of Bristol* ET Case No 1400780/2022 (re opposition to 'political Zionism' held a protected belief at para 238). Note that a 'lack of belief' in opposition to 'political Zionism' is therefore likely, prima facie, to also be legally protected under the mirror protection principle set out in s10(2) of the Equality Act 2010. See on this point *Maya Forstater v CGD Europe & ors* (UKEAT/0105/20/JOJ): 'The fact that the Claimant did not share the gender identity belief is enough **in itself** to qualify for protection'. per Choudhury P. at para 108 (emphasis added). See generally on this point the discussion at paras 105–109. While the new Advance HE guidance (*Protected beliefs in higher education* (May 2024) 17) notes that **support for** Zionism would possibly also qualify as a protected philosophical belief, it would appear not to need to for a claimant nevertheless to be protected on a 'lack of belief' basis: No doubt this issue will be clarified in future case law.

63 UCU, *Academic Freedom in the Digital University* (May 2024).

64 For a recent report (July 2024) on a UK law firm's introduction of an anonymous staff reporting tool including for the reporting of microaggressions see https://www.lawgazette.co.uk/news/city-firm-wants-staff-to-call-out-microaggressions/5120172.article and for an example of critical commentary regarding anonymous staff reporting tools more generally see: https://freespeechunion.org/dial-m-for-microaggression-law-firm-launches-interactional-bias-hotline/.

> and never meant them any harm, it is not an act of aggression, although the other person may *perceive* it as one.

They argue that

> it is not a good idea to start by *assuming the worst about people* and reading their actions as uncharitably as possible. This is the distortion known as mind reading; if done habitually and negatively, it is likely to lead to despair, anxiety and a network of damaged relationships.[65]

There is also a concern about not just whether words can be seen as offensive, but whether they can be seen as a form of violence. The equation of speech with violence has also been challenged by Lukianoff et al.: '[o]utside of cultures of safetyism, the word 'violence' refers to *physical* violence'.[66] Doyle also argues that '[t]he language of physical harm is a rhetorical device intended to strengthen the case for ideological submission'.[67]

The equation of speech with violence is roundly rejected, a conclusion with which Professor Ahmed concurs:

> Over a century and a half of persecution, political paranoia and Civil War, [England], like much of Europe, tore herself apart over religious disagreements. We learnt, although we have struggled to remember, that words are not a kind of violence. They are the alternative to violence; and if we as a society forget this then we as a society are finished.[68]

There is some echo of this fear of encouraging a culture of over sensitisation in the UK case law on harassment in a discrimination setting.

In *Richmond Pharmacology Ltd v Dhaliwal*,[69] the Employment Appeal Tribunal upheld a claim of racial harassment based on a senior colleague telling the claimant who had handed in her notice of resignation that their paths would probably cross once she left the organisation 'unless you are married off

65 G. Lukianoff, et al., *The Coddling of the American Mind: How Good Intentions and Bad Ideas Are Setting Up a Generation for Failure*, (Penguin 2018) 40–41 (original emphasis). See generally re microaggressions, 40–46.

66 ibid 85–86 (original emphasis).

67 A. Doyle, *The New Puritans: How the Religion of Social Justice Captured the Western World* (Constable 2023) 131. He argues (131) that '[e]mployers are unlikely to discipline workers over a simple difference of opinion, but once an allegation is made that personal safety has been jeopardised, they are obliged to take action'.

68 Office for Students, *Transcript of Arif Ahmed's speech at King's College London*, published 10 October 2023 (available at https://www.officeforstudents.org.uk/news-blog-and-events/press-and-media/transcript-of-arif-ahmeds-speech-at-kings-college-london/).

69 [2009] ICR 724.

in India'. A sum of £1,000 compensation was awarded by the Employment Tribunal.

In rejecting the claimant's appeal against the size of the compensation and also the employer's appeal against the liability finding, the EAT made a number of (obiter) comments about how Tribunals should approach harassment cases under the then relatively new statutory wording. (Note that this case was brought under the old Race Relations Act 1976 (as amended), but the case is still seen as very influential as the current wording in s26 of the Equality Act 2010[70] is very similar.) The case is important in part because it addresses the issue of unintentional offence.

Underhill J explained that:

> We accept that not every racially slanted adverse comment or conduct may constitute the violation of a person's dignity. Dignity is not necessarily violated by things said or done which are trivial or transitory, particularly if it should have been clear that any offence was unintended. While it is very important that employers, and tribunals, are sensitive to the hurt that can be caused by racially offensive comments or conduct (or indeed comments or conduct on other grounds covered by the cognate legislation …) it is also important not to encourage a culture of hypersensitivity or the imposition of legal liability in respect of every unfortunate phrase.[71]

In the university lecture or seminar room, one should always encourage civility, politeness and respectful debate. Deliberate offence giving should have no place whatsoever. Careless offence giving should be carefully guarded against. However, in pursing this goal, it is likely that the concept of 'micro-aggressions',

70 'S26(1) A person (A) harasses another (B) if – (a) A engages in unwanted conduct related to a relevant protected characteristic, and (b) the conduct has the purpose or effect of – (i) violating B's dignity, or (ii) creating an intimidating, hostile, degrading, humiliating or offensive environment for B … (4) In deciding whether conduct has the effect referred to in subsection 1(b), each of the following must be taken into account – (a) the perception of B; (b) the other circumstances of the case; (c) **whether it is reasonable for the conduct to have that effect**' (emphasis added).

71 Underhill J at para 22. The essential element of **objectivity** in s26(4) has also recently been confirmed by Eady J in *Omooba v Michael Garrett Associates Ltd & anor* [2024] IRLR 440 at paras 101 and 102. A caution, based on previous case law, against Tribunals finding in favour of genuine but unreasonably hypersensitive claimants is also included at para 103. Note that the OfS draft 'Regulatory advice 24: Guidance related to freedom of speech' (see further below) also sensibly mirrors the requirement for an objective element in any assessment of harassment. Para 62 notes that, as regards any university code of conduct on restricted speech, 'that definition should explain that the interpretation of that category includes an **objective element** (so that it does not depend only on the perception of the alleged victim)' (emphasis added).

particularly in relation to the asking of questions, or decision to debate important issues, has little to offer which is helpful.

Safeguards for Free Speech and Academic Freedom

In the United Kingdom, certain safeguards already exist which provide some protection for academics teaching controversial subjects.

The Equality Act 2010 makes clear that the discrimination provisions applicable to universities do not apply to 'anything done in connection with the content of the curriculum'.[72] The Equality and Human Rights Commission state in their Technical guidance on the Equality Act 2010:

> [Universities] are not restricted in the range of issues, ideas and materials [they] use in [their] syllabus and will have the academic freedom to expose students to a range of thoughts and ideas, however controversial. Even if the **material** causes offence to students with certain protected characteristics, this will not make it unlawful unless it is **delivered in a way** which results in harassment or subjects students to discrimination or other detriment.[73]

An example from the guidance makes the distinction clear:

> **Example**: A college English department teaches The Merchant of Venice. This would not be unlawful race or religion or belief discrimination even though the play itself could be viewed as being hostile towards Jewish people.
>
> **Example**: In the above example, while teaching The Merchant of Venice, a lecturer says that Jewish people are unethical money lenders who only have themselves to blame for the resentment they experience. This could amount to unlawful racial or religious discrimination or harassment because the comments would be related to how the education is delivered, not the content of the curriculum.[74]

A similar provision relating to schools was given a wide interpretation by Warby J who noted in a claim concerning injunctive relief that:

> The purpose of s89(2) [*i.e. the schools provision*] is to enable a school to teach controversial material without being accused of contravening the

72 S92(2) Equality Act 2010.

73 Equality and Human Rights Commission, *Equality Act 2010: Technical guidance on further and higher education* (2015), para 10.27, 146 (emphasis added).

74 Equality and Human Rights Commission, *Equality Act 2010: Technical guidance on further and higher education* (2015), para 10.27, 146 (emphasis added).

[EqA] ... The exemption is cast in broad terms; it does not just apply to decisions about the curriculum content, but to 'anything done in connection with' that content. This is consistent with an intention to protect against collateral attack.[75]

A key recent development in this area is the enactment of the Higher Education (Freedom of Speech) Act 2023. The Act largely amends some existing legislation (in particular the Higher Education and Research Act 2017) including by placing a duty on the governing body of a higher education provider to take reasonably practicable steps to secure academic freedom for academic staff at the provider.[76] (Note though that on 26 July 2024, the UK Government issued a press release confirming that it intended to halt the implementation of the 2023 Act pending a review of its adequacy.)[77]

The Act defines 'academic freedom', in relation to academic staff as meaning: 'their freedom within the law:

(a) to question and test received wisdom; and
(b) to put forward new ideas and controversial or unpopular opinions, without placing themselves at risk of being adversely affected [in their employment]'[78]

Murray considers that the revised law has significantly reduced the risk of academic speech breaching s26 of the Equality Act 2010 as regards unlawful harassment. He argues that:

unless the alleged harassment can be shown to be purposeful, it will be difficult to establish that a legitimate exercise of academic freedom, particularly if it also amounts to academic free expression, will meet the

75 *Birmingham City Council v Afsar* [2019] EWHC 3217 (QB) at para 50–51 (cited in A McColgan, *Discrimination Law: Text, Cases and Materials* (Hart 2023) 228–229).

76 Explanatory Notes to the Higher Education (Freedom of Speech) Act 2023, para 17.

77 See https://www.gov.uk/government/news/government-watchdog-to-help-stabilise-university-finances. In the release, the Education Secretary stated that: 'We are absolutely committed to freedom of speech and academic freedom, but the Free Speech Act introduced last year is not fit for purpose and risked imposing serious burdens on our world class universities. This legislation could expose students to harm and appalling hate speech on campuses. That is why I have quickly ordered this legislation to be stopped so that we can take a view on next steps'. Initial reaction to this has not been wholly positive. See for example: https://freespeechunion.org/government-has-just-declared-war-on-free-speech/ (26 July 2024). Though some welcomed the decision eg. https://www.researchprofessionalnews.com/rr-news-uk-universities-2024-7-labour-pause-on-free-speech-act-labelled-sensible/ (26 July 2024). By December 2024, over 660 UK based academics had signed an open letter to the Secretary of State urging her to implement the remaining provisions of the Act.

78 S1 of the Higher Education (Freedom of Speech) Act 2023, inserting new sA1(6) into the Higher Education and Research Act 2017.

> objective threshold for harassment contained in section 26(4) EqA when one considers the academic context and the question of whether it was reasonable for the impugned conduct to have the required harassing effect.[79]

In March 2024, the Office for Students (OfS) issued a new consultation on the issues raised by the new powers and duties.[80] At the time of writing, the OfS is yet to publish a summary of responses to the consultation.

In the consultation document, the OfS state it is their

> firm view that significant weight will always need to be placed on freedom of speech and academic freedom. In practice, this sets a **very high hurdle** and there will be very limited room for a [university] ... to create restrictions on lawful speech.[81]

Content or viewpoint restrictions are particularly frowned upon.

> In particular it is likely to be extremely difficult, if not impossible, for [universities] ... to comply with their free speech duties if they seek to directly or indirectly restrict the **particular content** of speech. ... However, there may be some scope for limited restrictions in respect of the time, place and manner of expression.[82]

The OfS also rejects the possibility of universities promoting a commonality of viewpoint in the academic faculty by carefully appointing candidates who agree with the consensus, explicitly referring to the prohibition of this in their draft guidance.[83]

Not all academics agree though that viewpoint discrimination has no place in certain decisions including academic hiring ones. In explaining her disagreement with one of the principles of the recently formed UK based Committee for Academic Freedom,[84] Srinivasan argues that 'academic freedom essentially involves view-point based discrimination – that indeed the whole point of academic freedom is to protect academics' rights to exercise their expert

79 J. Murray, 'The Higher Education (Freedom of Speech) Act 2023: an employment focused overview' *ILJ* 2023, 52(3), 791, section 4.

80 Office for Students, *Consultation on proposed regulatory advice and other matters relating to freedom of speech*, (26 March 2024).

81 ibid para 42 (emphasis added).

82 ibid paras 42–43 (emphasis added).

83 Office for Students, *Regulatory advice 24: Guidance related to freedom of speech* (March 2024 draft) para 46.

84 'I. Staff and students at UK universities should be free, within the limits of the law, to express any opinion without fear of reprisal'. See afcomm.org.uk under principles listed under 'Our Mission'.

judgement in hiring, peer review, promotion, examining, conferring degrees and so on'.[85]

However, an academic's expert judgement on whether a candidate has mastered a field of knowledge and has the ability to teach and research successfully in that field is clearly different from the issue of refusing to hire otherwise well qualified candidates whose views, beliefs and opinions (assuming lawfully expressed) are not to the liking of the selection panel.[86]

The OfS draft guidance (if implemented) should also be read in conjunction with recent cases such as *Mr S Corby v ACAS*.[87] The case is notable for the Tribunal's unanimous finding as a preliminary issue that Mr Corby's belief in opposing 'critical theory in general, and, on the issue of race, as the importance of character over race' was a legally protected philosophical belief.[88] This belief might be paraphrased as an opposition to critical race theory. The Tribunal set out a summary of his belief in more detail at para 9.1 of its decision.[89]

Stokes has noted how a number of universities currently include the expression of criticism of certain viewpoints which might be thought consistent with critical race theory as being examples of racial microaggressions.[90] Such categorisations might now need to be revised in the light of the *Corby* decision.

Indeed, beyond the area of microaggressions, there are no doubt important implications for institutional approaches to race equality more generally from this decision. For example, the new guidance on protected beliefs from Advance HE,[91] in reflecting specifically upon the implications of *Corby*, sensibly suggests that:

85 A Srinivasan, 'Open Letters and Campus Protests' *London Review of Books*, vol 46 number 10 (23 May 2024) 6.

86 Note the recent decision in May 2024 of Massachusetts Institute of Technology to ban the use of diversity statements in hiring academic staff: https://www.thefire.org/news/mit-stops-using-dei-statements-faculty-hiring. See too Harvard University's decision in June 2024 no longer to require mandatory DEI statements from aspiring tenure track faculty in the Faculty of Arts and Sciences.: https://www.goacta.org/2024/06/harvards-faculty-of-arts-and-sciences-to-stop-requiring-diversity-statements-for-tenure-track-positions/.

87 *Mr S Corby v Advisory, Conciliation and Arbitration Service* ET Case No 1805305/2022. At the time of writing (May 2024) it is believed the case is under appeal.

88 *Mr S Corby v Advisory, Conciliation and Arbitration Service* ET Case No 1805305/2022 at para 9.

89 *Mr S Corby v Advisory, Conciliation and Arbitration Service* ET Case No 1805305/2022 para 9.1: 'he believes that the "woke" approach to racism is misconceived in that its belief in structural racism is divisive because it tends to see white people as a problem that can result in separatism, segregation and ethnocentrism. The Claimant prefers the approach of Martin Luther King [sic] which he says desires a society where people are judged by the content of their character, rather than the colour of their skin. This approach, in the claimant's view emphasises what people of all races have in common, namely their humanity and capacity to support a shared national culture'.

90 D Stokes, *Against Decolonisation: Campus Culture Wars and the Decline of the West* (Polity Press 2023) 52.

91 Advance HE, *Protected beliefs in higher education*, (May 2024).

> Race and institutional race equality initiatives, may be viewed as related to societally relevant and contested debates. HEIs [higher education institutions] should be mindful that reasoned critique or academic discussion of race and race-related initiatives is likely to be lawful, and that the critical views of staff or students in relation to critical race theory or institutional initiatives may qualify as protected beliefs or lawful manifestations of a protected belief.[92]

Related to the issue of whether a commonality of viewpoint should be able to be bolstered by hiring practices, is the larger question of institutional neutrality in general. The enforcement by an educational body of a particular contested viewpoint has been alleged in Tribunal cases concerning philosophical belief.[93] This question also touches upon the issue of so called 'compelled speech'.[94]

However, arguably, a university which effectively adopts an institutional position on a matter of public controversy, may be acting detrimentally to the promotion of free speech and academic freedom.[95] The London Universities' Council for Academic Freedom argues in its 'London Principles for Academic Freedom' that:

> *It is not possible to combine support for individual freedom of conscience with the imposition of a collective ideology*. Taking a political stance includes not only overt statements but also the imposition of training for staff or students espousing particular ideological viewpoints, the adoption of political symbols and the flying of flags.[96]

92 Advance HE, *Protected beliefs in higher education*, (May 2024) 19. Previous cases such as *Charalambous v Barnsley College* ET Case No 1802552/2021 (re opposition to the BLM movement held, on the evidence, not to be a protected belief) might therefore be analysed differently if brought today on similar facts.

93 See for example *Charalambous v Barnsley College* ET Case No 1802552/2021 at para 74 re the claimant's belief that the college 'should not be supporting a political organisation which has the particular characteristics of the Black Lives Matter movement.' See too press reports in June 2024 of University of Exeter staff feeling forced to sign up to certain pledges: https://www.telegraph.co.uk/news/2024/06/08/exeter-uni-staff-feel-coerced-to-sign-stonewall-pledge/

94 See for example J. Rowbottom, 'Cakes, Gay Marriage and the Right against Compelled Speech' U.K. Const.L.Blog (16 October 2018) (available at https://ukconstitutionallaw.org/).

95 For a discussion of whether academic freedom is an individual or a collective right see J. Butcher, 'Academic Freedom Is an Individual Right' (Cielo, 11 June 2024) available at: https://www.cieo.org.uk/research/academic-freedom-is-an-individual-right/

96 London Universities' Council for Academic Freedom, 'London Principles for Academic Freedom' (March 2024) principle 5 Institutional Neutrality (extract) (emphasis added) Available at: https://nms.kcl.ac.uk/lucaf/viewdocument.php?id=2

With possible implications for cases of alleged 'misgendering' and appropriate pronoun usage and other contested issues such as the appropriate societal and individual response to climate change,[97] the Council further argues that

> Compelled speech violates freedom of conscience and expression. Compelled speech includes the requirement or pressure to express agreement with political or social causes in words or deeds, as well as the obligation to provide certain answers to ideological questions, or signal (even if only implicitly) agreement with certain ideas in order to gain or retain employment or advance in rank or status. *Neither education nor research can flourish where individuals are compelled to pretend to views which they do not truly believe.*[98]

Taking the example of employers encouraging employees to declare their pronouns, Doyle warns that 'it establishes a precedent for a socially acceptable form of compelled speech, the future consequences of which could well represent a serious threat to individual liberties'.[99]

Whether or not the enforcement of a common ideology is wise is a question which ultimate relates back to the very purpose of what a university is for. Some, such as Grant, argue that the modern university should become an active advocate for policy and political issues which matter to its communities.[100] However, arguably such an agenda for universities is misplaced and risks fundamentally weakening the existence and value of such institutions.

In 1967, the Kalven Report[101] on the University of Chicago's role in political and social action drew a clear distinction between the proper role of a university itself, compared to that of students or staff. Drawing from what they saw as the mission of a university as being 'the discovery, improvement and dissemination of knowledge', they observed that a university

97 On the issue of the use of the suffix 'denier' to close down debate as regards controversial issues such as the appropriate response to climate change, see M Hume, *Trigger Warning: is the fear of being offensive killing free speech?*, (William Collins 2015 concise edition) 113–114.

98 London Universities' Council for Academic Freedom, 'London Principles for Academic Freedom' (March 2024) principle 6 Freedom of belief and from compelled speech (extract) (emphasis added).

99 A Doyle, *The New Puritans: How the Religion of Social Justice Captured the Western World* (Constable 2023) 142. In Doyle's view, at 144, 'there appears to be little utility in announcing pronouns other than to endorse the notion of gender identity. But this is a specifically ideological stance, one that people should not be pressured into making against their will'. See generally, the discussion of pronoun usage and compelled speech at 141–147.

100 J Grant, *The New Power University: The Social Purpose of Higher Education in the 21st Century* (Pearson Education 2021).

101 H. Kalven et al., *Report on the university's role in political and social action* (University of Chicago 1967).

> will provide enduring challenges to social values, policies, practices, and institutions. By design and by effect, it is the institution which creates discontent with the existing social arrangements and proposes new ones. In brief, a good university, like Socrates, will be upsetting.

However, importantly, they explained that:

> the instrument of dissent and criticism is the individual faculty member or the individual student. *The university is the home and sponsor of critics: it is not itself the critic.* It is … a community of scholars. To perform its mission … a university must sustain an extraordinary environment of freedom of enquiry and maintain an independence from political fashions, passions, and pressures.[102]

In the committee's view, to 'be diverted from its mission into playing the role of a second-rate political force' would endanger the very conditions necessary for its existence and effectiveness. In short,

> there is no mechanism by which [the university] can reach a collective position without inhibiting that full freedom of dissent on which it thrives. It cannot insist that all of its members favour a given view of social policy; if it takes collective action, therefore, it does so at the price of censuring any minority who do not agree with the view adopted.[103]

A similar viewpoint has also been considered much more recently by Harvard University in the context of public pronouncements.[104] The independent non-profit American Council of Trustees and Alumni (ACTA) has also made institutional neutrality one of its campaigns.[105]

Further parts of the draft OfS guidance state, in relation to teaching, that: 'Academic staff should not be constrained or pressured in their teaching to endorse or reject particular value judgements'.[106] Academic freedom within the law is also protected in the area of university research.[107]

102 ibid (emphasis added).

103 ibid.

104 Feldman et al., *Report on Institutional Voice in the University* (Harvard University, May 2024) available at: https://www.harvard.edu/president/news/2024/institutional-voice/. Adopting a self described 'say less' policy, the report noted that if the university issues official positions on an issue **beyond its core functions** '[it] may make it more difficult for some members of the [university] community to express their views when they differ from the university's official position.'

105 See further https://www.goacta.org/kalven-report/.

106 Office for Students, *Regulatory advice 24: Guidance related to freedom of speech* (March 2024 draft) para 113.

107 Office for Students, *Regulatory advice 24: Guidance related to freedom of speech* (March 2024 draft) para 105. See too the concern raised by the Vice Chancellor of the University of

Further protection from accusations of harassment against academics based on what they say or do as part of their academic roles is envisaged by the OfS. As part of a new proposed condition of registration for higher education providers regarding harassment and sexual misconduct, the OfS planned to require providers to comply with 'freedom of speech principles'. It was proposed that providers would have to apply a rebuttable presumption to the effect that students being exposed to certain types of statement is unlikely to amount to harassment. The types of statement in question were: 'statements made and views expressed by a person as part of teaching, research or discussions about any subject matter which is connected with the content of a higher education course'.[108]

The Modern Paper Chase: Practical Suggestions for Teaching Controversial Issues

An increasing amount of work is being done to consider how to improve respectful debate and free speech at universities.[109] For example, Scott-Baumann et al. put forward a fourfold model for handling freedom of speech issues in a university using the approaches of Liberal, Libertarian, Guarded liberal or No-platforming.[110] They recommend the default position for university students and staff should be the Liberal approach. They explain that:

> This means upholding freedom of speech as far as possible within the law, including for offensive views, up to the point where it is clearly likely to harm others or infringe their rights. But it also means encouraging

Reading that Government and universities should guard against certain research avenues being rejected or undersupported due to not being consistent with currently favoured thinking and outlooks: https://www.theguardian.com/education/2024/feb/27/universities-must-overcome-echo-chamber-and-self-censorship-says-reading-vc. Note also the concerns raised in November 2023 by the London Universities' Council for Academic Freedom regarding the assessment of 'People, Culture and Environment' proposed for REF 2028: Consultation Response: Assessment of people, culture and environment in REF 2028 (kcl.ac.uk).

108 Office for Students, *Consultation on a new approach to regulating harassment and sexual misconduct in English higher education* (February 2023) 31 para 75. On 31 July 2024 the Office for Students published a new Condition E6: Harassment and sexual misconduct which will come into force on 1 August 2025.

109 See too N. Suttie, 'Cultivating Controversy … with Civility' HEPI Guest post (6 June 2023). See also F. Malcolm, et al., The Policy Institute, King's College London, *'Freedom of Speech in UK Higher Education: Recommendations for Policy and Practice'* (Sept 2023) 19-33 available at: https://www.kcl.ac.uk/policy-institute/assets/freedom-of-speech-in-uk-higher-education.pdf.

110 A. Scott-Baumann et al. *Freedom of Speech in Universities: Islam, Charities and Counter-terrorism* (Routledge 2021) 27.

> people to avoid language **(but not topics or ideas)** that many others are likely to find grossly offensive or hateful.[111]

The reality and indeed likelihood of someone being offended by something said when any politically contentious issue is debated is inevitable and not something to be surprised by or unduly feared. As Prof. Arif Ahmed notes:

> Of course it offends them: any disagreement over political or social questions that actually matters to people is likely to cause some of them to feel offence. Shutting down debate on that basis is not going to improve things for anyone.[112]

All of these commentators recognise that classroom culture is key to being able to sensibly but respectfully discuss controversial legal topics. Scott-Baumann et al. put forward the suggestion of adopting a Community of Inquiry approach. In their view, such an approach 'can help encourage a culture of reciprocity … when arguing against each other's views, participants are encouraged to see each other as collaborators in the learning process and to assume that everyone has well-intentioned rather than bad faith motives'.[113]

Ignoring difficult topics is not a feature of the best law teachers, as it does not serve the needs of their students. Hunter Schwartz et al. researched in depth the teaching practices of 26 of the most highly regarded professors from US law schools. They concluded that: 'the teachers we studied do not eschew controversy; instead, they find ways to encourage dissident voices, calm discussion, and foster respect among their students'.[114] Amongst some practical ideas highlighted were: getting students to take on roles of Supreme Court justices ('it's easier for students to speak in another's voice'); allowing students to take time out if they become uncomfortable about a topic; challenging vague student statements if they may imply for example racist or other discriminatory assumptions.[115]

Other lessons from across the Atlantic might be drawn from the ongoing *Harvard Dialogues* events and initiatives begun at Harvard University, designed to enhance people's ability to engage in respectful and robust debate.[116] ACTA also promotes the greater use of college debates as a way of

111 ibid 125 (emphasis added).

112 Office for Students, *Transcript of Arif Ahmed's Speech at King's College London*, published 10 October 2023 (available at https://www.officeforstudents.org.uk/news-blog-and-events/press-and-media/transcript-of-arif-ahmeds-speech-at-kings-college-london/).

113 A. Scott-Baumann et al., *Freedom of Speech in Universities: Islam, Charities and Counter-terrorism* (Routledge 2021) 126.

114 M. Hunter Schwartz et al., *What the Best Law Teachers Do* (Harvard University Press 2013) 248.

115 ibid 249–250.

116 See https://www.harvard.edu/harvard-dialogues/.

helping students to respectfully engage with controversial political and social issues.[117]

Some personal practical suggestions/considerations when teaching potentially controversial topics put forward by the present writer are:

- Have an educational purpose for including content
- Communicate the purpose clearly
- Tell students at the start of your module your expectations about respectful debate and explain the starting position of assuming good faith of other students[118]
- Be aware of/have copies of official case facts if relevant (beware press or partisan summaries of controversial cases or relying on your memory!)
- Ascertain what really needs to be included for your educational purpose
- Consider summarising/euphemising potentially offensive material[119]
- Continue to gauge and reflect on student perspective/reaction/feedback
- Be conscious and respectful of some students' disabilities (physical and mental) in a class
- Consider if advance notice of certain topics is appropriate[120]
- More generally, make clear to students at the outset of your module/programme that some topics to be discussed might be controversial/cause offence to some people[121]

117 See https://www.goacta.org/initiatives/college-debates/. See too the new Sheldonian Series debates launched by the University of Oxford in November 2024.

118 For examples of free to use resources intended for use by American universities when inducting first year students about free speech issues and created by the US non-partisan Foundation for Individual Rights and Expression (FIRE) and New York University see: https://www.thefire.org/research-learn/faq-adopting-free-speech-lessons-orientation-first-year-experience-programming

119 See too, for comparison, the list of factors to which regard should be had in carrying out the required balancing exercise relating to the manifestation of protected beliefs in an employment context set by Eady P. in *Higgs v Farmor's School* [2023] ICR 1071 at para 94: '(i) the content of the manifestation; (ii) the tone used; (iii) the extent of the manifestation; (iv) the worker's understanding of the likely audience; (v) the extent and nature of the intrusion on the rights of others and any consequential impact on the employer's ability to run its business; (vi) whether the worker has made clear that the views expressed are personal, or whether they might be seen as representing the views of the employer, and whether that might present a reputational risk; (vii) whether there is a potential power imbalance given the nature of the worker's position or role and that of those whose rights are intruded upon; (viii) the nature of the employer's business, in particular where there is a potential impact on vulnerable service users or clients; (ix) whether the limitation imposed is the least intrusive measure open to the employer.' Note an appeal on the *Higgs* case was heard in the Court of Appeal on 2 October 2024. At the time of writing (December 2024) its decision is awaited.

120 On the issue of trigger warnings, see L. Mitchell, 'Courting Controversy: The Use of Trigger Warnings in Teaching Human Rights Law' (2024) *The Law Teacher* 1.

121 This idea also mirrors the suggestion for briefings on issues of tolerance in student inductions put forward by Douglas-Oloyede in Advance HE, *Promoting Good Relations in Higher Education*, (May 2024) 19.

- In discussion, be prepared to offer a 'devil's advocate' viewpoint if no student offers one[122]
- Reassure students they do not need to personally agree with a viewpoint to play 'devil's advocate' before their classmates – this is an important skill for a lawyer in defending a client or anticipating opposing arguments
- Remember that not airing any counter arguments at all in a law class (where they clearly exist) fails students and is not worthy of a serious law school[123]
- Be prepared to challenge students' viewpoints/arguments
- Insist on and model respectful debate in class – no student (or staff member) comes to class to be harassed or bullied
- Students may feel very strongly about an issue – remember the value of allowing intellectual steam to be released before any challenge/counter argument is given
- Don't ignore real life or sell students short (their fees pay to learn both sides of an argument!) – beware unthinking self-censorship
- Remember students at university are adults who have chosen to enrol voluntarily, and remember the value of and duty to promote 'resilience'
- Discuss your approaches to teaching with other colleagues, swap ideas
- Check your university's policies, in particular its Freedom of Speech code of practice and ensure that you get appropriate training if needed or required[124]
- Don't ignore what your instinct tells you. It is a legitimate factor to consider too
- Tread carefully and respectfully but bravely.

Conclusion

Whether and, if so, how the law should protect philosophical beliefs in the workplace (and which beliefs) is a contentious issue. Often the cases brought before the Tribunals and courts involve parties who are passionate in their beliefs and may have genuine fears if the law does not protect those beliefs. Teaching such contentious material requires careful thought, a sense of

122 A practice also adopted by Prof. Arif Ahmed when teaching philosophy students. See Office for Students, *Transcript of Arif Ahmed's Speech at King's College London*, published 10 October 2023 (available at https://www.officeforstudents.org.uk/news-blog-and-events/press-and-media/transcript-of-arif-ahmeds-speech-at-kings-college-london/)

123 Remember that students also have a right to hear alternative arguments, as well as to express their own. As the formerly enslaved anti-slavery campaigner Frederick Douglas argued: 'To suppress free speech is a double wrong. It violates the rights of the hearer as well as those of the speaker.' (cited in M. Hume, *Trigger Warning: is the fear of being offensive killing free speech?*, (William Collins 2015 concise edition) 72).

124 In the case of *Meade v Westminster City Council (1) and Social Work England (2)* ET Case No.s 2200179/2022 & 2211483/2022, the Tribunal issued a formal recommendation that the Council employer 'ensures that all of its managers and human resources staff receive training on freedom of expression and protected belief, to include the implications of the EAT's judgment in Forstater (sic)', (para 91).

balance and mindfulness of the different needs and reasonable expectations of students.

In concluding her examination of academic freedom, Williams offers both a prescription and a warning which is worth serious reflection:

> To breathe life back into academic freedom, those working in universities need to see students … as intelligent, rational and autonomous individuals, capable of engaging in reasoned debate … Most importantly of all, academic freedom can only survive through being **continually exercised** in the classroom, in writing and in the public square. If not exercised, academic freedom quickly becomes reduced to rhetoric or dead dogma.[125]

Ultimately, as academics in the Law School, we should not shy away from grappling with the detail of controversial cases and issues, the discussion of which is central to our educational mission.

References

Adekoya, R. et al. *Academic Freedom in the UK: Protecting Viewpoint Diversity* (Policy Exchange 2020)

Advance HE, *Microaggressions. Call it Racism* available at: https://wZAQww.advance-he.ac.uk/tackling-racism-campus/resources as part of pack 1

Advance HE, *Protected Beliefs in Higher Education* (May 2024)

Advance HE, *Promoting Good Relations in Higher Education* (May 2024)

Berstein, D.E. *You Can't Say That! The Growing Threat to Civil Liberties From Antidiscrimination Laws* (Cato Institute 2003)

Bhambra, G.K. et al. 'Introduction: Decolonising the University?' in G.K. Bhambra et al. (eds), *Decolonising the University* (Pluto Press 2018)

Birmingham City Council v Afsar (2019) EWHC 3217 (QB)

Butcher, J. 'Academic Freedom Is an Individual Right' *Cieo* (11 June 2024) available at: https://www.cieo.org.uk/research/academic-freedom-is-an-individual-right/

Byrne, E. et al. *The University Challenge: Changing Universities in a Changing World* (Pearson 2020)

Charalambous v Barnsley College ET Case No. 1802552/2021

Commission on Race and Ethnic Disparities. *Commission on Race and Ethnic Disparities: The Report ('Sewell Report')* (Commission on Race and Ethnic Disparities, March 2021)

Cowan, S. et al. 'Should "Gender Critical" Views about Trans People Be Protected as Philosophical Beliefs in the Workplace? Lessons for the Future from *Forstater, Mackereth* and *Higgs*' (2022) 55(1) *Industrial Law Journal* 1–37

Dame Sara Khan, D.B.E. *Threats to Social Cohesion and Democratic Resilience: A New Strategic Approach* ('the Khan Review') (March 2024)

125 Williams, J. *Academic Freedom in an Age of Conformity: Confronting the Fear of Knowledge* (Palgrave Macmillan 2016) p198 (emphasis added).

Doyle, A. *The New Puritans: How the Religion of Social Justice Captured the Western World* (Constable 2023)

Dr David Mackereth v Dept for Work and Pensions & anor (2022) EAT 99

Equality and Human Rights Commission. *Equality Act 2010: Technical Guidance on Further and Higher Education* (Equality and Human Rights Commission 2015)

Equality and Human Rights Commission. *Freedom of Expression: A Guide for Higher Education Providers and Students' Unions in England & Wales* (Equality and Human Rights Commission 2019)

Equality and Human Rights Commission Scotland. *Tackling Racial Harassment in Universities* (undated article)

Fanshawe, S. *The Power of Difference: Where the Complexities of Diversity and Inclusion Meet Practical Solutions* (Kogan Page 2022)

Foran, M 'Discrimination and Manifestation of Belief: *Higgs v Farmor's School* (2024) ILJ 53(2) 285–304

Goodwin, M. *Is Academic Freedom Under Threat?* (Legatum Institute 2022)

Goodwin, M. *Values, Voice and Virtue: The New British Politics* (Penguin 2023)

Grainger plc v Nicholson [2010] ICR 360

Grant, J. *The New Power University: The Social Purpose of Higher Education in the 21st Century* (Pearson Education 2021)

Griffiths, R. (ed). *Political Correctness: Dyson and Goldberg v Fry and Peterson (The Munk Debates)* (Oneworld Publications 2018)

Higgs v Farmor's School & anor [2023] EAT 89

Hillman, N. *You Can't Say That!' What Students Really Think of Free Speech on Campus* (HEPI Policy Note 35, June 2022)

House of Commons Education Committee Report. *The Forgotten: How White Working Class Pupils Have Been Let Down, and How to Change It* (June 2021) HC 85

House of Commons/House of Lords Joint Committee on Human Rights. *Freedom of Speech in Universities* (March 2018)(HC 589/HL Paper 111)

Hume, M. *Trigger Warning: Is the Fear of Being Offensive Killing Free Speech?* (William Collins 2015 concise edition)

Hunter Schwartz, M. et al. *What the Best Law Teachers Do* (Harvard University Press 2013)

Joanna Phoenix v The Open University Case No 3322700/2021 & 3323841/2021

Johnson, A. et al. 'Are You Supposed to Be in Here?' Racial Microaggressions and Knowledge Production in Higher Education' in J. Arday et al (eds), *Dismantling Race in Higher Education: Racism, Whiteness and Decolonising the Academy* (Palgrave Macmillan 2018)

Kalven, H. et al. *Report on the University's Role in Political and Social Action* (University of Chicago 1967)

Keyishian v Board of Regents of the University of the State of New York, 385 U.S. 589 (1967)

Lister v Swindon College ET Case No. 1404223/2022

London Universities' Council for Academic Freedom. 'London Principles for Academic Freedom' (March 2024) available at: https://nms.kcl.ac.uk/lucaf/viewdocument.php?id=2

Lukianoff, G. et al. *The Coddling of the American Mind: How Good Intentions and Bad Ideas Are Setting Up a Generation for Failure* (Penguin 2018)

Malcolm, F. et al. *Freedom of Speech in UK Higher Education: Recommendations for Policy and Practice* (The Policy Institute, King's College London, September 2023)

Maya Forstater v CGD Europe & ors (UKEAT/0105/20/JOJ)
McColgan, A. *Discrimination Law: Text, Cases and Materials* (Hart 2023)
McEleny v Ministry of Defence S/4105347/2017
Meade v Westminster City Council (1) and Social Work England (2) ET Case No.s 2200179/2022 & 2211483/2022
Miller v University of Bristol ET Case No 1400780/2022
Mitchell, L. 'Courting Controversy: The Use of Trigger Warnings in Teaching Human Rights Law' (2024) *The Law Teacher* 58(2), 168-185
Mr S Corby v Advisory, Conciliation and Arbitration Service ET Case No. 1805305/2022
Ms Allison Bailey v Stonewall Equality Ltd & ors Case No. 2202172/2020
Murray, J. 'The Higher Education (Freedom of Speech) Act 2023: an employment focused overview' ILJ 2023, 52(3), 791, section 4
Niehoff, L. et al. *Free Speech: From Core Values to Current Debates* (Cambridge University Press 2022)
Office for Students. *Consultation on a New Approach to Regulating Harassment and Sexual Misconduct in English Higher Education* (Office for Students, February 2023)
Office for Students. *Consultation on Proposed Regulatory Advice and Other Matters Relating to Freedom of Speech* (Office for Students, 26 March 2024)
Office for Students. *Regulatory advice 24: Guidance related to freedom of speech* (Office for Students, March 2024 draft)
Office for Students. *Transcript of Arif Ahmed's speech at King's College London* (Office for Students, 10 October 2023) available at: https://www.officeforstudents.org.uk/news-blog-and-events/press-and-media/transcript-of-arif-ahmeds-speech-at-kings-college-london/
Olivier v Dept for Work and Pensions ET/1701407/2013
Omooba v Michael Garrett Associates Ltd & anor [2024] IRLR 440
Orwell, G. 'The Freedom of the Press', (1945) cited in Appendix I to George Orwell, *Animal Farm* (Secker & Warburg 1987)
Orwin v East Riding of Yorkshire Council ET Case No. 6000146/2022
Patten, K. 'Protected Beliefs under the Equality Act: Grainger Questioned' (2024) 53(2) *Industrial Law Journal* 239–267
Prime Minister's Office. *The King's Speech 2024 Background Briefing Notes* (Prime Minister's Office, 17 July 2024)
Richmond Pharmacology Ltd v Dhaliwal (2009) ICR 724
Rowbottom, J. 'Cakes, Gay Marriage and the Right against Compelled Speech' (UK Constitutional Law Blog, 16 October 2018) available at: https://ukconstitutionallaw.org/
Scott-Baumann, A. et al. *Freedom of Speech in Universities: Islam, Charities and Counter-terrorism* (Routledge 2021)
Srinivasan, A. 'Open Letters and Campus Protests' (23 May 2024) 46(10) 3–6 *London Review of Books*
Stokes, D. *Against Decolonisation: Campus Culture Wars and the Decline of the West* (Polity Press 2023)
Suttie, N. 'Cultivating Controversy … with Civility' (*HEPI Guest Post,* 6 June 2023)
Sweezy v State of New Hampshire, 354 U.S. 234 (1957)
Waltham-Smith, N. and Murray, J. 'Academic Freedom and Philosophical Belief: Strengthening the Legal Analysis' ILJ (2024) (advance publication 4 Oct 2024)
Wieman v Updegraff, 344 U.S.183 (1952)

Williams, J. *Academic Freedom in an Age of Conformity: Confronting the Fear of Knowledge* (Palgrave Macmillan 2016)
Zelinsky, N.A.G. et al. *Campus Speech in Crisis: What the Yale Experience Can Teach America* (Encounter Books 2016)

Legislation

Equality Act 2010
European Convention on Human Rights 1950 (in force 1953)
Higher Education (Freedom of Speech) Act 2023
Higher Education and Research Act 2017
Human Rights Act 1998
Race Relations Act 1976

13 "But It's All About Women Though" Socio-Legal and Gender Research in the Core Curriculum

Jessica Guth

Introduction

I have always been a socio-legal scholar, one of the, at the time at least, rare lawyers also trained in empirical research methods.[1] This wasn't by design. I did not know that what I did was rare really and I also did not really know that what I therefore wanted to bring to my teaching was in any way unusual.[2] In the early years of my teaching I co-designed and co-taught a module named Law and Society which was aimed at introducing students to different ways of thinking about law and legal education. It foregrounded justice, rights and our experience of those things and introduced students to a variety of perspectives on law. As part of that module I taught a couple of sessions on feminist approaches to law. The rest of the law school curriculum was very traditional and mostly black letter law focused and underpinned by doctrinal legal methodologies. For most students choosing the module, it offered a welcome break from that tradition and a space to explore some of the tensions and contradictions between their experience of law and what they were being taught.[3] One year though, I was walking into the lecture theatre to start my session as two male students were walking out. I asked them where they were going and their response was 'it's all about women today though isn't it, so we don't need to be here'. Their comment now forms part of the title of this chapter more than a decade and a half later because what they said stuck with me. What they said informed my approach to teaching about gender and diversity generally and

1 Nuffield Inquiry on Empirical Legal Research (2006) *Law in the Real World: Improving Understanding of How Law Works,* https://www.ucl.ac.uk/judicial-institute/sites/judicial-institute/files/law_in_the_real_world_-_improving_our_understanding_of_how_law_works.pdf (last accessed 11th May 2024).

2 Anthony Bradney, 'The Place of Empirical Legal Research in the Law School Curriculum' in P. Cane and H.M. Kritzer (eds) *The Oxford Handbook of Empirical Legal Research* (OUP 2010); Caroline Hunter (ed), *Integrating Socio-Legal Studies Into the Law School Curriculum'* (Palgrave 2012).

3 For work stressing the importance of this see Foluke Adebisi, *Decolonisation and Legal Knowledge* (Bristol University Press 2023); Foluke Adebisi, Shraiya Jivraj and Ntinta Tzouvala (eds), *Decolonisation, Anti-Racism, and Legal Pedagogy* (Routledge 2024).

DOI: 10.4324/9781003457985-13

my desire and ambition to teach from a standpoint that authentically reflected me, my biases, my concerns, my research and my experiences of life and law. That is not to say that I wanted students to think like I did, have the same views as me or perceive what I had to share as objective or authoritative. It simply meant that I wanted to make explicit much of what often goes unsaid about law. I wanted to highlight that when we position law as neutral and objective we are in fact taking a position.[4] I wanted students to feel able to express their discomfort when the law they encountered in books did not match the law as they experienced it and I wanted them to learn to think critically about systems that, while sometimes a force for good, can also uphold an inherently biased, harmful and discriminatory status quo.[5]

Foregrounding alternative approaches to law, exploring different theoretical perspectives and introducing students to feminist, queer or critical race theories in an optional module where they had signed up for exactly that was one thing: Students embraced the opportunities to think differently and question all they had studied before in the light of their new found ways of analysis.[6] They thrived on debate and inhaled bodies of literature that had seemingly remained closed to them before they appeared on my reading list. They wanted to read about research in the area, they wanted to understand how it was conducted, what the flaws might be and how they themselves might undertake research projects that tackle difficult issues. It was a joy to work with interested and engaged final year students in this way, but cohorts were small and represented a tiny fraction of the students on the course.

But law doesn't just become contested in an optional module. Law taught in core subjects is contested and problematic and experienced differently by each of us. In fact, core modules may leave less space to explore the contested nature of law because there are more fixed ideas about what should or should not form part of a core module and about how core modules should be taught.[7] Introducing alternative approaches to core subjects therefore seemed

4 See a plethora of feminist writing on law here but also critiques of what it means to think like a lawyer: John O. Mudd, 'Thinking Critically About "Thinking Like a Lawyer"' (1983) 33 J. Legal Educ. 704; Susan A Bandes, 'Feeling and Thinking Like a Lawyer: Cognition, Emotion, and the Practice and Progress of Law' (2020–2021) 89 Fordham L. Rev. 2427; Rebecca Huxley-Binns, 'Tripping over Thresholds: A Reflection on Legal Andragogy' (2016) 50(1) *The Law Teacher* 1–14; and the work on decolonisation cited at above n 3.

5 There is a huge variety of writing on law as causing harm from feminist, queer, critical race and other perspectives. For a recent example containing critiques from several perspectives see Dragica Vujadinović, Antonio Álvarez del Cuvillo and Susanne Strand (eds), *Feminist Approaches to Law* (Springer 2023). See also above n 3.

6 See also Morag McDermont, Bronwen Morgan and David Cowan, 'Socio-Legal Studies Module: The Bristol Experience' in Caroline Hunter (ed), *Integrating Socio-Legal Studies Into the Law School Curriculum'* (Palgrave 2012).

7 Richard Ball and Christian Dadomo '*UKCLE Law* Subject Survey: European Union Law' (UKCLE 2010); P. Birks, 'Compulsory Subjects: Will the Seven Foundations Ever Crumble?"' (1995) 1 *Web Journal of Current Legal Issue;* available at: https://www.bailii.org/uk/other

a different thing entirely. It seemed riskier and more difficult, and it took me a while to find my voice in that space. This chapter is about some of the journey to finding my voice and being confident using it in the classroom. It explores the tensions arising from the introduction of approaches to teaching core subjects such as European Union (EU) Law and Public Law which embed discussions of gender, gender politics and themes around diversity and social justice throughout the module. In this chapter I am particularly focused on how using my own research around EU citizenship, as well as the courts and the importance of judicial diversity, helped me in this process and provided a way of introducing perspectives and ways of thinking without alienating students (or colleagues) who were expecting something different and more traditional and generally more black letter law based.

The chapter proceeds as follows. The next section summarises the problem, as I perceived it, with traditional teaching in two core subjects: EU Law and Public Law. The second section then outlines some of my early initiatives introduced to try and address those problems together with the challenges I experienced in making those changes. This section explains why I had to go back to the drawing board and think of other ways of achieving what I wanted to achieve. The third section provides a brief overview of my research on judicial diversity at EU level and the section after explains how I used that research in a variety of context to create better modules that would engages students and help them to challenge dominant narratives. The fifth section outlines key challenges and the final section offers some brief thoughts on the importance of persevering with the incorporation of socio-legal research and alternative approaches in core modules.

EU Law and Public Law: Content Heavy and Technical = Boring?

While I have taught many undergraduate subjects, my background and real expertise lie in EU Law and Public Law. Over the last 20 years I have taught one or the other, if not both, every academic year. Both are often perceived to be content heavy and technical. Both have similar critiques levelled at them: They are difficult to make relevant to students, they are a bit dull, key cases are old and/or difficult to understand, key concepts feel alien. Nothing is intuitive or captures the imagination of undergraduate students in any meaningful way. My approach to law has always been one that 'covers the theoretical and empirical analysis of law as a social phenomenon'[8] and while Simon Halliday

/journals/WebJCLI/1995/issue1/birks1.html; William Twinning, *Blackstone's Tower: The English Law School* (Sweet & Maxwell 1994) S. Boyes, (2019), '"Do We Still Have to Do This Now We're Leaving?" The Future of European Union Law in the Curriculum After Brexit' (2019) 53(3) *The Law Teacher* 378–382. James, C., & Koo, J, 'The EU law "Core" Module: Surviving the Perfect Storm of Brexit and the SQE' (2017) 52(1) *The Law Teacher* 68–84.

8 Economic and Social Research Council *Review of Socio-Legal Studies: Final Report* (ESRC 1994).

contends that Public Law does not belong to the 'claustrophobic world of doctrinal legal scholarship' and that 'many aspects of what could easily be called a 'socio-legal' approach have long been integrated into the study of public law in the UK',[9] that was not my experience. As both a student and then a teacher inheriting modules, my sense of both Public Law and EU Law was that they

> manifest in curricula as dry, alienating and most bizarrely of all dusty… Students are expected to trawl through a lot of institutional information – disregarding not only socio-legal but also analytical skills, with an emphasis on description that would not be entertained in a history syllabus at primary school level.[10]

I wanted to do better for my students, and I wanted the modules I taught to be about our lives and our rights and how we experience them. I did not want my students to have to go through what O'Brien called an 'unpleasant but necessary right of passage'.[11] I knew that both subjects could be engaging, important and fun. I knew this because while I had not enjoyed either of them as an undergraduate, my PhD on highly skilled migration in the EU had given me a glimpse at how a different way of looking at law can raise interesting question, can encourage different thinking and can help us understand law as one of many social phenomena shaping our lives.[12] As such any legal subject can be made relevant to students and can be a powerful driver for student learning and engagement on a variety of issues. The problem is not the subjects but our approach to them and the assumptions we make about what students do and should already know.

As long ago as 2004, Cownie noted that legal academics are as likely as not to consider themselves socio-legal in their approach.[13] However, she also noted that students tend to be more vocationally oriented than their counterparts[14] and Bradney noted that there is very little teaching of empirical legal research in UK Law Schools.[15] He goes on to say that while empirical legal research should be in the curriculum, this can only be achieved 'if students not only use and understand such studies but also understand the methods used

9 Simon Halliday, 'Public Law' in Caroline Hunter (ed), *Integrating Socio-Legal Studies Into the Law School Curriculum'* (Palgrave 2012) 143.

10 Charlotte O'Brien, 'European Union Law' in Caroline Hunter (ed), *Integrating Socio-Legal Studies Into the Law School Curriculum'* (Palgrave 2012) 184.

11 ibid 184.

12 Jessica Guth, 'Evaluating Law and Policy in the Context of Doctoral Mobility in the European Union'. University of Liverpool Doctoral thesis (University of Liverpool 2011).

13 Fiona Cownie, *Legal Academics: Culture and Identities* (Hart Publishing 2004).

14 ibid.

15 Bradney above n 2 1028; Hunter above n 2.

and theories on which they are based'.[16] I therefore felt a little stuck. I knew that trying to incorporate more of the huge variety of research was probably the answer to more engaging modules, but I was keenly aware of the difficulties of introducing socio-legal work and empirical work in particular. I was further hampered by textbooks. Textbooks in EU Law and Public Law tend not to include much, if any, socio-legal, contextual or empirical work. Their focus is doctrinal or sometimes contextual insofar as the context relates to legal practice. Students often see textbooks as the authoritative sources for what they need to know. Auchmuty puts it like this:

> How are we to persuade students that the textbook account is inadequate? The textbook is *the* Authority in many of our classrooms; for most students, what appears in a book published by Oxford University Press *must* be more reliable than something said by their obviously biased lecturer in class.[17]

I was therefore faced with modules which were unpopular amongst the student body, which had a reputation for being boring and difficult and with a lack of easily available materials or examples I could draw on but with a strong commitment to make my students experience of those modules better than mine had been and to somehow share the fun, intellectual challenge and genuine interest in the subject. I just wasn't sure how.

Trying to Make EU Law and Public Law Engaging

My first attempts at making my core subjects more engaging had only limited success. I revised reading lists having spent hours searching for what I thought might be the most accessible texts, I provided case summaries in text and podcast format, I searched the internet for content that was accessible, entertaining **and** accurate and I played with module structures. For example in EU Law I decided to swap the teaching of free movement of goods and free movement of people round and do the latter first. Previous cohorts had always struggled with free movement of goods more, so I thought the introduction of key principles in a context they could identify with more easily might help. Anecdotally, it did help students do better but it didn't help them engage more overall or consider the subject less boring and technical. It also did not help them to 'spot, use and contest points of EU Law'[18] from a practical perspective and the whole module remained as far removed from their daily lives as ever. I had not reduced content, I had just re-ordered it so the module

16 Bradney above n 2 1036.

17 Rosemary Auchmuty, 'Land Law and Equity and Trusts' in Caroline Hunter (ed), *Integrating Socio-Legal Studies Into the Law School Curriculum* (Palgrave 2012) 77 emphasis original.

18 O'Brien above n 10 186.

remained content heavy. I still had a lot of coverage of institutions and I was still teaching in neat categories of institutions, principles and substantive law. Although it felt like I had done a lot of work and made a lot of changes, the module was still largely the same.

My efforts in Public Law to move away from A V Dicey and think about how our constitution functions now by focusing on current affairs, big news stories and politics resulted in some great and sometimes heated debates in the classroom but did not necessarily lead to a greater understanding of the Constitution, Constitutional Principles or Judicial Review and led to some students to comment that they were not studying a law degree to just talk about politics. I had thrown the proverbial baby out with the bathwater and focused too much on contemporary issues, ignoring our rich constitutional history and how we can learn from that. The same criticisms levelled at my attempts to change EU Law can also be levelled at Public Law. The changes were superficial and did not actually fundamentally disrupt the modules in ways that would get us to the often difficult, controversial but important discussions.

There is also no evidence to suggest that those early attempts resulted in better pass rates or a better learning experience for the students. It seemed it was mainly more of the same – just in a different order and with different reading, still chosen by me with little input from the students. In addition, in my efforts to try and find accessible reading that I thought might speak to students' interest, I sacrificed some coherence, and it is possible that students could no longer see the links between topics or threads running through the module which, in Public Law in particular, seemed key to success in the module overall.

In my efforts to be innovative and different I had also removed textbooks from my modules which students really seemed to struggle with. My attempts to get away from tradition and think differently about the topics removed an important safety net for students making it even harder for them. I also learned quickly that Bradney[19] was right, introducing reading that was based on empirical studies, or drawing on political science literature or statistical evidence caused anxiety and sometimes confusion because students were not taught how to read, understand and use this sort of literature and information. I therefore had to go back to the drawing board.

Gender and the Court of Justice of the European Union: A Way In

At the same time as struggling with how best to teach the two core subjects I was involved in and trying to understand why my interdisciplinary and research-based approach worked in my optional module, but did not work at all in the core modules, I was involved in a variety of research projects

19 Bradney above n 2.

about the Court of Justice of the European Union (CJEU). Starting in 2012 I turned my attention from substantive law around EU Citizenship and EU migration[20] to focus more on the EU institutions and the Court in particular. I started exploring how gender played out in the Court at all levels thinking about the composition of the court, the ways of working and processes as well as the outcomes in the forms of case law. I began to really understand the Court as a legal and political institution and began to build up a body of writing in the area.[21] In my research I was particularly interested in gender and how gender might play out in the composition of the Court, its ways of working and its decisions.

I had also found my confidence in the classroom. I had been teaching for a few years and I was searching for my own authentic voice. These things came together to provide the opportunity to re-think how my research and teaching could re-enforce each other and provide students with a more engaging way to explore the core subjects.[22] At the same time I would be able to introduce different perspectives and allow my voice to be heard which would hopefully inspire students to also let theirs be heard. Changing the modules became much more about changing classroom dynamics and positioning of content than it did about content.

Using my Research to Create Better Modules

As my research was rooted in EU Law, I started there. In a similar way that O'Brien talks about moving away from the pillars of institutions, principles and

20 Jessica Guth, Louise Ackers and Bryony Gill, 'Migration Processes and Their Determinants: "Professional" Factors' in Louise Ackers and Bryony Gill, *Moving People and Knowledge* (Edward Elgar 2008); Jessica Guth, 'Evaluating Law and Policy in the Context of Doctoral Mobility in the European Union'. University of Liverpool Doctoral thesis (University of Liverpool 2011); Jessica Guth and Edward Mowlam 'The Evolution of European Union Citizenship: Where Does Zambrano Take Us?' (2012) 46(1) *The Law Teacher* 75; Jessica Guth, 'When Is a Partner Not a Partner? Conceptualisations of "Family" in EU fFree Movement Law' (2011) 33(2) *Journal of Social Welfare and Family Law* 193.

21 Jessica Guth, 'Law as the Object and Agent of Integration: Gendering the Court of Justice of the European Union, Its Decisions and Their Impact' in Gabriele Abels and Heather McRae, *Gendering European Integration Theory* (Barbara Budrich Verlag 2016); Jessica Guth, 'Transforming the European Legal Order: The European Court of Justice at 60+' (2016) 12(1) *Journal of Contemporary European Research* 455; Jessica Guth and Sanna Elfving, *Gender and the Court of Justice of the European Union* (Routledge 2018); Jessica Guth, 'The EU Legal Order After Brexit: A Shame to Lose the Contribution?' in Scott L. Greer and Janet Laible (eds), *Europe After Brexit.* (MUP 2020); Jessica Guth and Sanna Elfving 'Court of Justice of the EU and Judicial Politics' In Gabriele Abels et al (eds), *Routledge Handbook of Gender and EU Politics.* (Routledge 2021); Jessica Guth, 'The Court of Justice of the European Union, Women, and Leadership' in Henriette Müller and Ingeborg Tömmel (eds), *Women and Leadership in the European Union* (Oxford University Press 2022).

22 McDermont et al above n 6; Barbara Zamorski 'Research Led Teaching and learning in higher education: a case' (2002) 7(4) *Teaching in Higher Education* 411.

substantive law and instead thinking about EU Law in terms of themes and problems,[23] I thought about how I could completely re-design the module using the Court of Justice as the central point around which a rights focused content would be structured. Using my own work on gender I wanted to encourage students to think about differential access to and impact of law. At this point I had the luxury of being in charge of the module and the only teacher on it. Instead of starting the module with an exploration of the EU's history and the institutional set up and then talking about key principles before moving on to substantive law, I started with telling the story of third-country nationals in an EU Member State and their stateless children who became EU citizens.[24] I contrasted that with nationals living in their home state but with dual (EU) nationality and a third-country spouse wanting to join them.[25] We jumped straight into substantive law but not with abstract treaty provisions to be logically applied but with two potentially EU Law related problems that hinged on our conceptualisation of Citizenship and the enjoyment of rights and might well have been influenced by questions of gender and race. Contrasting the two cases allowed us to explore questions around equity in application of rights, the purpose of the EU and how that might shape the application and also processes of enforcing rights. At this early stage I had my early thinking and some research work, but I did not yet have a record of publications in this area. The conversations with students through these teaching sessions undoubtedly sharpened my thinking and helped shaped the research. This is most obvious in what eventually became a co-authored chapter in the *Gender and the Court of Human Rights* book where a dissertation student took up the themes explored in her second-year EU course to focus on them in greater depth.[26]

Once we had established a story telling approach which introduced real cases not as abstract legal documents but as the real lives of the people involved, we opened up the discussions around why legal solutions were important for those families or individuals. Students engaged much more with EU Law overall as this seemed to bring the subject alive and make it relevant. On the first run through, I went too fast and still had too much content leading to students feeling a little bit anxious and confused about expectations and what to focus on. Some students also struggled to be able to understand some of the basic principles or how institutions worked. After that first year, I was more careful to provide more information through the virtual learning environment (VLE) for background which I could direct students to and to

23 O'Brien above n 10.

24 *Gerardo Ruiz Zambrano v Office national de l'emploi* (Case C-34/09), EU:C:2011:124, [2011] ECR I-1177, 8 March 2011.

25 *Shirley McCarthy v Secretary of State for the Home Department* (Case C-434/09), ECLI:EU:C:2010:718.

26 Jessica Guth and Sanna Elfving with Sophie Mayat, 'European Union Citizenship – Free Movement for All? In Guth and Elfving above n 21.

allow more time for discussions around institutions and principles. As well as students no longer finding these boring because they had context and could see why it mattered, this teaching also helped shaped my thinking around how and why processes and ways of working matter in EU Law and have gendered and racialised implications. Student engagement, attendance and satisfaction with the module increased, the number of dissertation students choosing EU Law topics, particularly around citizenship rights and around institutional power, increased from 0 to between 6 and 8 annually (in a cohort of around 85), and student outcomes in terms of pass rates also increased. Importantly though this was not only the case for those students who clearly enjoyed the same things and same approach I enjoyed, but also for others. My starting points may have been 'all about women' but most students understood it as a way in to talk about all sorts of questions that were meaningful to them. By starting with my research and sharing what questions I was asking of the case law and why, I empowered students to take a critical approach to all areas. While my work was focused on gender and provided the way into discussions around equality, rights, power and fairness, students naturally took the conversations in other directions to explore how characteristics and intersections of them played out in the legal arena. I had been concerned about whether I would be able to teach free movement of goods in a similarly engaging way and keep the focus on rights and questions of (social) justice, but I need not have worried. Students soon asked really interesting questions around national protectionism, impacts of regulations on small businesses and why and how consumer protection arguments seemed to vary in success. As the module progressed over the next few years and new case law emerged, we looked back on arguments I and others had made in our research to see if that still held true. Had we over-estimated the impact of cases or had there been unintended consequences? The module worked well and outcomes and feedback were excellent. In addition there was a direct link between what I was teaching and the direction my research was developing in which made the work so much more enjoyable.

I then moved institutions and joined a much larger EU Law team as a seminar tutor. I therefore had no direct responsibility over the module and had to work within parameters given. I was therefore back to teaching in an institutions, principles, substantive law pillar structure with a doctrinal focus. The focus on rights had gone and it was difficult to see a space for my work within the module. While the module leader was not willing to change the module significantly and incorporate some of the key things I had successfully implemented, she was happy for me to supplement the materials available to students. To ensure that all students and not just those in my seminar class could benefit, I shared some of my writing with podcast commentary and in my classes I tried to ensure that discussions centred on cases as stories of peoples' lives and why the rights we were considering were important. Students were not convinced and pushed back against my approach because they failed to see the relevance of it and saw it, perhaps rightly, as a distraction from doing the things that would get them good grades. Student comments alluded to the fact that they saw my gendered reading of EU Law at best as an interesting side note and at worst as some nonsense that would make it harder for them to score well on the examination. Some students opted not to attend my seminar and moved to other tutors instead. That is not to say though that what I was doing was not important. Every year I had a few students who were inspired by my different approach or who were helped in their understanding of the CJEU through our contextual discussions and every year I would end up with one or two dissertation students wanting to explore a variety of legal topics from socio-legal and often feminist perspectives. I may not have been able to win over a cohort or persuade colleagues to try something different, but I did reach some students and empower them to find their voice.

As I could do little on the EU Law module to introduce the more contextual and rights-based approach that brought the subject to life to my previous cohorts, I turned my attention to the Public Law module I was leading. My hope was that if I could introduce first year students to a rights-based and contextual approach grounded in research, I may also have more traction with my more limited scope in the second-year EU law module. If I could show how a gendered approach was a legitimate and helpful way of thinking about law, then maybe that would carry through into later modules and give me more traction later. My approach here had to be different to the one I took at my previous institution though because I was not the only teacher on the module. In fact there was a team of 6 of us. Therefore I could not just go with the student cohort and see where discussions would take us, because we needed to ensure some consistency across our different groups and because seminar tutors would need some structure and guidance for the sessions. My goal for Public Law was to structure it around the notion of power and to take account of which voices were amplified and which were silenced, and to examine how this played out in our constitutional set up. While my own research work was not directly relevant here, I could draw on general ideas around diversity including judicial diversity which underpinned some of it and there is plenty of work out there which allows for a similar approach.[27] The module seemed

27 See 'Part III Public Law: International Law, Human Rights and the Courts' in Adebisi et al. above n 3 for excellent recent examples. See further the following for examples I have used previously: Susan Millns and Noel Whitty, *Feminist Perspectives on Public Law* (Routledge 2013); Se-shauna Wheatle and Elizabeth O'Loughlin, *Diverse Voices in Public Law* (Bristol University Press 2023); VE Munro, 'Feminist Critiques of the Rule of Law' in J. Meierhenrich, M. Loughlin (eds), *The Cambridge Companion to the Rule of Law*. Cambridge Companions to Law (Cambridge University Press 2021) 340–356. Halliday above n 9; Hazel Genn, 'When Law is Good for Your Health: Mitigating the Social Determinants of Health through Access to Justice' (2019) 72(1) *Current Legal Problems* 159–202; Varda Bondy, Linda Mulcahy with Margaret Doyle and Val Rei, 'Mediation and Judicial Review: An Empirical Research Study' (The Nuffield Foundation 2009); B. Baines, D. Barak-Erez, T, Kahana, (eds), *Feminist Constitutionalism: Global Perspectives* (Cambridge University Press 2012).

perfect to allow an examination of the feminist assertation that 'the personal is political'.

Interestingly it was much more difficult to engage students with other's research than with my own. Students were overall less likely to read the materials I set and my podcast summaries, videos on how to read the articles or look at the research were accessed by less than 25% of the students in every cohort and students were retreating to whatever textbook they could find in the library. I therefore changed my approach again slightly and worked with a textbook and a relatively traditional structure but included in each lecture questions to be asked of the core narrative. We therefore discussed who had power and who did not, who benefitted from particular structures and processes, how we all experience State power and how and why that might be different depending on who we are. I also structured seminar activities around those questions and themes. This had more success as both students and colleagues seemed to find it easier to engage with alternative perspectives and challenges to the dominant narrative as long as the mainstream Public Law curriculum formed the core of the module. Everyone felt comfortable teaching the core ideas with the help of the textbook, and I then provided questions to challenge that core supported with research that I discussed with colleagues in preparation for seminars. Colleagues found this approach far easier and it helped them embrace new ideas and empowered them to bring additional research and ideas to the table. Both students and colleagues pushed back far less than when I had tried to put what we often call 'perspectives on…' at the core. Taking this approach was a compromise but one which allowed me to engage most of the students in some meaningful discussions and thinking about issues of power relationships, rights and differential impacts of State Power, Human Rights and access to things like Judicial Review. It also allowed me to create an atmosphere of inclusion and empower students who might be alienated by a traditional Public Law Curriculum. One student came to me after one of my first Public Law lectures to her cohort and said: 'Thank you for seeing me'.

Barriers to Integrating Research and Gender Perspectives

Introducing a more contextual, socio-legal and in particular gendered approach to teaching core subjects isn't easy. Several barriers seem to pop up again and again. First, there is still, even more than a decade after a volume on socio-legal studies highlighted the point repeatedly, a lack of textbooks which include these perspectives.[28] While there are specialist textbooks offering contextual or feminist approaches to legal subjects, they sit outside the mainstream and rarely seem used as the key text.[29] Mainstream textbooks mostly cling to the doctrinal tradition and do not provide alternative approaches or ways of

28 Hunter above n 2.

29 See Millns and Whitty above n 27, Baines Barak-Erez and Kahana above n 27.

thinking about law. This makes it very difficult to convince students that the alternative approaches are worthy of their time and consideration rather than just my opinion which can be ignored. This is particularly the case where students follow textbook structures in their other modules.

Second, colleagues who have 'been brought up' in the doctrinal tradition and have no training or experience of socio-legal or interdisciplinary approaches might, like the Nuffield Enquiry[30] suggested nearly 2 decades ago, lack the knowledge and experience and therefore confidence to introduce such research into the classroom. It is not only the students who need to understand the studies, methodologies and theories, it is us as teachers, too. Colleagues can therefore be reluctant to use unfamiliar literature, studies or types of evidence with students or in some cases may not see the relevance of them to the study of undergraduate law. If the teacher is part of a larger teaching team then this can make a different approach really difficult to implement. As module leader, the team needs to be convinced, as a team member, the module leader has to be convinced to include the approach in a way that makes it meaningful and possible for the students to engage with it. The most successful teaching of rights focused EU Law which took gender as well as other characteristics into account throughout the curriculum rather than as an alternative to the norm, was where I had complete control and was the only one doing the teaching. The students in this context already had experience of my teaching in their Legal Skills classes and we had already looked at socio-legal material together to build those skills. The least successful attempts have been in contexts where almost everything else studied before or alongside has been traditional doctrinal law, where skills teaching has not involved any consideration of research about law (as opposed to legal method) and where I have been part of larger teaching teams where colleagues have no experience with and sometimes no interest in deviating from mainstream module structures.

Third, while progress has been made, assessments in law schools are often still quite traditional exams and problem questions or essays.[31] More recently there has been a move towards authentic assessment which seems to focus on tasks which students might encounter in legal practice.[32] Examining key issues

30 Nuffield Enquiry above n 1.

31 See *The Law Teacher* journal for a plethora of articles about assessment in Law Schools. See also Maribel Canto-Lopez, Daniel Bansal and Jessica Guth 'Special Issue: Assessment in Legal Education: Towards an Inclusive, Diverse, and Authentic Strategy' 59(1) *The Law Teacher: The International Journal of Legal Education*.

32 N. McNamara, 'Authentic Assessment in Contract Law: Legal Drafting' (2016) 51(4) *The Law Teacher* 486–498; D. Berger and C. Wild, 'Enhancing Student Performance and Employability Through the Use of Authentic Assessment Techniques in Extra and Co-curricular Activities (ECCAs)' (2016) 521(4) *The Law Teacher* 428–439; N. Bedford, W. Bonython, and A. Taylor, 'Law As It Is, and How It Could Be: Law Reform Participation As Authentic Assessment and a Pedagogical Tool' (2024) 58(1) *The Law Teacher* 58–73.

from a variety of perspectives does not lend itself to problem based or scenario questions or legal practice based tasks. Where subjects are taught in different ways with different emphasis, they must also be assessed in different ways. A problem question which requires the doctrinal application of Treaty provisions and case law is not going to serve students who studied my EU Law module particularly well in the same way that a questions asking students to critique a judgment or article using a lens of their choosing is not going to result in high marks for students on a doctrinal course. Freedom in assessment was key in the modules I designed so that they became a way for students to share their ideas, experience and voice. I did not use problem questions at all and where I set essay questions, they tended to be broad, offer a choice of at least 3 different ones and the opportunity for students to write their own question (to be approved by me). Assessment was meant to be an extension of the teaching overall and empower rather than constrain. Where I was part of a teaching team and the assessment was set by the module lead, questions raised in my research or the research I was highlighting to students did not really feature, so students, in many ways rightly and unsurprisingly, paid little attention to it.

Finally, for many students studying law, the focus appears, at least initially to be to forge a path into the legal profession and they often appear more interested in grades than in content or the knowledge and skills they are actually developing.[33] If anything what Cownie identified as a vocational focus in 2004[34] has only got more prevalent.[35] They often want to learn those things that they perceive as important for and relevant to their future careers. For many that means learning legal rules and how to apply them. Engaging with research, particularly if that research is not focused on mainstream questions or provide answers relevant to the employment market, are seen as less important. Some of the highest scoring students across all their modules have been the most vocal about the irrelevance of some of my content and approach and it is from them that most comments like 'it's all about women though' have come. This is perhaps particularly the case where it is just one module in a level that takes a different approach to the others.

Why Do We Bother?

Given the pushback from colleagues and students, the considerable work involved and the risks around student satisfaction metrics, why do I keep trying and why do I think we should all be trying to introduce research to our students which opens up opportunities to talk about law as a problem as well

33 A. Nicholson and P. Johnston, 'The Value of a Law Degree – Part 3: A Student Perspective' (2020) 55(4) *The Law Teacher* 431–447.

34 Cownie above n 13.

35 Nicholson above n 33.

as a solution to some of the world's big problems and to acknowledge our different experiences of law, State power, rights and the application of laws?

It is of course a joy to work with engaged students on optional modules who have made a more or less considered choice to engage with the themes I suggest. Equally it is a joy to run a core module structured around my research and introduce an entire cohort to gendered discussions of EU institutions and EU Law in a way that engaged the majority of them and avoided gendered (and other 'alternative' perspectives) being seen as an aside or something that a few weird academics do. But in some ways the other work in modules that I have not led or where I have worked with a team as module leader is more important. Introducing gendered perspectives, socio-legal research considering the impact of law, asking questions that acknowledge gendered, queer, racialised and intersectional issues makes sure that we empower all of our students. Offering space for discussions so that all of our students can explore their experience of law, how they feel about law and legal issues and how that fits with dominant narratives is really important. Using research that focuses on one or more of those themes can open the door for those wider conversations that help students find their voice and their place in law. It can help narrow awarding gaps for all key characteristics because it allows students to see themselves in the discipline leading to better engagement with and understanding of the law, how it works (or doesn't) and why that matters to all of us.

Conclusion

Introducing my research into core modules has been challenging at times because my research is socio-legal, interdisciplinary and focused on gender. It is not something many of my EU Law and Public Law colleagues have always been familiar with or keen to integrate into modules they were running. Leading my own modules was full of joy because it allowed me to build them around my research to help empower students and at the same time make my research better. While I didn't really know what to say to the students all those years ago when they pointed out that the session was 'all about women', I think I would now suggest that it was about time given that so much law is really all about men. Bringing my research and other socio-legal work into my teaching has only partly been about bringing an awareness of gendered issues to students. It has turned out to be more about using it as a vehicle for opening up discussion, for reducing the power imbalance in the classroom through making clear that students' experiences are important and valid even if they don't fit the mainstream narratives about law and how it works. It has allowed me to say 'here are my questions of the law, what are yours?' That has made even those subjects often portrayed as technical and boring about our lives. Therefore, in the feminist tradition, the personal has become the socio-legal, interdisciplinary political cornerstone of our shared understanding of law.

Bibliography

Adebisi, F., *Decolonisation and Legal Knowledge* (Bristol University Press 2023)

Adebisi, F., Jivraj, S., and Tzouvala, N. (eds), *Decolonisation, Anti-Racism, and Legal Pedagogy* (Routledge 2024)

Auchmuty, R., 'Land Law and Equity and Trusts' in Caroline Hunter (ed), *Integrating Socio-Legal Studies Into the Law School Curriculum* (Palgrave 2012) 69–103

Baines, B., Barak-Erez, D., and Kahana, T. (eds), *Feminist Constitutionalism: Global Perspectives* (Cambridge University Press 2012)

Ball, R., and Dadomo, C., *UKCLE Law Subject Survey: European Union law* (UKCLE 2010)

Bandes, S.A., 'Feeling and Thinking like a Lawyer: Cognition, Emotion, and the Practice and Progress of Law' (2020–2021) 89 *Fordham Law Review* 2427

Bedford, N., Bonython, W., and Taylor, A., 'Law as It is, and How It Could Be: Law Reform Participation as Authentic Assessment and a Pedagogical Too' (2024) 58(1) *The Law Teacher* 58–73

Berger, D., and Wild, C., 'Enhancing Student Performance and Employability Through the Use of Authentic Assessment Techniques in Extra and Co-curricular Activities (ECCAs)' (2016) 51(4) *The Law Teacher* 428–439

Birks, P., 'Compulsory Subjects: Will the seven Foundations Ever Crumble?' (1995) 1 *Web Journal of Current Legal Issues*, https://www.bailii.org/uk/other/journals/WebJCLI/1995/issue1/birks1.html

Bondy, V., Mulcahy, L., Doyle, M., and Reid, V., *Mediation and Judicial Review: An Empirical Research Study* (The Nuffield Foundation 2009)

Boyes, S. 'Do We Still Have to do this Now We're Leaving? The Future of European Union law in the curriculum After Brexit' (2019) 53(3) *The Law Teacher* 378–382

Bradney, A., 'The Place of Empirical Legal Research in the Law School Curriculum' in P. Cane and H.M. Kritzer (eds), *The Oxford Handbook of Empirical Legal Research* (OUP 2010) 1026–1043

Canto-Lopez, M., Bansal, D., and Guth, J. (eds), 'Special Issue: Assessment in Legal Education: Towards an Inclusive, Diverse, and Authentic Strategy' (2024) 59(1) *The Law Teacher: The International Journal of Legal Education*

Cownie, F., *Legal Academics: Culture and Identities* (Hart Publishing 2004)

Economic and Social Research Council, *Review of Socio-Legal Studies: Final Report* (ESRC 1994)

Genn, H., 'When Law is Good for Your Health: Mitigating the Social Determinants of Health through Access to Justice' (2019) 72(1) *Current Legal Problems* 159–202

Guth, J., 'The Court of Justice of the European Union, Women, and Leadership' in Henriette Müller and Ingeborg Tömmel (eds), *Women and Leadership in the European Union* (OUP 2022) 273–289

Guth, J., 'The EU Legal Order after Brexit: A Shame to Lose the Contribution?' in Scott L. Greer and Janet Laible (eds), *Europe After Brexit* (MUP 2020) 113–127

Guth, J., 'Evaluating Law and Policy in the Context of Doctoral Mobility in the European Union' (University of Liverpool Doctoral thesis, University of Liverpool 2011)

Guth, J., 'Law as the Object and Agent of Integration: Gendering the Court of Justice of the European Union, Its Decisions and Their Impact' in Gabriele Abels and Heather McRae (eds), *Gendering European Integration Theory* (Barbara Budrich Verlag 2016) 175–196

Guth, J., 'Transforming the European Legal Order: The European Court of Justice at 60+' (2016) 12(1) *Journal of Contemporary European Research* 455

Guth, J., 'When Is a Partner not a Partner? Conceptualisations of "Family" in EU Free Movement Law' (2011) 33(2) *Journal of Social Welfare and Family Law* 193

Guth, J., Ackers, L., and Gill, B., 'Migration Processes and their Determinants: "professional" factors' in Louise Ackers, and Bryony Gill (eds), *Moving People and Knowledge* (Edward Elgar 2008)

Guth, J., and Mowlam, E., 'The Evolution of European Union Citizenship: Where does Zambrano Take Us?' (2012) 46(1) *The Law Teacher* 75

Guth, J., and Sanna, E., 'Court of Justice of the EU and Judicial Politics' in Gabriele Abels et al. (eds), *Routledge Handbook of Gender and EU Politics* (Routledge 2021) 170–180

Guth, J., and Sanna, E., *Gender and the Court of Justice of the European Union* (Routledge 2018)

Halliday, S., 'Public Law' in Caroline Hunter (ed), *Integrating Socio-Legal Studies Into the Law School Curriculum'* (Palgrave 2012) 141–160

Hunter, C., (ed), *Integrating Socio-Legal Studies Into the Law School Curriculum* (Palgrave 2012)

Huxley-Binns, R., 'Tripping Over Thresholds: A Reflection on Legal Andragogy' (2016) 50(1) *The Law Teacher* 1–14

James, C., and Koo, J., 'The EU Law "Core" Module: Surviving the Perfect Storm of Brexit and the SQE' (2017) 52(1) *The Law Teacher* 68–84

McDermont, M., Morgan, B., and Cowan, D., 'Socio-Legal Studies Module: The Bristol Experience' in Caroline Hunter (ed), *Integrating Socio-Legal Studies Into the Law School Curriculum* (Palgrave 2012)

McNamara, N., 'Authentic Assessment in Contract Law: Legal Drafting' (2016) 51(4) *The Law Teacher* 486–498

Millns, S., and Whitty, N., *Feminist Perspectives on Public Law* (Routledge 2013)

Mudd, J., 'Thinking Critically About "Thinking Like a Lawyer"' (1983) 33 *Journal of Legal Educucation* 704

Munro, V.E., 'Feminist Critiques of the Rule of Law' in J. Meierhenrich and M. Loughlin (eds), *The Cambridge Companion to the Rule of Law* (Cambridge University Press 2021) 340–356

Nicholson, A., and Johnston, P., 'The Value of a Law degree – Part 3: A Student Perspective' (2020) 55(4) *The Law Teacher* 431–447

Nuffield Inquiry on Empirical Legal Research (2006) 'Law in the Real World: Improving Understanding of How Law Works' https://www.ucl.ac.uk/judicial-institute/sites/judicial-institute/files/law_in_the_real_world_-_improving_our_understanding_of_how_law_works.pdf

O'Brien, C., 'European Union Law' in Caroline Hunter (ed), *Integrating Socio-Legal Studies Into the Law School Curriculum* (Palgrave 2012) 184–201

Twining, W., *Blackstone's Tower: The English Law School* (Sweet & Maxwell 1994)

Vujadinović, D., del Cuvillo, A.Á., and Strand, S., (eds), *Feminist Approaches to Law* (Springer 2023)

Wheatle, S., and O'Loughlin, E., *Diverse Voices in Public Law* (Bristol University Press 2023)

Zamorski, B., 'Research Led Teaching and Learning in Higher Education: A Case' (2002) 7(4) *Teaching in Higher Education* 411

Index

Made in the USA
Las Vegas, NV
19 September 2026

e76a8287-33dc-4859-a83b-ba661b39ae04R01